# TOP TRAILS
# UTAH

## INCLUDES ZION, BRYCE, CAPITOL REEF, CANYON-LANDS, ARCHES, GRAND STAIRCASE, CORAL PINK SAND DUNES, GOBLIN VALLEY, AND GLEN CANYON

by Eric Henze

Gone Beyond Guides
Publisher

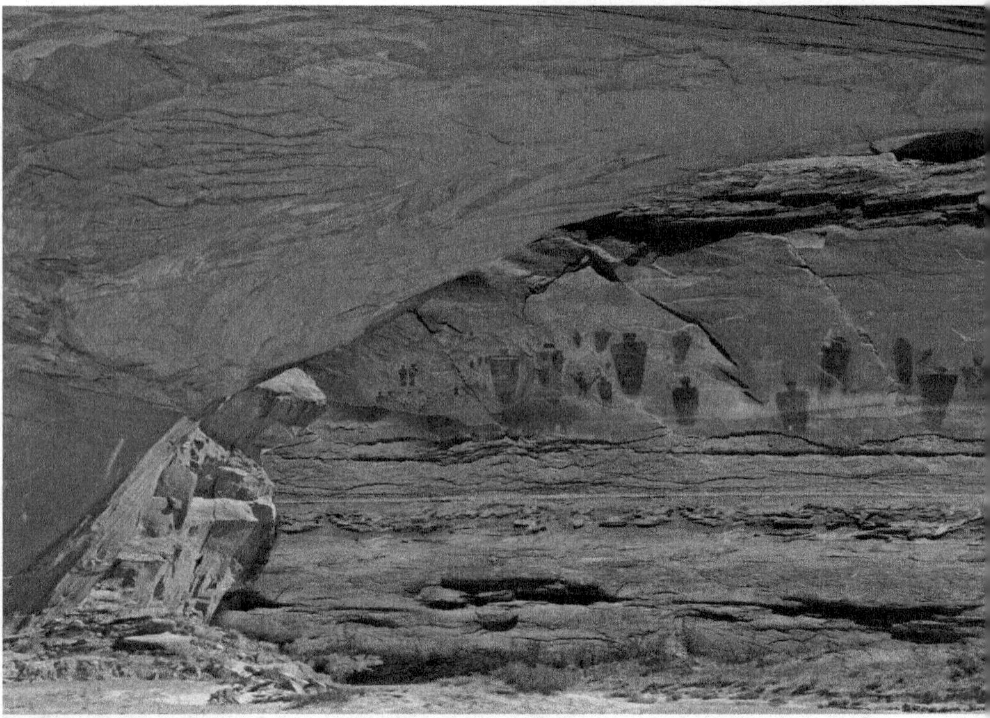


## General Information 8

## Southwest Utah ......... 17

Zion National Park ............... 18

Quail Creek State Park ............... 36

Sand Hollow State Park ............... 37

Coral Pink Sand Dunes State Park ............................... 38

Snow Canyon State Park ............... 42

Gunlock State Park ............... 47

Frontier Homestead State Park Museum ............... 48

Cedar Breaks National Monument ............... 49

## South Central Utah 53

Bryce Canyon National Park 55

Grand Staircase-Escalante National Monument ............... 62

Escalante Petrified Forest State Park .............................. 76

Kodachrome Basin State Park 77

Anasazi State Park Museum 79

Capitol Reef National Park 80

Glen Canyon National Recreation Area 93

Rainbow Bridge National Monument ............. 100

## Southeast Utah ....... 101

Goblin Valley State Park ............. 103

Canyonlands National Park Island in the Sky District 106

Canyonlands National Park Needles District ............. 114

*The Great Gallery, Horseshoe Canyon, Maze District of Canyonlands National Park*


Canyonlands National Park
Maze District ........................... 121

Dead Horse Point
State Park ........................... 123

Arches National Park ............ 126

Goosenecks State Park ............ 134

Edge of the Cedars
State Park ........................... 136

Natural Bridges
National Monument ............ 137

Hovenweep
National Monument ............ 142

Four Corners Monument ........... 145

## South West Colorado . 147

Mesa Verde
National Park ........................... 148

Canyons of the Ancients
National Monument ............ 158

Yucca House
National Monument ............ 159

## Northern Arizona ...... 160

Monument Valley
Navajo Tribal Park ............ 161

Navajo
National Monument ............ 164

Antelope Canyon ............ 168

Vermilion Cliffs
National Monument ............ 171

Grand Canyon
National Park - South Rim ......... 182

Grand Canyon
National Park - North Rim......... 193

Havasu Falls ........................... 199

# Parks Covered in This Book

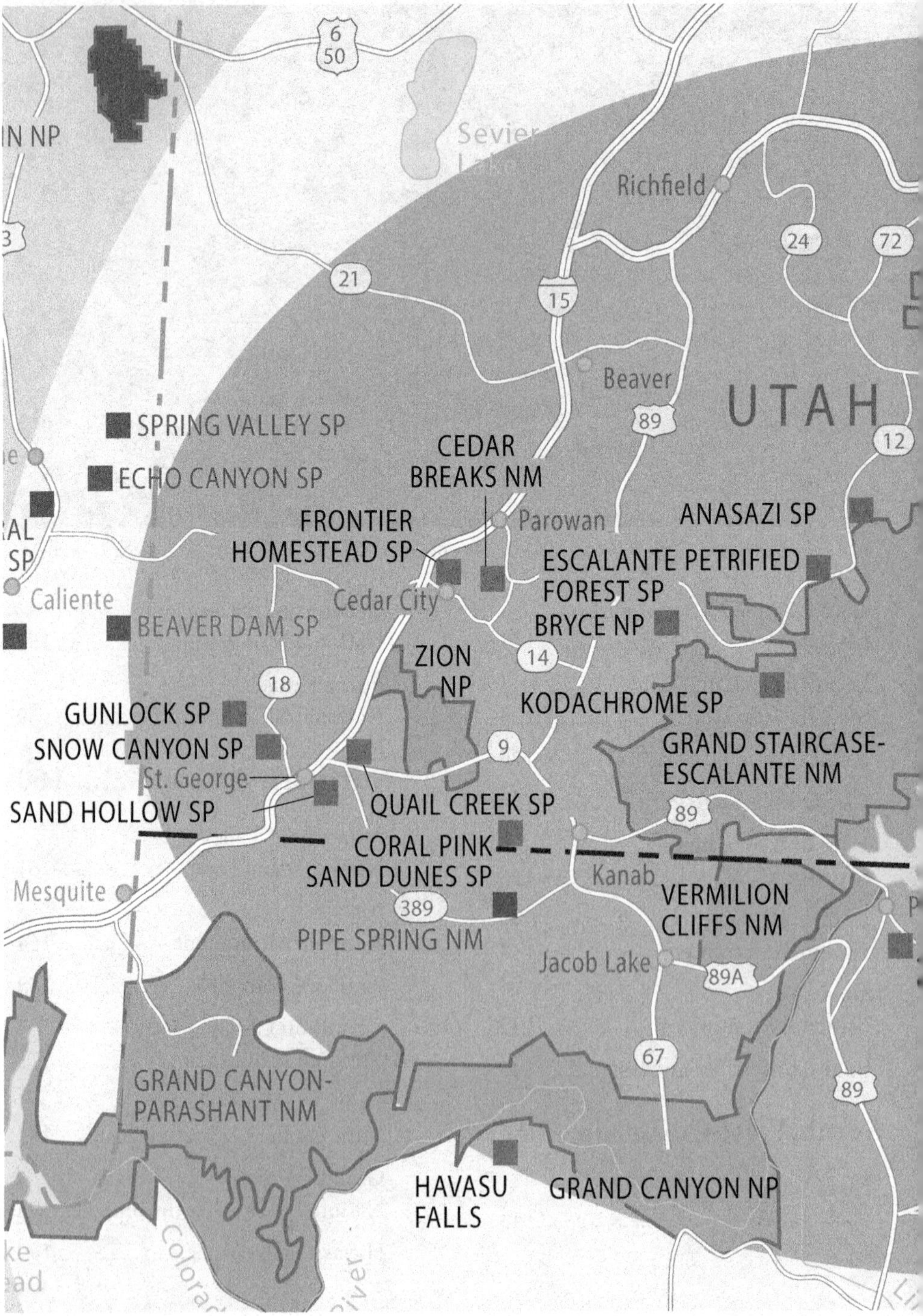

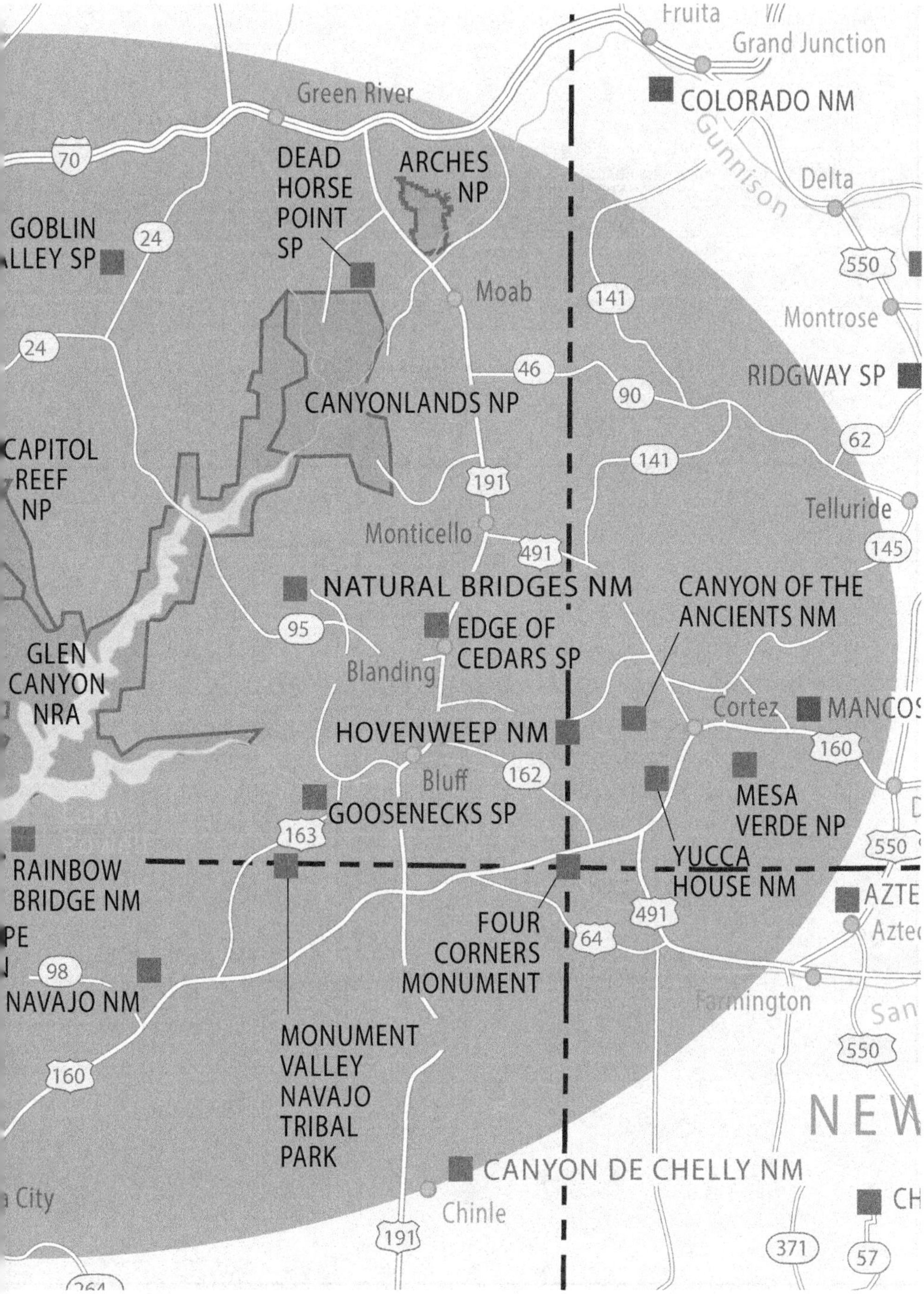
Fruita
Grand Junction
COLORADO NM
Gunnison
Delta
550
Montrose
RIDGWAY SP
62
Telluride
145
Green River
70
DEAD HORSE POINT SP
ARCHES NP
GOBLIN VALLEY SP
24
Moab
141
46
90
CANYONLANDS NP
141
191
CAPITOL REEF NP
Monticello
491
NATURAL BRIDGES NM
CANYON OF THE ANCIENTS NM
95
EDGE OF CEDARS SP
Blanding
GLEN CANYON NRA
Cortez
MANCOS
HOVENWEEP NM
160
Bluff
162
MESA VERDE NP
GOOSENECKS SP
163
550
RAINBOW BRIDGE NM
YUCCA HOUSE NM
FOUR CORNERS MONUMENT
491
64
Aztec
98
NAVAJO NM
Farmington
MONUMENT VALLEY NAVAJO TRIBAL PARK
550
160
NEW
CANYON DE CHELLY NM
Chinle
191
371
57

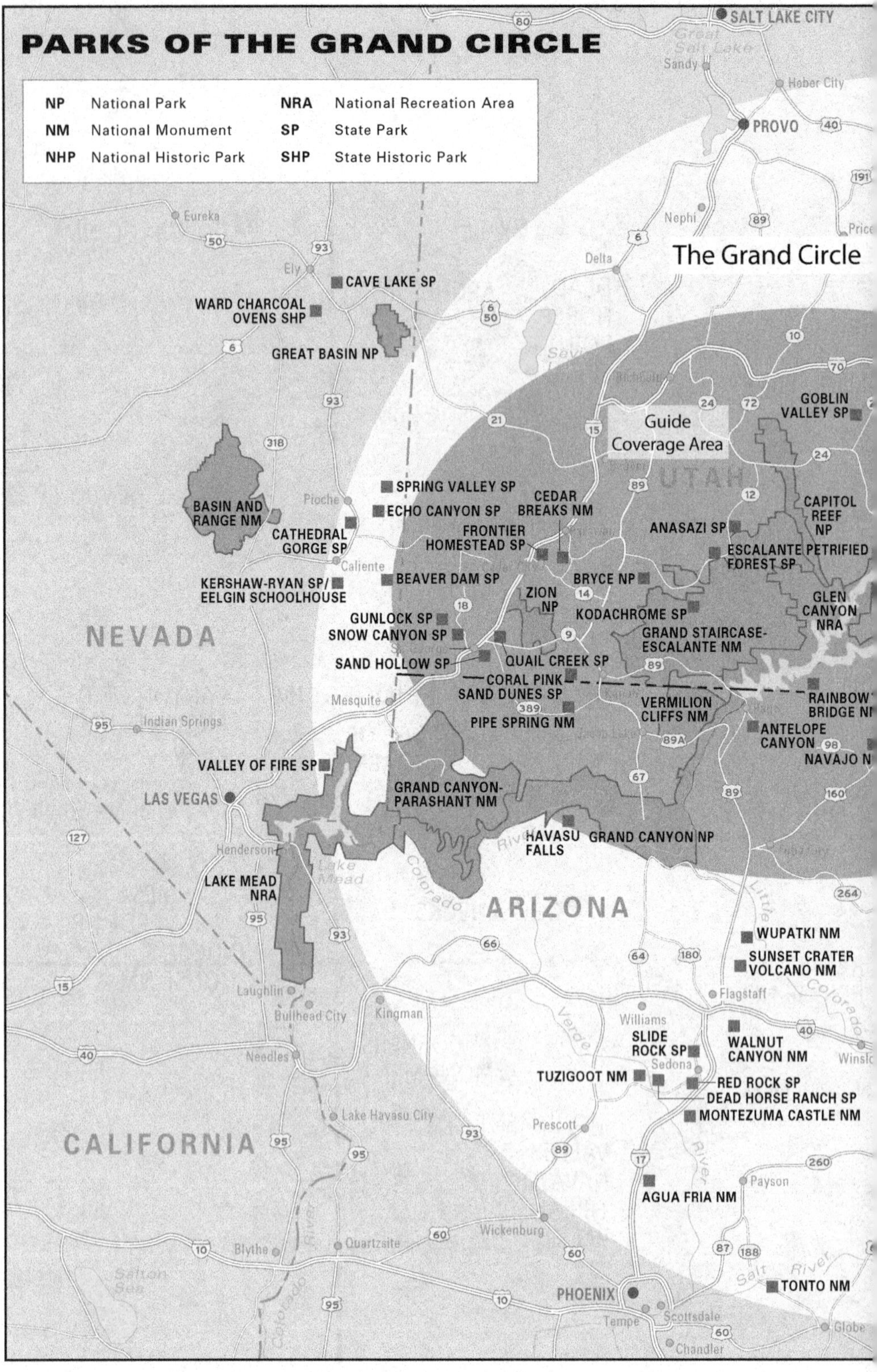
PARKS OF THE GRAND CIRCLE
NP National Park
NM National Monument
NHP National Historic Park
NRA National Recreation Area
SP State Park
SHP State Historic Park
The Grand Circle
Guide Coverage Area
SALT LAKE CITY
PROVO
NEVADA
UTAH
ARIZONA
CALIFORNIA
LAS VEGAS
PHOENIX
CAVE LAKE SP
WARD CHARCOAL OVENS SHP
GREAT BASIN NP
BASIN AND RANGE NM
SPRING VALLEY SP
ECHO CANYON SP
CATHEDRAL GORGE SP
KERSHAW-RYAN SP/ EELGIN SCHOOLHOUSE
BEAVER DAM SP
CEDAR BREAKS NM
FRONTIER HOMESTEAD SP
GUNLOCK SP
SNOW CANYON SP
SAND HOLLOW SP
ZION NP
BRYCE NP
KODACHROME SP
QUAIL CREEK SP
CORAL PINK SAND DUNES SP
PIPE SPRING NM
GOBLIN VALLEY SP
CAPITOL REEF NP
ANASAZI SP
ESCALANTE PETRIFIED FOREST SP
GLEN CANYON NRA
GRAND STAIRCASE-ESCALANTE NM
VERMILION CLIFFS NM
RAINBOW BRIDGE NM
ANTELOPE CANYON
NAVAJO NM
VALLEY OF FIRE SP
GRAND CANYON-PARASHANT NM
HAVASU FALLS
GRAND CANYON NP
LAKE MEAD NRA
WUPATKI NM
SUNSET CRATER VOLCANO NM
WALNUT CANYON NM
SLIDE ROCK SP
TUZIGOOT NM
RED ROCK SP
DEAD HORSE RANCH SP
MONTEZUMA CASTLE NM
AGUA FRIA NM
TONTO NM
Eureka
Ely
Pioche
Caliente
Mesquite
Indian Springs
Henderson
Laughlin
Bullhead City
Kingman
Needles
Lake Havasu City
Blythe
Quartzsite
Wickenburg
Prescott
Williams
Flagstaff
Sedona
Payson
Scottsdale
Tempe
Chandler
Globe
Nephi
Delta
Sandy
Heber City
Lake Mead
Colorado River
Verde River
Salt River

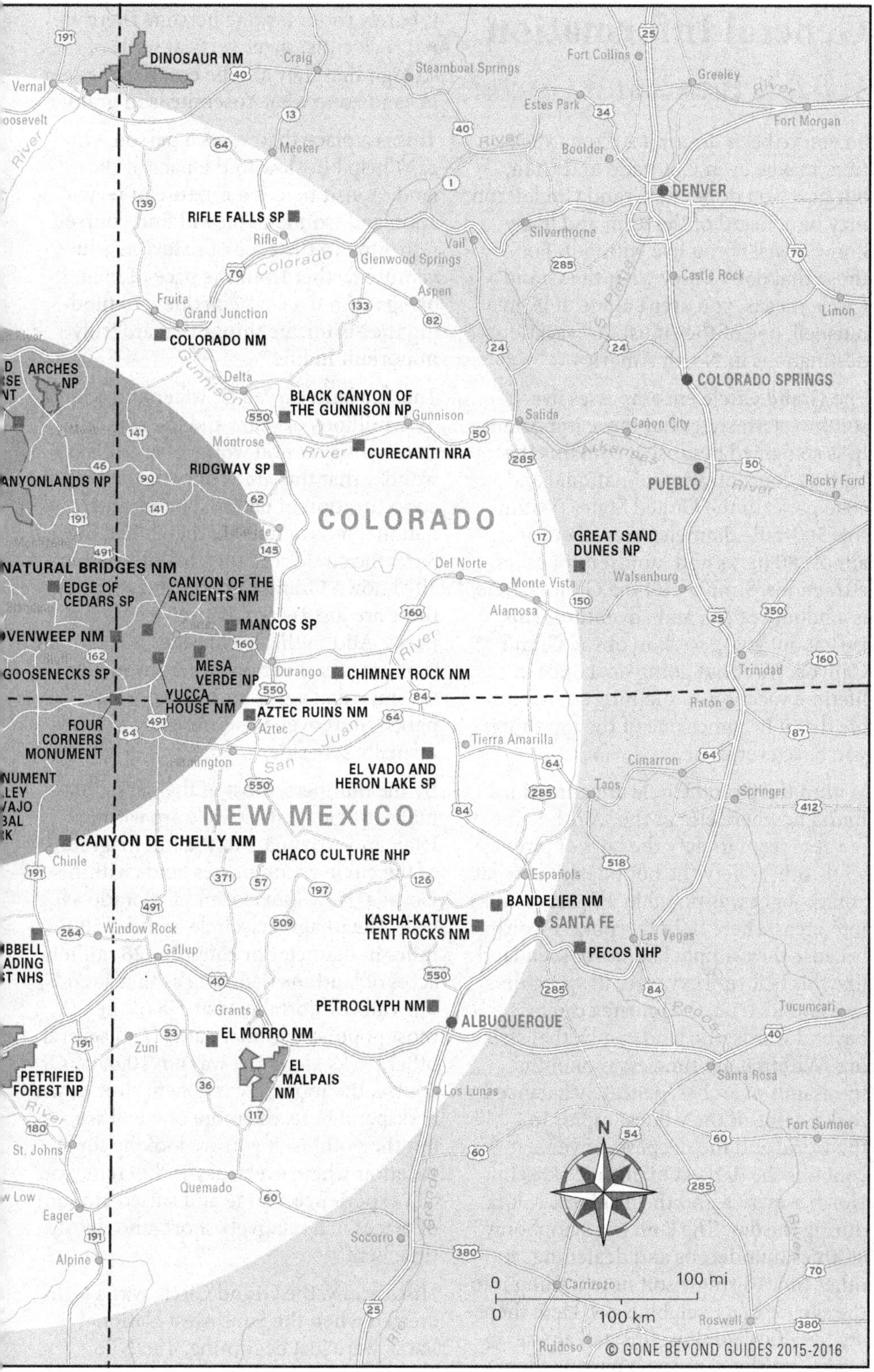
DINOSAUR NM
Craig
Steamboat Springs
Fort Collins
Greeley
Vernal
Estes Park
Fort Morgan
Meeker
Boulder
DENVER
RIFLE FALLS SP
Rifle
Silverthorne
Vail
Colorado
Glenwood Springs
Castle Rock
Aspen
Fruita
Grand Junction
Limon
COLORADO NM
ARCHES NP
Delta
Gunnison
COLORADO SPRINGS
BLACK CANYON OF THE GUNNISON NP
Gunnison
Salida
Montrose
Cañon City
CURECANTI NRA
RIDGWAY SP
PUEBLO
Rocky Ford
Arkansas River
ANYONLANDS NP
COLORADO
GREAT SAND DUNES NP
NATURAL BRIDGES NM
Del Norte
Monte Vista
Walsenburg
EDGE OF CEDARS SP
CANYON OF THE ANCIENTS NM
Alamosa
MANCOS SP
VENWEEP NM
MESA VERDE NP
Trinidad
GOOSENECKS SP
Durango
CHIMNEY ROCK NM
YUCCA HOUSE NM
Raton
FOUR CORNERS MONUMENT
AZTEC RUINS NM
Aztec
Tierra Amarilla
San Juan
Cimarron
EL VADO AND HERON LAKE SP
Taos
Springer
NEW MEXICO
CANYON DE CHELLY NM
Chinle
CHACO CULTURE NHP
Española
BANDELIER NM
KASHA-KATUWE TENT ROCKS NM
SANTA FE
Window Rock
Las Vegas
Gallup
PECOS NHP
PETROGLYPH NM
Tucumcari
Grants
ALBUQUERQUE
EL MORRO NM
Zuni
Santa Rosa
PETRIFIED FOREST NP
EL MALPAIS NM
Los Lunas
St. Johns
Fort Sumner
N
Quemado
Eager
Socorro
Alpine
Carrizozo
0
100 mi
0
100 km
Roswell
Ruidoso
© GONE BEYOND GUIDES 2015-2016

# General Information

## What is the Grand Circle?

So you've been done an Arizona vacation, maybe even Colorado and Utah, but have you done the Grand Circle? You may have heard of the term and likely know it well if you live within it. For those that don't know what the Grand Circle means, you aren't alone. It is, in a nutshell, one of the "must do" vacation destinations in North America.

The Grand Circle encompasses five southwestern states but more importantly, is so named because it contains the highest concentration of national and state parks in the United States. Within this 500-mile diameter area, there are almost 80 parks and hundreds of other attractions. Simply put, the Grand Circle is a bounty of fun and adventure. This isn't about going to Zion or the Grand Canyon, it's about going on a once in a lifetime vacation, something so incredible that it becomes one of the top things you have ever done.

Within the Grand Circle are attractions found nowhere else in the world. Some of these seem to defy the laws of physics while others defy the boundaries of what you thought was possible. I've taken folks into areas where nobody spoke a word because they simply had never seen land like this before. They were in speechless awe and it's true, the journey can be beyond words, the land can be that striking. Within it are timeless monoliths, thousands of arches, delicately balanced rocks, some of the wildest rapids in the world and the deepest canyons. It contains the darkest nighttime skies in North America and the brightest colors during the day. The land is a symphony, at times thunderous and deafening, at other times a single soft note trailing into the silence of a deep blue sky. Here there are hoodoos, goblins, fins, tall alpine peaks and slot canyon so narrow there is barely room for one person. There are red rock cliffs, sheer vertical walls of rock so high that they are the emotional equal in sandstone what Yosemite is in granite.

This is a place that resets a person. One can't help but slow to the pace of the land. A visit here is a mixture of relaxation and wonder. You will find yourself returning to the pace of nature as you venture farther from the pace of man. It brings with it a connectedness reminding the visitor the things that are truly important in life.

This is a land carved by water and wind over millions of years and the results are astounding natural works of art. It is no wonder that this area contains the largest concentration of national parks and national monuments in the United States. Sure, the circle contains the internationally known Grand Canyon and Zion, but these are just two of its twelve national parks. Add to this list another 30 national monuments, 3 national recreation areas, several tribal parks and 29 more state parks. Moreover, these are just the lands formally set aside.

By the numbers, most of the parks that make up the Grand Circle are within Utah and Arizona, but the full magnitude of the circle encompasses lands within Nevada, New Mexico, and Colorado as well. The imaginary circle is about 500 miles in diameter or roughly 126 million acres of land. As daunting as that sounds, one can comfortably visit 7-8 of the most popular national parks (and several other parks along the way) in 10 days. Of course, the more one is able to slow down and spend here, the more one will see, but the point is, if you are looking for a vacation where every day is different, you can experience a large and varied amount of places in a relatively short amount of time here.

Historically, the Grand Circle was a term created when the Southwest National Parks were just beginning. The NPS worked with the Union Pacific Railway and created trips by rail and bus up until the 1970's. Back then, a trip to the Grand Circle was a time of great adventure and romance. There were dance bands at the stops and as your tour bus would drive away from the lodge, employees would line up and "sing away" the visitors. Today, it remains one of the best vacations in North America that one can take. This is a vacation destination of adventure, relaxation, and wonder. It is a land that humbles, inspires, and refreshes the spirit and for those that know of it, they have the Grand Circle as a bucket list place to experience at least once in their lives. The term Grand Circle is a great term to describe this land.

*Thors Hammer, Bryce Canyon NP*

## When to Go

There are really only two factors on when to go, do you like temperate climates or would you prefer less people. Weather plays a hand in both but in different ways.

In general, the Grand Circle is a blisteringly hot place in the summer, starting in mid to late June and going full force through August. That doesn't seem to keep folks away, particularly if you have kids out for the school year. Temperature wise though, the best time to go is during the spring/early summer and fall/early winter. Elevation is another consideration. High elevation parks such as Bryce and Great Basin are typically cooler in the summer than say Canyonlands or Lake Powell.

In terms of going at a time when the crowds have thinned, the best times to go are the dead of winter, followed by the dead of summer. Winter receives a lot fewer crowds for the obvious reasons. It's colder, snowier, and wetter. In fact, it tends to be the antithesis of what folks have in mind when they think of the southwest. That said, these parks in winter are perhaps when they are at their most spectacular. There is something transformative about a dusting of snow across the layered mesas and canyons or topping each hoodoo of Bryce. In fact, for places like Bryce, which receive tons of visitors each summer, the arguably best time to go is winter. I've been out on trails covered in snow on a crisp clear day with the entire park practically to myself.

Winter at any of the parks can be magical, but it does run the risk of being miserable. In fact, you could be snowed in, which isn't the worst thing that could happen to a person, but can be difficult if your boss is expecting you back at work. In addition, some of the parks are simply closed in the winter.

The dead of summer is a good second choice as it is usually too hot for most. That said, given kids are out of school at this time, there are many whose lifestyles gives them nothing else to work with, so it can still be crowded. The parks in summer can be too hot to hike in during the heat of the day, so for those that take this tactic, get in the habit of hitting the trails in the cool of early morning.

## Where to Go

If you think about it, there is a fair amount of irony in guidebooks that tell you the best places to go to avoid crowds. They are basically saying, we've learned all these secret cool places that no one goes to and we are now publishing this information in a globally available guidebook for anyone to read. If you see one of these sections, don't believe it, the word is already out on all these "secret places". In fact, places such as Havasu Falls are so impacted, it is nearly impossible to get a permit to hike the trail.

That said, there are some general tips to getting an otherwise crowded national park or monument to yourself. Take the Grand Canyon for example. This park receives some 4.5 million visitors to the South Rim alone. The vast majority of these folks don't hike any farther than to the overlooks. So simply getting out on any trail cuts the population of the park down by about 90%. If you've purchased this book, that means you like to hike, so you are on good footing right from the start.

There are other tips to share. In general, I've found that the more strenuous the hike is, the harder the trail is to get to, and the longer the trail's length, the greater the chances you will have the trail to yourself. If the trail is a short little paved walkway with interpretive signs, be prepared to share it. If it is one of the routes described in these guides, so rugged there isn't even a trail, be prepared to survive on your own because you are likely the only one out that way.

The same can be said about weather. Heat, rain, snow, and cold tend to filter out a fair amount of people. What's amazing about this is sometimes inclement weather will bring out the most unique views of a trail you will likely ever see. Now keep you in mind that you should add in a large degree of common sense. You don't want to have a slot canyon "all to yourself" in a thunderstorm or hike in the direct heat of a summer's day unless you are fully prepared and acclimated. Don't be stupid in your quest to have the place to yourself. The point here is, in general I've found a rather obvious truth. If a guidebook says it's secret, it isn't. The more remote a place is, the longer the hike, the steeper the inclines, the more extreme the journey, these all act as filters to minimizing the crowd factor.

## Being Prepared

Hiking in the Grand Circle can be highly rewarding. However, don't let the desert fool you. This is an extreme environment, and one shouldn't just venture out without some forethought and preparation. This section seems straightforward, but as the rangers at the Grand Canyon can attest to, there are literally dozens of people that venture out into the wilderness with nothing more than enthusiasm. Since enthusiasm alone can really put a damper on your hike, here are some tips to make your hikes safer and more enjoyable.

### Water

Rule of thumb; bring three quarts per person per day. Some folks prefer two 1.5-liter bottles; some find they can balance their day or backpacks out better with three 1.0-liter bottles. Make sure the bottles do not leak by turning them upside down to see if water comes out. If it's only a drip, it's still a problem.

Water is pretty heavy, but bringing more rather than less keeps you hydrated and allows you to go farther.

If you are traveling with small children, you will likely need to carry their water for them beyond one quart. Keep this in mind as you are packing.

### Clothing

Bring layers as appropriate for the hike. This means if the temperatures are cooler when you are at rest; bring a layer or two to keep you warm. Windbreakers are great allies in keeping warmth in and cold out and are also lightweight. In really cold temps a good beanie helps as well as some 15% of your body temperature is lost through your head. If it looks like rain, bring a waterproof version of that windbreaker.

In the heat, most folks go with the t-shirt and shorts, which is fine, but definitely bring a hat. The heat can be oppressing, especially with no shade and that hat will definitely help. I also recommend a full brimmed hat over a baseball cap. This will provide more shade and definitely helps keep the back of your neck from getting sunburned.

In either hot or cold weather, bring another warm layer if you can. This is your emergency backup layer should you find

*Tower of Babel, Arches National Park*

*Springtime in Zion National Park*

yourself having to spend the night in the wilderness for whatever reason. A windbreaker that can be rolled up or a long sleeve shirt can make a big difference if you find yourself facing the setting sun with nothing but a t-shirt and shorts on a summer trip. I've also found it to be a good thing to have on hand for others that may need some warmth when you don't.

## Boots, Tennis and Water Shoes

Most people will tend to go for their tennis shoes because they are comfortable and easier to lace up. That said, boots are preferred because they offer a lot more protection, especially around the ankles. Tennis shoes are great for flat surfaces, but boots are made for uneven terrain. It's like taking a sedan tire on a 4WD road instead of an all-terrain tire. You wouldn't do it to your car, don't do it to your feet. Where a good boot and also, be the boot. Wear it in before you start your hiking adventures so you don't get blisters.

If the trail involves some hiking in water, it really helps to have a pair of water shoes. They are lightweight and keep your boots dry. A dry boot makes for a happy hiker, whereas a wet boot can destroy your feet in short order.

## Daypack

A decent no nonsense day back to hold everything is essential. At the end of the day, you just want something that will last a long time. The more parts the pack has, the more parts that can fail. Zipper quality is number one. Most otherwise solid daypacks fail because of the zipper.

Also, a little tip on the daypack. If you get one that zips like an upside down U, put the zippers on one side or the other, not at the top. I have seen and personally had a branch find its way between the two zippers at top and open the entire contents of the pack onto the trail. In my case, it opened on brushy 30-degree incline I was scrambling up and I watched my lunch and water roll downhill out of sight forever.

## Other Gear

At this point, you have three quarts of water, a bunch of layers, some food, and no room for anything else right. Well, it can seem that way. What to bring is a balancing act. On the one hand, you want to be lightweight. The more stuff you have on your back, the more burdensome it will feel. On the other hand, you do want to be prepared. In the excellent book, Climbing Ice by Yvon Chouinard, he says something that is about as true a piece of advice I've ever heard in this context.

If you bring it, you will use it.

What this means is if you bring a sleeping bag, you will likely spend the night in it. If you bring rope, you will likely use that rope. So start with packing only what you need for the hike.

## Essentials include:

- Water and some food
- A hat
- Extra clothing as appropriate
- Sunscreen
- A map and possibly this trail guide (if you feel you will need it to navigate the trail)

On top of this, I would seriously consider also bringing:

- Some form of fire, a lighter, or fire starter of some kind
- Compass
- Small first aid kit, a whistle, and reflector mirror (for emergencies)
- A sharp knife
- Moleskin (for blisters)
- Ibuprofen (to help if you aren't acclimated to the heat)
- Water purification tablets
- Small flashlight
- Cell phone
- GPS device

It's hard to come up with a list that works under all conditions and the above list is more geared towards summer hiking than winter, so adjust what you bring for cold, rain, or snow. Also, be sure to bring something fun, a little treat goes a long way and is much better appreciated on the trail. This falls under "being kind to yourself" which is described below.

# Know Yourself

## Gung Ho-ness

Many of these trails are steep and long. Add in that you are at high elevations and the temperatures are hot means many of the hikes in this book can be challenging. With that in mind, choose a hike that is appropriate for you. You will enjoy the hike more and plus; you will be able to go on another hike the next day. Know your physical limitations and don't test them to the point that you will need to be rescued.

## Find your pace

Great hiking partners are not only experienced; they are great for each other because they both travel at the same pace. Start by finding your own pace and ask others to share that pace with you. If you are the faster traveler, slow down to the pace of the other person or group.

## Take Breaks, Eat Snacks

Taking a ten-minute break every hour actually improves your stamina, allowing you to enjoy the hike more and go longer. Resting helps remove metabolic waste products such as lactic acid and gives your body time to flush them out. Eating snacks and drinking fluids helps refuel your body so you can continue onwards happy and content.

## Time Flies

Being stuck on the trail after the sun sets isn't much fun, well unless there's a full moon out and no canopy to block the light. That can actually be a lot of fun and is highly recommended. Wait, the point I'm trying to make here is if you are out in the wilderness, watch your time and be aware of how long it took you to get to your turn around point. If the trail starts as a major descent, some of the steeper trails require twice as much time for returning up then it took getting down. The Grand Canyon is a good example of this. Being stuck in areas where the temperature drops dramatically at night is also a concern. Here, the The Narrows hike in Zion is a great example. Also, if you think you might be caught out in the dark, having a little flashlight, per person, can be a lifesaver.

## Don't be afraid to abort the trip

If you or another hiker is showing signs of exhaustion, heat stroke, hypothermia or if the weather doesn't look like its adding up right, don't hesitate to turn back. Typically, these trips are planned far in advance and there is plenty of anticipation and excitement, but nothing is worth serious health issues or worse from not making the right decision. If someone doesn't feel they are up to a hike or someone in the group feels they may be putting themselves in danger, take their concerns seriously. Heat stroke and hypothermia can get serious and can lead to death.

Hypothermia, altitude sickness, and heat exhaustion have nothing to do with physical ability. I've seen firsthand the symptoms of each of these health issues and everyone that experienced them started out in terrific shape. It can hit hard and quickly. The typical "first signs" that I've seen are loss of mental sharpness and generally just out of it. The victim appears drunk and off, but otherwise may seem "themselves" at times. Don't second-guess here, if your buddy isn't acting like his or her normal self; stop, assess and remediate the issue. Don't keep pressing on.

# The Hazardous H's + Altitude Sickness

The below is put out by the National Park Service and gives a good overview of some of the health issues to look out for while hiking. Since some of the trails within the Grand Circle are at altitude, a description of altitude sickness or acute mountain sickness (AMS) is also included.

## Heat Exhaustion

The result of dehydration due to intense sweating. Hikers can lose one or two quarts (liters) of water per hour.

Symptoms: pale face, nausea, vomiting, cool and moist skin, headache, cramps.

Treatment: drink water with electrolytes, eat high-energy foods (with fats and sugars), rest in the shade for 30-45 minutes, and cool the body by getting wet.

## Heatstroke

A life-threatening emergency where the body's heat regulating mechanisms become overwhelmed by a combination of internal heat production and environmental demands. Your body loses its ability to cool itself. Grand Canyon has two to three cases of heatstroke a year. Untreated heat exhaustion can lead to heatstroke.

Symptoms: flushed face, dry skin, weak and rapid pulse, high core body temperature, confusion, poor judgment or inability to cope, unconsciousness, seizures.

Treatment: the heatstroke victim must be cooled immediately! Continuously pour water on the victim's head and torso, fan

*Canyonlands National Park*

to create an evaporative cooling effect. Immerse the victim in cold water if possible. Move the victim to shade and remove excess clothing. The victim needs evacuation to a hospital. Someone should go for help while attempts to cool the victim continue.

## Hyponatremia (water intoxication)

An illness that mimics the early symptoms of heat exhaustion. It is the result of low sodium in the blood caused by drinking too much water and losing too much salt through sweating.

Symptoms: nausea, vomiting, altered mental states, confusion, frequent urination. The victim may appear intoxicated. In extreme cases seizures may occur.

Treatment: have the victim eat salty foods, slowly drink sports drinks with electrolytes, and rest in the shade. If mental alertness decreases, seek immediate help!

## Hypothermia

A life-threatening emergency where the body cannot keep itself warm, due to exhaustion and exposure to cold, wet, windy weather.

Symptoms: uncontrolled shivering, poor muscle control, careless attitude. Look for signs of the "umbles" - stumbling, mumbling, fumbling, grumbling.

Treatment: remove wet clothing and put on dry clothing, drink warm sugary liquids, warm victim by body contact with another person, protect from wind, rain, and cold.

## Altitude Sickness

Altitude sickness is your body not being able to acclimate to altitude. If untreated, it can lead to high altitude pulmonary oedema (HAPE) which is a life threatening condition where your lungs fill with fluid, making it difficult to breath. It can also lead to high altitude cerebral oedema (HACE), which is a buildup of fluid in your brain. Both can cause death within hours if not treated.

Symptoms: The most common symptom is typically a headache similar to that felt with a hangover. Some folks will feel nausea and may vomit as well as a general malaise feeling, and dizziness.

Treatment: If you are experiencing AMS, the best and only treatment is descending. Altitude sickness is not uncommon, especially if you have ascended in elevation too fast, starting at elevations of 8200 feet (2500 m). While it is common, some people are only slightly affected, while others feel so bad they have to turn around. For all, even those slightly affected, be self-aware as it can lead to pulmonary and cerebral oedema, which are very serious conditions.

## If You Get Lost

Daniel Boone once said, "I have never been lost, but I will admit to being confused for several weeks." If you do get lost, you will quickly realize you aren't Daniel Boone and wished you had of paid more attention to all those nifty tricks you might have seen on those survival shows. Never fear, this book might just save you. Read the following tips if you happen to get lost.

- Stay calm. The sun's setting and you still haven't found the trail, let alone your car. This is not a time to freak out. Take some deep breaths and stay calm. You will get through this. I realize if you are freaking out, reading this won't help one bit. I recommend rereading the first sentence in this bullet point until it makes sense. Once you are thinking rationally, continue to the next bullet.
- Ration water and food. Stay hungry, ration your water, don't eat and drink everything at once.
- Readjust your schedule to maximize for hydration. Water loss has now become your biggest enemy. This means hiking during the cool of the morning and evening, while hunkering down at mid-day. Aim for shade and stay put during the heat of the day. Remember, the power of threes when it comes to survival. Though you will be incredibly hungry, you can survive three weeks without food. For water, that time period is only three days (and for air, three minutes). Water loss is the biggest barrier to you surviving or not if you are lost in the desert.
- Make a plan. If you have a compass, see a landmark, can get a sense of direction from the sun, use all these things to help make a plan of action. This starts by staying calm. With calmness, you can think. In thought, you can assess what you know (and what you don't know). From this catalog of observations, you can make a plan. Try to remain rational and fact based in your observations, its okay to make an assumption, but assess how confident you are of these assumptions.
- Stay at an even calm pace, pick your path. Look ahead to where you want to go, aim for paths of least resistance and effort versus paths that are harder to get through, if possible. Don't rush your walking, stay calm.
- Follow a road, a trail, or a route. If you see a road or a trail, take it. You have greatly increased your chances of being found or finding a way out yourself.
- Stay off the ground during the day. Finding shade is important when resting as the ground temperature can by 30 degrees hotter than the air temperature.
- Hike together at the pace of the slowest member and only separate if someone is injured.
- Stay with your car. If you are near your car, stay with it. It will make finding you easier and will provide shade, shelter and hopefully some food.

# Southwest Utah

Zion National Park ........ 18
Quail Creek State Park ........ 36
Sand Hollow State Park ........ 37
Coral Pink Sand Dunes State Park ........ 38
Snow Canyon State Park ........ 42
Gunlock State Park ........ 47
Frontier Homestead State Park Museum ........ 48
Cedar Breaks National Monument ........ 49


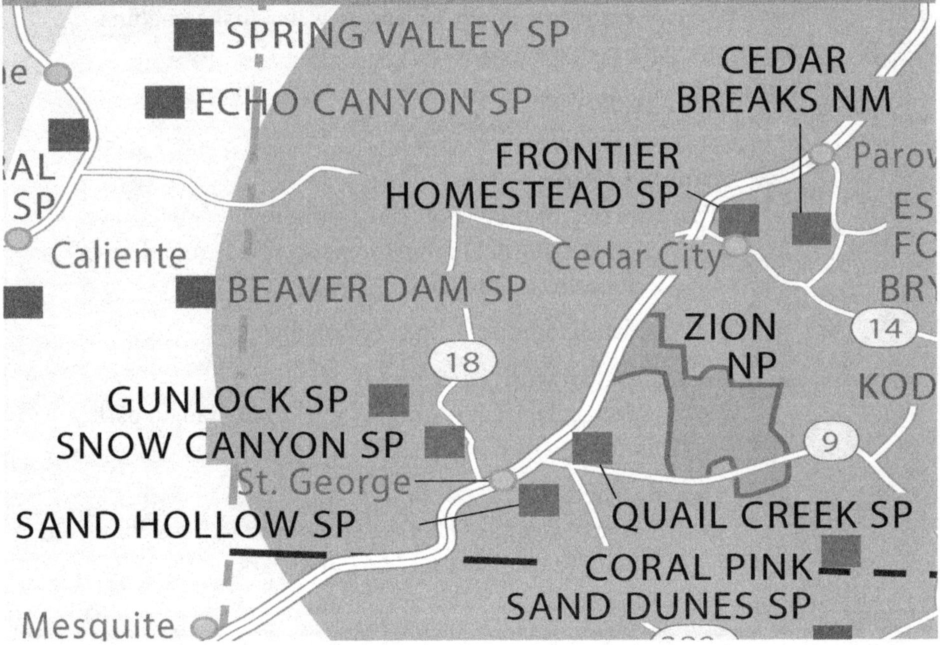

# Zion National Park

## Quick Facts

**Official Park Website:** www.nps.gov/zion

**Visitor Center:**

(435) 772-3256

**Park Accessibility:**

- Okay for 2WD and RVs
- Day and Overnight Use

**Experience Level:**

- Family Friendly to Experienced Hiker

*Within The Narrows*

**Camping in Park:**

- Watchman: 176 T/RV, 2 ADA, 6 group sites, host on site, water, hookups, reservations at www.recreation.gov or by calling (877) 444-6777
- South: 127 T/RV, 3 ADA, host on site, water, no hookups, first come/first served, open seasonally
- Lava Point: 6T, Pit Toilets, no water, first come/first served, open seasonally

**Lodging in Park:**

- Zion Lodge: (888) 297-2757

**Dining in Park:**

There are two options, both at Zion Lodge

- Red Rock Grill Dining Room, open year round, reservations recommended, (435) 772-3213
- Castle Dome Café, open seasonally

**Nearest Town with Amenities:**

- Springdale, Utah is within 1 mi / 2 km of main park entrance

**Getting There:**

- From St George, UT: Take I-15 North to UT-9 East. Total distance is 41 mi / 66 km to park

## What Makes Zion Special

- The afternoon light striking wall after wall of massive 2,000-foot red rock cliffs extending into a deep river canyon
- The Narrows, a hike whose trail is the Virgin River itself in a slot canyon over fifteen hundred feet tall
- Hiking Angels Landing, a hike hewn into cliff walls to the top of the canyon for stunning views

Zion National Park has a lot of "Wow" factor and for good reason. The entire Colorado Plateau was once a massive sand dune in line with the current Sarah Desert. As with any set of sand dunes, there is one area where the winds are just right and the dunes are at their highest. For the Colorado Plateau, those highest dunes were where Zion sits today and as a result, when the mechanics of geology turned those dunes into sandstone, it left the area with some really big chunks of rock to play with. Enter water and wind, which cut into the stone over millions of years, leaving sheer cliffs of epic rock in hues of reds, oranges and tans. There are many singular words to describe Zion, stunning, humbling, majestic, and even heavenly. Whatever one word that comes to mind, there are really no words that give this place a proper description. You just have to go and see it.

*Angels Landing*

## Hiking in the Main Park

### Pa'rus Trail

Easy – (3.5 mi / 5.6 km), round trip, allow 2 hours, elev. Δ: 50 ft / 15 m, trailheads at South Campground and Canyon Junction

Pa'rus, which is from the Paiute language, means bubbling, tumbling water. The name describes this trail well as it meanders along the Virgin River. The trail is paved and thus accessible for those with wheelchairs. Pa'rus starts at the visitor center and heads upstream at a very slight incline. The surrounding cliffs and valley open up throughout the journey.

There are several places along the way that provide beach access to the river and it is not uncommon to see families enjoying the heat of the day by cooling off in the water. Pa'rus trail crosses six bridges as it makes its way to trail's end at Canyon Junction. From here you can hike back (downhill all the way) or pick up the shuttle to your next destination. Dogs and bikes are welcome on this trail.

### Watchman Trail

Moderate – (3.3 mi / 5.3 km), round trip, allow 2 hours, elev. Δ: 368 ft / 112 m, trailhead near visitor center

If you are looking to get higher up for better views but don't want to climb the 2,000 feet or so to the top of the rim, the Watchman Trail is a good alternative. The trail starts at the Zion Canyon Visitor Center and ends at a mesa top that gives some commanding views of Zion NP and even a glimpse of the Towers of the Virgin and the town of Springdale.

The trail begins by following along the banks of the North Fork of the Virgin River and then juts away from the water to connect to a series of moderate switchbacks that wind their way to the top of the mesa. There is a nominal 368 feet elevation gain, but the views are worth every step. Once at the mesa top there is a half-

# ZION NATIONAL PARK

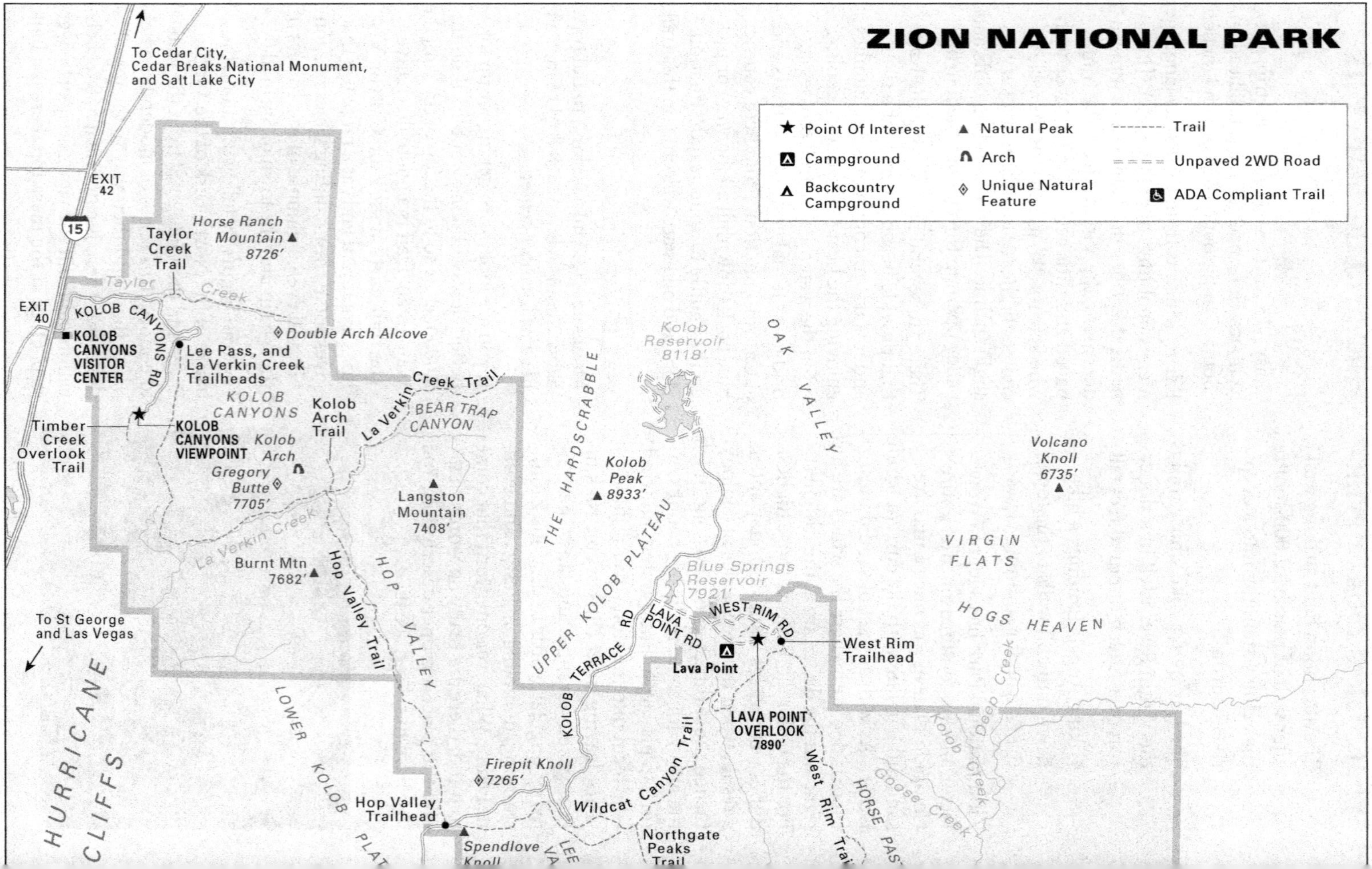
Point Of Interest
Campground
Backcountry Campground
Natural Peak
Arch
Unique Natural Feature
Trail
Unpaved 2WD Road
ADA Compliant Trail
To Cedar City, Cedar Breaks National Monument, and Salt Lake City
EXIT 42
15
EXIT 40
Horse Ranch Mountain 8726'
Taylor Creek Trail
Taylor Creek
KOLOB CANYONS RD
KOLOB CANYONS VISITOR CENTER
Double Arch Alcove
Lee Pass, and La Verkin Creek Trailheads
KOLOB CANYONS
Kolob Arch Trail
La Verkin Creek Trail
BEAR TRAP CANYON
Timber Creek Overlook Trail
KOLOB CANYONS VIEWPOINT
Kolob Arch
Gregory Butte 7705'
Langston Mountain 7408'
La Verkin Creek
Burnt Mtn 7682'
Hop Valley Trail
HOP VALLEY
To St George and Las Vegas
HURRICANE CLIFFS
LOWER KOLOB PLATEAU
Hop Valley Trailhead
Spendlove Knoll
LEE VALLEY
Firepit Knoll 7265'
Wildcat Canyon Trail
Northgate Peaks Trail
KOLOB TERRACE RD
UPPER KOLOB PLATEAU
THE HARDSCRABBLE
Kolob Peak 8933'
Kolob Reservoir 8118'
OAK VALLEY
Blue Springs Reservoir 7921'
LAVA POINT RD
WEST RIM RD
Lava Point
LAVA POINT OVERLOOK 7890'
West Rim Trailhead
West Rim Trail
HORSE PASTURE
Goose Creek
Kolob Creek
Deep Creek
Volcano Knoll 6735'
VIRGIN FLATS
HOGS HEAVEN

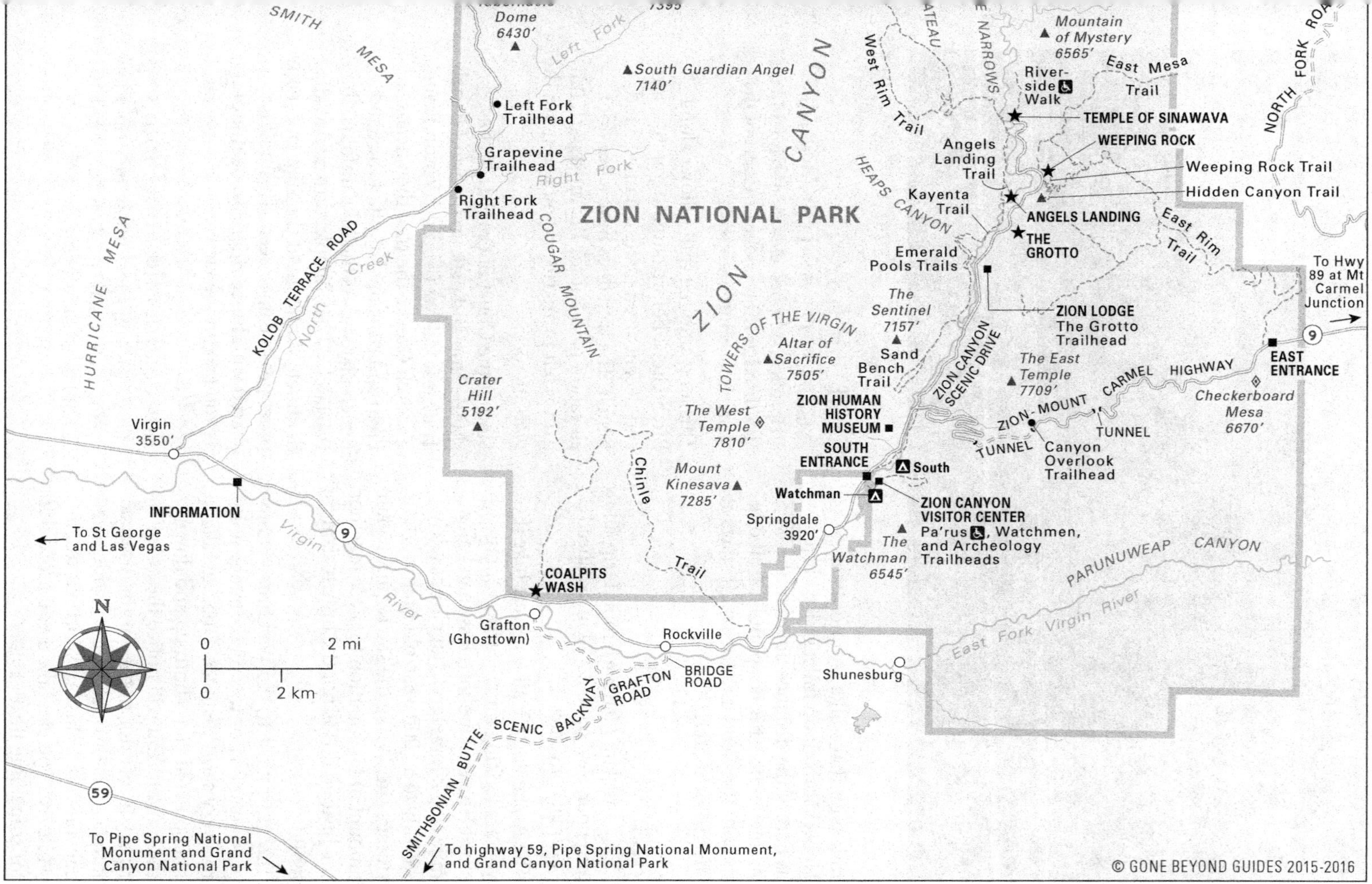
ZION NATIONAL PARK
ZION CANYON
SMITH MESA
HURRICANE MESA
KOLOB TERRACE ROAD
North Creek
Dome 6430'
Left Fork
South Guardian Angel 7140'
Left Fork Trailhead
Grapevine Trailhead
Right Fork
Right Fork Trailhead
COUGAR MOUNTAIN
Crater Hill 5192'
West Rim Trail
HEAPS CANYON
NARROWS
Mountain of Mystery 6565'
East Mesa Trail
Riverside Walk
TEMPLE OF SINAWAVA
WEEPING ROCK
Weeping Rock Trail
Hidden Canyon Trail
Angels Landing Trail
ANGELS LANDING
Kayenta Trail
THE GROTTO
East Rim Trail
NORTH FORK ROAD
Emerald Pools Trails
ZION LODGE
The Grotto Trailhead
To Hwy 89 at Mt Carmel Junction
9
EAST ENTRANCE
The Sentinel 7157'
TOWERS OF THE VIRGIN
Altar of Sacrifice 7505'
Sand Bench Trail
ZION CANYON SCENIC DRIVE
The East Temple 7709'
ZION-MOUNT CARMEL HIGHWAY
Checkerboard Mesa 6670'
TUNNEL
Canyon Overlook Trailhead
The West Temple 7810'
ZION HUMAN HISTORY MUSEUM
SOUTH ENTRANCE
South
Mount Kinesava 7285'
Chinle Trail
Watchman
ZION CANYON VISITOR CENTER
Pa'rus, Watchmen, and Archeology Trailheads
Springdale 3920'
The Watchman 6545'
PARUNUWEAP CANYON
East Fork Virgin River
Virgin 3550'
INFORMATION
To St George and Las Vegas
Virgin River
COALPITS WASH
Grafton (Ghosttown)
Rockville
BRIDGE ROAD
GRAFTON ROAD
Shunesburg
N
0
2 mi
0
2 km
SMITHSONIAN BUTTE SCENIC BACKWAY
59
To Pipe Spring National Monument and Grand Canyon National Park
To highway 59, Pipe Spring National Monument, and Grand Canyon National Park
© GONE BEYOND GUIDES 2015-2016

*Sunrise in Zion Canyon*

mile loop that walks around the edge. Note that the loop mileage isn't listed as part of the distance noted in the NPS hiking guide. This is a popular trail due to both the views and the fact it starts at the visitor center.

## Archeology Trail

Easy – (0.4 mi / 0.6 km), round trip, allow 0.5 hour, elev. Δ: 80 ft / 24 m, trailhead near visitor center

The Archeology Trail is a great hike if you are looking for an early evening stroll. The trail is short, less than half a mile (0.6 kilometers), but climbs fairly steadily to a 1000-year-old prehistoric storage site. While the site requires a fair amount of imagination to piece together the history, this is not the only reason for going.

The site is close to the Watchman campground and rises to a nice vantage point in a very short distance. One can take in phenomenal views both up and down the canyon. You will notice the green riparian corridor of the Virgin River as it meanders through an ever-widening canyon. In all, this is a short but worthwhile trek you can take if you are looking for something near camp.

## Sand Bench Trail

Moderate – (7.6 mi / 12.2 km), round trip, allow 5 hours, elev. Δ: 466 ft / 142 m, trailhead at Zion Lodge or Court of the Patriarchs shuttle stops

This long ambling trail follows along Birch Creek before climbing up to a long and decent sized plateau named Sand Bench. The trail does have a 466-foot elevation gain but for the most part, the gain is felt primarily as you ascend to the plateau.

Start at the Court of the Patriarchs shuttle stop and pick up the Sand Bench Trail as it follows from the Virgin River up Birch Creek. The trail then heads up to and runs the length of the Sand Bench plateau. As the hike unfolds, the Patriarchs, East Temple, Streaked Wall, Sentinel, Mountain of the Sun, and many other peaks can be seen. This trail is shared with horse riders, so be mindful as you take in the views.

## Lower Emerald Pool Trail

Easy – (1.2 mi / 1.9 km), round trip, allow 1 hour,, elev. Δ: 69 ft / 21 m, trailhead at Zion Lodge shuttle stop

There are two trails described in the Zion hiking guide that make up the Emerald Pools, the lower pools and upper pools. Lower Emerald Pools is flat, is paved much of the way, is short in distance and provides incredible views of waterfalls and shallow pools. You do climb a bit on the lower trail, which allows for some nice views of the valley.

The two pools on the lower trail are nice enough, but as is almost always the case, the best pool is at the top. As the canyon is surrounded on both sides by steep cliffs, it will be well into morning before the sun hits the western side of the canyon. By mid-afternoon, the sun will have passed over the other side, providing more shade. In warm weather, plan on hitting the trail either in early morning or late afternoon to stay cool.

## Upper Emerald Pool Trail

Moderate – (1.0 mi / 1.6 km), round trip from lower pools, allow 1 hour, elev. Δ: 200 ft / 61 m, trailhead at Zion Lodge shuttle stop

Here the trail continues from the Lower Emerald Pool Trail for the final mile. The paved trail is now dirt and the trail climbs more steeply. If you are doing this trail in the morning, the sun may have passed over the monolith walls and is now part of the climb up. The views do get better as you gain elevation, and the pool at the top is by far the biggest, sitting at the base of the western cliff faces. It is well worth the effort for the views. These pools are not intended for swimming.

## Kayenta Trail

Moderate – (2.0 mi / 3.2 km), round trip, allow 2 hours, elev. Δ: 150 ft / 46 m, trailhead at Grotto shuttle stop

Kayenta Trail is often done along with the Grotto Trail and the Emerald Pools Trail to create a loop. The trail is great in its own right, giving some great views deeper into the canyon near the Zion Lodge. The trail has a small 150-foot elevation gain.

*Waterfall at Emerald Pools*

The trail can be picked up easily from The Grotto shuttle stop. From the shuttle stop cross the Virgin River via a bridge and follow along its upper banks for a short distance. The trail then enters into Behunin Canyon from the North side before meeting up with the Emerald Pools Trail. To make a loop of it, continue along and down the Emerald Pools Trail until it ends at the Zion Lodge and then pick up the Grotto Trail back to where you started.

## The Grotto Trail

Easy – (1.0 mi / 1.6 km), round trip, allow 30 minutes, elev. Δ: 35 ft / 11 m, trailhead at Grotto shuttle stop

The Grotto Trail is a simple little flat jaunt that connects the Zion Lodge with the Grotto Picnic Area. It is used by many to connect the Emerald and Kayenta Trails to make a 2 ½ mile loop. The Grotto area itself contains picnic tables and grates for grilling. It also contains the Grotto Museum, which is the oldest building in Zion. If you are a fan of the historical stonework of the Zion Lodge, be sure to include the Grotto Trail to the mix to see both the museum and the artist in residence house.

## Angels Landing via West Rim Trail

Strenuous – (5.4 mi / 8.7 km), round trip, allow 4-5 hours, elev. Δ: 1,488 ft / 453 m, trailhead at Grotto shuttle stop

The views are unparalleled from the unique Angels Landing trail. Built during the wake of the Great Depression by the CCC, it comprises a series of switchbacks cut into solid rock. The final half mile is along a narrow knife-edged ridge that uses chains and carved footholds to assist you to the final destination. It is strenuous, but the end result is well worth it. You will have climbed from the bottom of the canyon to close to the top, giving you a view that will most certainly become a life moment. It is a world famous hike and one of the most popular in Zion.

The trail's name was coined by Frederick Fisher in 1916 when he looked up at the monolith and exclaimed, "only and angel could land on it." With the help of the CCC, (Frederick Fisher) forged a trail to the top.

The trail is composed of six distinct parts. The first follows a paved path along the river before dog legging west from the river toward a cliff wall. If you look carefully at this point in the trail, you will see the second portion of the journey, a series of switchbacks up this cliff wall. Even from a distance, the switchbacks are impressive if not audacious. The trail builders carved a fairly wide paved trail into solid rock and while you are indeed climbing up a cliff face, this portion is merely strenuous and no more dangerous than any well-established trail with exposure.

There is a reprieve at the third portion. At the top of the switchbacks, the trail goes between two massive monolithic columns through what is aptly named Refrigerator Canyon. The monoliths climb high enough to block out the sun and there is a cool breeze that greets visitors as soon as they reach the top of the switchbacks. This lasts for only a short half mile before you arrive at the fourth portion, called Walter's Wiggles. The Wiggles are a series of 21 short but consistently steep switchbacks that wind back and forth until you get to the next respite, called Scout's Lookout.

The lookout is the fifth portion of the journey and a great place to take a rest. The Wiggles are below you and from the lookout, you can see the final half mile pitch ahead of you to Angels Landing. The area offers incredible views. There is also a pit toilet and plenty of places to relax before your final leg. Up to this point you have been on the West Rim Trail, so make sure you follow the signs to the top of Angels Landing, as the West Rim Trail does continue onward.

The final pitch is a bit exciting as it has the adventure of chains that you can grab onto to ensure you get up the last leg. This portion is a razor back ridge. It is fairly narrow with steep drop offs on either side. The trail is well marked by the chains and crosses the back of the ridge several times as you climb. Many hikers have made this journey and in the end, it is not as scary as it sounds. That said, this is not a place to test yourself; a handful of people have fallen to their deaths on this trail. I've seen teenagers on this trail but only two children who were in the single digit age bracket. Use caution, for both yourself and your fellow hikers.

Once at the top, there is a somewhat narrow but flat area to take in the lofty vista. To the north is a grand view of the end of Zion Canyon. You will find yourself gazing at an enormous cul-de-sac of towering rock. As the eye travels from the edge of Angels Landing down the canyon, the citadel of rock stands as one complete sentry extending to the horizon. The red cliff walls meet the green of the desert, culminating in a dense riparian snake of vegetation that surrounds the Virgin River. At times swallows soaring at incredible speeds up to 40 miles per hour (64 km/hour) can be seen. They will soar seemingly straight into the cliff walls only to stop at the last second and land in their nests.

## Weeping Rock Trail

Easy – (0.4 mi / 0.6 km), round trip, allow 30 minutes, elev. Δ: 98 ft / 30 m, trailhead at Weeping Rock shuttle stop

This is a short paved trail that ends at an alcove called Weeping Rock. True to its name, water seeps through the sandstone and then falls gently like a soft rain once it reaches the overhang. It is possible to stand underneath and watch the magic of water and stone, even on a sunny day. The trail is great for kids and casual hikers looking for a great view of the Great White Throne. There is about 100 feet of elevation gain and some trailside exhibits.

## Hidden Canyon Trail

Strenuous – (2.4 mi / 3.9 km), round trip, allow 2-3 hours, elev. Δ: 850 ft / 259 m, trailhead at Weeping Rock shuttle stop

If you don't mind exposure to steep drop offs, this is a really cool hike. Mind you, there are long drops and chains are put in places to assist in some areas, so if you do have a fear of heights, this trail may not be for you. Hidden Canyon starts from the Weeping Rock shuttle and follows a paved trail steeply upwards along a set of well-constructed switchbacks. At the trail junction for Hidden Canyon, East Rim Trail and Observation Point, keep to the right and head up a series of short and steep switchbacks not unlike Walters Wiggles found over at Angels Landing.

*Climbing up Angels Landing*

After the switchbacks, the trail clings at various times to the edge of a steeply sloping rock face. In some areas there are chains to assist the hiker, in others, the trail looks a little intimidating but is wide and safe enough. In one part, steps have been carved directly into the sandstone. This whole part of the hike is akin to being Indiana Jones looking for some ancient treasure. This is truly a fun and exhilarating hike. That said, if you aren't a fan of heights, this might not be the best trail.

The hike ends at the mouth of Hidden Canyon. With some basic scrambling, it is possible to continue up the canyon a bit to a small 10-foot arch along a sandy stream-bed section of the trip. Hidden Canyon throws off a lot of the visitors due to its exposure and while it can be dangerous under wet conditions, is quite fine for those who have figured out how far to trust the grip of sandstone under one's feet. The other plus is the hike is typically in the shade for most of the day, which helps in the heat of the summer. Elevation gain for this trail is 800 feet.

## East Rim Trail

Strenuous – (10.6 mi / 17.1 km), one way, allow 6 – 7 hours, elev. Δ: 1,365 ft / 415 m, two trailheads, described below

Like the West Rim Trail, most hikers start at the upper end with the descent in front of them. For this trail, that is done by starting at the East Rim Trailhead, located at the Zion East Entrance Ranger Station and heading to the Weeping Rock shuttle stop. This is a great backpacking destination due to the numerous spur trails, including Deertrap Mountain and Cable Mountain Trails.

Starting from the East Entrance, views of Checkboard Mesa and the head of Jolly Gulch can be seen. This initial portion of the trail does have some elevation gain as the trail navigates the contour of the plateau. There are some very dramatic views along this portion. At 6 miles in there is a trail to the left that leads to Cable Mountain and Deertrap Trails as well as a trail junction farther on for Observation Point. The trail then comes to the top of Echo Canyon, where it heads swiftly downwards 1,000 feet (see Observation Point for more details here).

*The magic of color at Zion*

## Observation Point via East Rim Trail

Strenuous – (8.0 mi / 12.9 km), round trip, allow 6 hours, elev. Δ: 2,148 ft / 655 m, trailhead at Weeping Rock shuttle stop

Okay, if you found yourself wanting to get to the top of Zion Canyon from the moment you arrived, this is one of the trails that will get you there. The trail climbs some 2,148 feet over four miles with some serious drop offs along the way and is all done in full sun. While strenuous, this is a hike to remember.

Start at the Weeping Rock shuttle stop and proceed up the shared trail to Hidden Canyon, East Rim Trail, and Observation Point following a series of well-built switchbacks. At the junction, stay left and continue through Echo Canyon, a narrow and steep canyon with little pools of running water carved into the sandstone. As the climb continues, the trail starts to bring the white Temple Cap formation closer into view. Zion Canyon, Angels Landing, Cathedral Mountain, and Three Patriarchs are in full view. The views from the top as well as the trip through Echo Canyon make this steep hike well worth the effort.

## Cable Mountain Trail

Strenuous – (17.5 mi / 28.2 km from East Entrance), round trip, allow 8-10 hours, elev. Δ: up 1,000 ft, down 2,000 ft

Strenuous (15.5 mi / 25.0 km from Weeping Rock shuttle stop), round trip, allow 7-9 hours, elev. Δ: 2,100 ft / 640 m

Moderate (7.5 mi / 12.1 km from Zion Ponderosa Ranch, round trip, allow 5 hours, elev. Δ: 300 ft / 91 m

There are three ways to get to Cable Mountain Trail. See the trail descriptions for Observation Point and East Rim Trail for additional information on the routes to Cable Mountain Trail. For the Zion Ponderosa Ranch route, head out to the East Entrance and make a left to North Fork Road. Follow the signs to Zion Ponderosa and once at the resort, look for signs to Cable Mountain Trail, making a left at the main entrance, and then going straight past the resort buildings. The trailhead connects with the East Rim Trail and onwards to Cable Mountain Trail.

In 1901, there was a tram that carried lumber from the top of Zion Canyon to the valley floor. This engineering marvel, built by pioneer David Flanigan contained 3,300 feet of cable and could supply lumber to the valley floor in several minutes, which was a massive improvement over the 3-day journey by wagon that it took prior. Many of the original buildings in Zion were built with this lumber. The frameworks were destroyed twice by fire and in 1930; the park service removed the cables. The draw works still sits at the top of Cable Mountain at the end of the trail.

## Deertrap Trail

Strenuous – (19.5 mi / 31.4 km from East Entrance), round trip, allow 11-12 hours,, elev. Δ: up 1,000 ft, down 2,000 ft

Strenuous (17.5 mi / 28.2 km from Weeping Rock shuttle stop), round trip, allow 8-10 hours, elev. Δ: 2,100 ft / 640 m

Moderate (9.5 mi / 15.3 km from Zion Ponderosa Ranch, round trip, allow 6 hours, elev. Δ: 300 ft / 91 m

This is certainly a long day hike or as an add on within the East Rim Trail. Use the East Rim, Observation Point and Cable Mountain Trail descriptions to initiate the three routes, as appropriate.

Once on the side trail from East Rim Trail, continue past Cable Mountain Trail for another two miles to a series of overlooks collectively referred to as a sky island. Each view is slightly different, offering expansive views into the north and south portions of Zion Canyon as well as the outer peaks and terrain.

## Canyon Overlook Trail

Moderate – (1.0 mi / 1.6 km), round trip, allow 1 hour, elev. Δ: 163 ft / 50 m, trailhead near east Zion Tunnel entrance

This is another in the list of "great views without too much effort" category. The trail starts right before the Zion Tunnel as you head into the park. There are parking lots on either side of the Zion-Mount Carmel Highway. The trail gets a fair amount of "impulse hiking" as folks wait for the directed traffic of the tunnel to open up. After all, hiking in Zion does beat out being stuck in traffic in Zion. The hike has a modest 163-foot elevation gain and climbs some steps cut into the sandstone. At the end of the trail is an overlook with a railing at the cliff's edge giving great views of the lower portions of Zion Canyon and Pine Creek immediately below, as well as an interesting perspective of the Zion Tunnel.

## Riverside Walk

Easy – (2.2 mi / 3.5 km), round trip, allow 90 minutes, elev. Δ: 57 ft / 17 m, trailhead at Temple of Sinawava shuttle stop

Riverside Walk starts at roads end of the wide main portion of the Zion box canyon. From here, the canyon begins to narrow but is still wide enough for the paved Riverside Walk trail that meanders until it reaches The Narrows proper. The trail is fairly flat, with several rolling ups and downs as it contours to the land. There are also a few spots with watery grottoes as well as multiple spots for river beach access. The trail ends at a stonework terrace where you can gaze at the mouth of The Narrows and the various hikers beginning or ending their hike of this landmark trek.

## The Narrows

Imagine walking up a river flowing clearly and gently around your feet. At times there is no shore, only river and massive sandstone walls that run from the edge of the water and rise swiftly straight up 2000 feet into the sky. There are places where the canyon is wide enough to permit a view of distant sandstone monoliths and other places where the canyon is delightfully slender, only 20-30 feet wide. Each turn gives a different view, all wondrous and grand. For a bit, the river stretches out, allowing a chance to walk on soft sand. You see deer grazing on the banks. Waterfalls come sliding down curved walls from unreachable heights. There is no trail but the river. If you think about it, each step up and down is a step no one has ever taken before in exactly the same way.

Be warned, it is possible that you won't be able to hike the Narrows. If the Virgin River is running too high, either due to winter/spring runoff or to summer flash floods, you will not be able to go on this hike. That said, if the river is running favorably, then make it a point to add this to your itinerary. The park service actively controls access to the Narrows, which does take the guesswork out of the safety of hiking this trail.

### Going Upstream from the Bottom of the Canyon

Easy to Strenuous – (9.4 mi / 15.1 km), round trip, allow up to 8 hours depending on distance traveled, elev. Δ: 334 ft / 102 m, trailhead at Temple of Sinawava shuttle stop

*Into the Narrows*

The Narrows is found by taking the shuttle to the very end of the canyon via the Riverside Walk Trail. It will take about 40–45 minutes from the campground to the end of the canyon via the shuttle. It will take another hour to 90 minutes to walk the 2.2 miles (3.5 km) needed to complete the Riverside Walk Trail. Make sure you add in this time when you plan your hike.

The Riverside Walk Trail is flat, easy and paved. The trail follows the Virgin River up along its banks, and there are plenty of places to drop off the trail to explore the river itself. At the end of the trail is a small set of steps down to the river where The Narrows begins and where the hike gets really interesting.

There are a few trails, but for the most part, you walk in the river itself. You will be walking upstream on uneven ground at times, so be prepared to get wet. Depending on how far up you decide to go, you will need to wade and even swim in some stretches. If you feel confident that the trail will be open, it's best to pick up water shoes beforehand and bring them on the trip for this hike. It will make your hike more enjoyable.

Depending on the time of year, the water may be swift and cold. In the summer, usually by June, the river slows down to a steady but not terribly swift pace, and the temperature is more refreshing than cold.

There are restrictions to how far up you are allowed to travel upstream without a permit. There is a tributary creek called Orderville Junction, which is a common destination for most hikers and is the limit of how far up you can travel without a permit. Orderville Junction is about two hours from the trail. That said, it is possible to never make it this far and still have an amazing hike. Each bend offers a different experience and new view with another bend at the end that beckons you farther.

Returning will take slightly less time since you are going downstream with the flow of water. If you are doing the hike in late afternoon, make a note of when

## If You Hike the Narrows

- Have a full understanding of the weather before you go. Flash floods can originate from storms that aren't close to where you are hiking.
- Carry a gallon of water per person and some food, sunscreen and a first aid kit.
- Bring a pullover if the weather is temperate. It is colder in the canyon.
- Bring waterproof bags for cameras and other items that you need to keep dry.
- The only restroom on the hike is at the beginning of the Riverside Walk. There are no other places to go, even if you "have to." This is a popular destination and there are no discreet bushes. Make sure everyone goes prior to beginning the hike.
- Walking sticks are preferred by most folks for added stability, as are sturdy hiking boots. Water shoes and tennis shoes are okay for the casual hike up river. Sandals are not recommended though hiking sandals are okay.
- This is not a great hike for young children. My 9-year-old did fine, but keep in mind it is over two miles of walking just to get to the beginning of The Narrows. While the current is typically fine for adults, it may be too much for smaller ones.

you start the hike from the shuttle drop off and how much time you have left before sunset. If you have 3 hours, hike up for 90 minutes and turn around. The Narrows is not an easy hike in the dark especially if you don't have a flashlight.

## Going Downstream from the Top of the Canyon

Strenuous – (16 mi / 25.7 km), one way, full day hike, elev. Δ: 1,400 ft / 427 m, trailhead at Zion Narrows parking area

Going downstream can be done with a National Park Service wilderness permit. Allow a full day for this 16-mile hike. You can find private jeep shuttles that regularly go up to the drop off spot. This is a strenuous day's hike. There are ample stories of folks that find themselves having to stick it out for the night because they thought it would be an easier hike. Hiking in streambeds is slow work and is more tiring than walking on even pavement. Underestimating this hike in the wrong conditions can be dangerous as well. Flash floods and exposure from the night's elements are serious matters.

*West Temple and Altar of Sacrifice*

## Chinle Trail

Strenuous – (6.8 mi / 10.9 km), round trip to Huber Wash, allow 3 – 5 hours, elev. Δ: 650 ft / 198 m, two trailheads off SR-9

This is a very different hike than most of Zion, showing off the diversity of Lowland Desert Ecology as well as crossing through a petrified forest. The trail is well exposed and will be very hot in the full sun of summer. The trail is more welcoming in spring and fall, with wildflowers present in the spring.

The hike has two trailhead entrances, both from Highway 9. The entrance closest to the town of Springdale requires parking in the designated lot labeled "Trailhead Parking". Parking in the subdivision will get you towed. From the trailhead wind through the local neighborhood to the park's boundary and continue through a forested area with absolutely remarkable views. After 3.2 miles, the trail meets up with Huber Wash. Head back from here.

It is also possible to continue to make this somewhat of a loop trail; however, as some of the loop is Highway 9, it's best to have two cars. Taking the full loop to Coalpits Wash from Chinle Trailhead is a total of 15 miles.

## Right Fork Trailhead

Strenuous – (10.6 mi / 17.1 km), round trip from bottom up, allow 8 – 12 hours, elev. Δ: 1,000 ft / 300 m, trailhead on Kolob Terrace Road

Like the Left Fork Trailhead, this is more route than maintained trail. The first couple of miles were hit by a fire in 2006 and the area is in a cycle of recovery. The hike within the streambed is pretty slow going, so allow extra time. That said, while the Right Fork is a bit more rugged to navigate, the scenery is quite peaceful and meandering with the route ending at a set of pretty incredible double waterfalls. Like the Left Fork, this trail can get hot in the summer despite the lure of water.

Start the hike at the Right Fork Trailhead on Kolob Terrace Road. The first quarter mile crosses the fire area to a bluff overlooking North Creek. From here head steeply down and into the creek bed. Do make note of this entrance, as it is easy to miss on the way out. Once at North Creek, start heading upstream passing the confluence of Left Fork. Cross the stream on the left side here and follow the path that crisscrosses the creek multiple times.

At about 2.5 miles into the hike, pass Trail Canyon on the right. A short spur trip up this canyon about one quarter of a mile will lead to a set of cascades. Back in North Creek, at close to 4 miles in, the hiker will encounter a very cool five-foot waterfall pouring through the slickrock into a nice pool. About a half mile further up, the canyon narrows and holds multiple waterfalls, pools, and hanging gardens. Further up another mile is Double Falls, another picturesque set of cascades.

From here, the end of the journey without ropes is Barrier Falls, about a third of a mile further upstream. The going here is tougher, requiring one to scramble up slick rock, bushwhack and otherwise navigate slowly to the falls. There is a set of falls in between, but you will know you are at Barrier Falls, its name holds true.

Unlike the Left Fork Trail, a permit is not required for Right Fork. Coming back, be glad you made note of the trail you came down as getting back up to the rim without the trail can be dangerous.

## Left Fork Trailhead

Strenuous – (7.0 mi / 11.3 km), round trip, allow 5 - 8 hours, elev. Δ: 1,000 ft / 300 m, trailhead on Kolob Terrace Road

The Left Fork of North Creek is most popular for a stretch labeled The Subway, a short and rather amazing section of the creek that looks more like a worm tunnel than a streambed. This is one of the best hikes in the park and is more route than actual trail. The whole journey is alongside and often in the creek, which makes for slow going. Unlike The Narrows, which can be cooler in the summer heat, this hike is definitely a hot hike when temperatures are high. Start early if it looks to be a hot day.

*The Subway*

It is possible to enter from the top and make your way down stream, but this is longer and requires a bit of rappelling and swimming (and carrying your rappelling gear). A permit is required no matter which direction you travel. From bottom to top is described here.

From the bottom, the trail starts by picking ones way down a 400 foot gully starting from the Left Fork Trailhead on Kolob Terrace Road. Once in the creek, head upstream for about two to three hours. The Subway section is a tight section of the creek with several twists and turns right above a cascading set of falls called Red Waterfalls. The Subway itself is spectacular with clear pools and an almost subterranean feel.

It is possible to continue upwards but be mindful of time. Shortly after The Subway you will be met with large black pools that you must swim to get across to continue exploring the slot canyon. Further up is a soothing little waterfall with a secret natural room behind a watery curtain. Journeying from here requires bouldering and rappelling experience. Enjoy and head back down before dark.

Like The Narrows, this slot canyon does experience extreme changes in water volume due to flash floods. The permit process helps provide education along the way for this route, but do enter well informed as to the weather for the day.

# Hiking in the Kolob Canyon Section

## Hop Valley Trail

Strenuous – (15 mi / 24.1 km), round trip, allow 10 hours, elev. Δ: 1,050 ft / 320 m, trailhead off Kolob Terrace Road

The Hop Valley Trail, located in the Kolob Canyons section of Zion is typically done as part of the Trans Zion hike, a 48 mile, 5-day trek that crosses Zion from the Kolobs at Lee Pass to the East Rim. Lacking the fame of the main Zion and Kolob Canyons, the Hop Valley trail is a hidden gem. It is possible to use Hop Valley as a longer and more remote method to Kolob Arch. The route described here is from Kolob Terrace Road to Kolob Arch and back.

From the Hop Valley Trailhead on Kolob Terrace Road pick up the northern trailhead into Hop Valley. The trail starts out in a wide and open valley filled with deep sand and plenty of sagebrush. Walking in deep sand is a consistent trait of this trail. In areas, grazing has left its mark on the vegetation. As you continue, the valley narrows and travel is along a pleasant stream. The trail does have a fair amount of creek crossings; look for NPS trail markers to keep you on the trail. Campsites are about five miles in at an NPS boundary gate. The vegetation is more pristine once you cross into the park. Take a series of switchbacks downhill to connect to La Verkin Creek and follow it downstream to the Kolob Arch Viewpoint.

Overall, this hike has about 1,000 feet elevation gain, mostly felt on the return. That said, the trail is more strenuous due to its length than the elevation.

## Northgate Peaks Trail

Easy – (4.5 mi / 7.2 km), round trip, allow 3 hours, elev. Δ: 50 ft / 15 m, trailhead off Wildcat Canyon trail

If you wondered if you could find a hike that wasn't too hard but also wasn't shared with millions of other tourists, this trail is a good bet. Northgate Peaks Trail is off the beaten path and isn't in the popular NPS hiking brochures so it doesn't get as much traffic. The hike also shows a different view of Zion, ambling through large ponderosa pine forests found in the higher elevations. The hike is cooler and walks amongst the white Temple Cap monoliths dotting the landscape.

While the name of this there and back hike makes it sound like it climbs some massive Zion mountain, the elevation gain is only 250 feet. The trail ends at a craggy volcanic knob offering views that

*Kolob Canyon*



are distinctively different from the main portions of Zion and the Kolob Canyons. Access to Northgate Peaks Trail is from the Wildcat Canyon parking lot on Kolob Terrace Road.

## Wildcat Canyon Trail

Moderate – (12.0 mi / 19.3 km), round trip, allow 4-7 hours, elev. Δ: 450 ft / 137 m, two trailheads off Kolob Terrace Road

Normally done as a connector trail, this is a great day hike in its own right. The hike is incredibly pleasant with only modest elevation gain/loss. The trail passes through groves of ponderosa pines and high meadows before dropping down into Wildcat Canyon. The trail offers a leisurely way to see the countryside, with plenty of opportunities to find wildflowers and wildlife along the way. This trail is not the standard Zion high red rock cliffs and there are no striking viewpoints to be found at trail's end, but the entire feel that the journey is the destination is what makes this hike so special.

## West Rim Trailhead

Strenuous – (12.9 – 14.4 mi / 20.7 – 23.1 km), one way, allow 10 hours, elev. Δ: 3,600 ft / 1097 m, trailhead at Lava Point

This is a long day hike or a pleasant overnight backpacking trip. The hike is best if started from the West Rim Trailhead at Kolob Terrace Road and heading towards the other end at The Grotto shuttle stop. Since the shuttle doesn't go to both ends of the trail, you will need a means of transportation back to your car.

Starting near Lava Point on Kolob Terrace Road pick up the trail and keep straight to avoid the Wildcat Canyon Trail. The trail heads along the Horse Plateau through sparsely forested ponderosa pines. After 4.5 miles, the trail descends into a happy little meadow named Potato Hollow. Here there is a small pond and a spring that is usually running. This is a good place to relax and fill up canteens, (be sure to treat or filter). There are some great views into Imlay canyon by taking a short side spur to the east.

The trail then climbs about 500 feet out of the hollow and back onto Horse Plateau proper over a distance of 1.5 miles. At this point, the hike offers two routes. There is the primary West Rim Trail, which is 1.5 miles longer, and the Telephone Canyon Trail. The West Rim variation gives great views of Phantom Valley and the southern Zion canyons. The Telephone Canyon variation is named by settlers trying to establish a telephone line into Zion Canyon. The route here is shorter and sticks more to the interior of Horse Plateau.

Both variations meet up at Cabin Springs, a small seep that collects into a small pool. There are campsites nearby. This water is fine to drink given you filter or treat it and have a strong amount of patience. From Cabin Springs, the real fun begins as the trail heads steeply down into Zion Canyon. There are long drop-offs here, but this is a well-maintained trail. Take the path cut into the slick rock and head downwards until you reach a respite at Lookout Point. From here, the trail is an inverse of what is described for the Angels Landing Trail. Follow down Walters Wiggles, through Refrigerator Canyon and down until you end at The Grotto shuttle stop. It is completely possible and recommended to add the Angels Landing to the journey. If you do, be sure to allow another 45 minutes to the overall duration of the hike.

## La Verkin Creek Trail (and Kolob Arch)

Strenuous – (14.0 mi / 22.5 km), round trip, allow 8 hours, elev. Δ: 1,037 ft / 316 m, trailhead at Kolob Canyon Road

La Verkin Creek Trail, in the Kolob Canyons section, is a fun trail all around, offering great views including Kolob Arch, one of the largest free-standing arches on earth. The hike itself does have some elevation gain, a little over 1,000 feet; however, the surroundings are amazing enough to help keep your mind off the inclines. Most folks get a permit and camp overnight; however, it is possible to do this as a long day hike to Kolob Arch.

*Kolob Arch*

The trail starts at Lee Pass and crosses in front of the southern portion of the Kolob Canyon cliffs. The trail meets up quickly with Timber Creek and follows along its banks, giving some spectacular views in a pinyon juniper forest setting. After about two miles, the trail veers away from the creek into the woods as it heads towards La Verkin Creek. The trail then descends down into the creek's clear waters, with each step putting you into a more immersive Kolob Canyon experience. Cliffs are now towering around you on either side with the sound of water adding to the magic of this hike.

The end of the trail is Kolob Arch viewpoint where the arch can be seen by hiking up about 150 feet to a viewing area. While the official end of the trail listed here is 7 miles, La Verkin Creek Trail does continue up stream for another two miles. There are many side canyons to explore, some of which require canyoneering techniques that lead to triple waterfalls and other delights. If backpacking, it is possible to connect to the Hop Valley Trail, which leads southeast to the Lower Kolob Plateau.

## Timber Creek Overlook Trail

Moderate – (1.0 mi / 1.6 km), round trip, allow 30 minutes, elev. Δ: 100 ft / 30 m, trailhead at end of Kolob Canyon Road

This is one of those trails that could labeled as "Easy" without much argument; however, the park lists it as moderate. It does have a 100-foot elevation gain, but is otherwise a straightforward trail. The trail is picked up at the very end of Kolob Canyon Road. From there the trail follows a small ridgeline to an overlook of Kolob Canyon, looking south. On a clear day, it is possible to see all the way to the north rim of the Grand Canyon.

This trail is located within the Kolob Canyon section. Groups are limited to a maximum size of 12 people at a time. Look for wildflowers in season, which can be abundant on this trail.

## Taylor Creek Trail

Moderate – (5.0 mi / 8.0 km), round trip, allow 4 hours, elev. Δ: 470 ft / 143 m, trailhead at Kolob Canyon Road

This trail lies within the Kolob Canyons Wilderness and ambles up the Middle Fork of Taylor Creek. This entire area gets less visitation than the main Zion Canyon and this trail in particular has strict limits on prohibiting groups larger than 12 people. Taylor Creek Trail heads into a narrow box canyon of red Navajo Sandstone along a normally gently flowing creek. There is a welcome interplay of the green vegetation and the red hue of the rocks here and the hike overall is one of delight and wonder. Before the trail begins to fade as it nears the end of the box canyon, look for Double Arch Alcove, an impressive set of alcoves, one on top of the other.

## Trans- Zion Hike

Strenuous – (47.3 mi / 76.1 km), one way, allow 3 - 5 days

This hike is a wondrous way to get an immersive multi-day experience that covers the broad spectrum that makes up Zion. The route typically starts from Lee Pass in the Kolobs and cuts down into La Verkin Creek before climbing up to the top of Zion Canyon via the West Rim Trail. From here, the trail heads steeply down, crosses the Zion Valley floor, and heads up the other side via the East Rim.

The trip can be done at a nice pace over five days, but one can hoof it in less. That said, the National Park Service allows camping only in designated areas, so plan your camping junctures carefully. The typical route and stops are given below.

The best part of this trek is there is a net elevation gain of just 325 feet! Don't let that fool you though, one ascends and descends over a whopping 6,000 feet getting to that net elevation number.

### Trans-Zion Hike Route:

- La Verkin Trail via Lee Pass Trailhead
- La Verkin Trail to Hop Valley Trail
- Hop Valley Trail to Connector Trail
- Connector Trail to Wildcat Canyon Trail
- Wildcat Canyon Trail to West Rim Trail
- Short side trip to Angels Landing (a must for any Trans Zion hike)
- West Rim Trail down to The Grotto shuttle stop
- Hard core walk or shuttle bus ride to Weeping Rock shuttle stop
- East Rim Trail to East Entrance

### Typical Itinerary:

Mileage is approximate, as it will depend on what campsites you get or where designated camping isn't a requirement such as on the East Rim and Echo Canyon, where you can find a campsite.

- Day 1 – 6.9 miles: Camp near Kolob Arch along La Verkin Creek Trail
- Day 2 – 16 miles: Camp at Lava Point Campgrounds or Sawmill Spring
- Day 3 - 8 miles: Camp at West Rim, (Potato Hollow or campsite #6)
- Day 4 – 10 miles: West Rim to Echo Canyon
- Day 5 – 6.5 miles: Exit to East Entrance

# Quail Creek State Park

## Parks Near Zion

Quail Creek and Sand Hollow State Parks offer camping, relaxation and water filled recreation for those traveling to and from Zion National Park. Both parks are located between St. George, UT and Zion NP on State Route 9. Quail Creek is a bit more on the mellow laid back side, whereas Sand Hollow is all about water filled fun in the middle of the desert.

**Official Park Website:** http://stateparks.utah.gov/parks/quail-creek//

**Visitor Center:** (435) 879-2378

**Park Accessibility:**

- Okay for 2WD and RVs
- Day and Overnight Use

**Camping in Park:**

- Quail Creek Campground: 22 T/RV, drinking water, restrooms, showers, no hookup, reservable at www.reserveamerica.com/

**Lodging and Dining in Park:**

- None

**Nearest Town with Amenities:**

- Washington, UT is 8 mi / 13 km from park

**Getting There:**

- From St George, UT: Take I-15 North to State Hwy 9 East. Total distance is 17 mi / 27 km to park

## What Makes Quail Creek State Park Special

Quail Creek State Park manages a deep reservoir for camping, boating, fishing, and swimming. The park is off Interstate 15 just north of the Highway 9 junction to Zion. Peaceful sweeping views of red rocks with the Pine Valley Mountains in the distance. A good place to stop for the night if you are heading to Zion NP.

*Quail Creek Reservoir.*

# Sand Hollow State Park



**Official Park Website:** http://state-parks.utah.gov/parks/sand-hollow//

**Visitor Center:**

(435) 680-0715

**Park Accessibility:**

- Okay for 2WD and RVs
- Day and Overnight Use

**Camping in Park:**
2 campgrounds in park, all sites reservable at http://utahstateparks.reserveamerica.com

- Westside Campground: 40 + 3 ADA T/RV, drinking water, showers, restrooms, hookups, some pull thru sites, dump station
- Sand Pit Campground: 29 T/RV, drinking water, showers, restrooms, hookups, some pull thru sites, dump station

**Lodging and Dining in Park:**

- None

**Nearest Town with Amenities:**

- Washington, UT is 10 mi / 16 km from park

**Getting There:**

- From St George, UT: Take I-15 North to State Hwy 9 East to Sand Hollow Road. Total distance is 18 mi / 29 km to park

## What Makes Sand Hollow State Park Special

Although Sand Hollow is very close to Quail Creek State Park and despite both being water themed recreational parks, Sand Hollow is very different. Whereas Quail Creek is peaceful and serene, with wandering vistas, Sand Hollow is playful and fun amidst red rock formations. There are sand dunes to dig your ATV into as well as slick rock to jump off into the waters below. Besides boating, fishing, and swimming, there are two campgrounds.

Sand Hollow is working through an issue with Swimmer's Itch, an allergic reaction to an otherwise harmless parasite found mainly in the summer months. The problem is more prevalent in the warmer shallower areas and can lead to secondary infections. The issue is unfortunately most prevalent with small children who prefer the shallow ends of the waters. For all the details on Swimmer's Itch, go here for more information: http://stateparks.utah.gov/parks/sand-hollow/swimmers-itch/.

# Coral Pink Sand Dunes State Park

*Mid Afternoon at Coral Pink Sand Dunes*

## Quick Facts

**Official Park Website:**

http://state-parks.utah.gov/parks/coral-pink/

**Visitor Center:**

(435) 648-2800

**Park Accessibility:**

- Okay for 2WD and RVs
- ATVs, 4WD needed for some areas
- Day and Overnight Use

**Experience Level:**

- Family Friendly to Experienced Hiker

**Camping in Park:**

- Coral Pink Sand Dunes Campground: 16 T/RV plus 1 group site, drinking water, showers, restrooms, no hookups, many pull thru sites, reservable at www.reserveamerica.com/

**Lodging and Dining in Park:**

- None

**Nearest Town with Amenities:**

- Kanab, UT is 20 mi / 32 km from park

**Getting There:**

- From St George, UT: Take I-15 North to State Hwy 9 East/State St to UT-59 South to AZ-389 East to Co Hwy 237 to Co Rd 43. Note that final 4 miles is a dirt road. Typically, passable by 2WD and smaller RV's. Total distance is 62 mi / 100 km to park.
- From Page, AZ: Take US-89 West to Hancock Road to Coral Pink Sand Dunes Road. Note that final leg from Hancock Road to park is on an unpaved gravel road, suitable for all vehicles.

## What Makes Coral Pink Sand Dunes Special

- The cool color of the sand dunes, especially at dawn and dusk
- The ability to hike in a Zion like world with all the wonder but with less fellow tourists
- Knowing you can put that ATV you brought to great use

The first thing to note about this park is while the color is distinctly different from other sand dunes; it may not be the pink color you envisioned when you first pull up. The color is more of a sandstone red much of the time and requires the right soft and low but direct lighting to bring out the picture perfect coral color.

The elusive pink color aside, the park is a great stay over spot within the typical route of the Grand Circle. Here there are nice campgrounds, good restroom facilities and a playground of sand nearby. Perhaps the only downside if you aren't riding an ATV is all the ATV's in the dunes area. One definitely needs to be mindful of these high-speed vehicles in this multiuse area. That said, if you do have an ATV, the area allows exploration into canyons that are very much like Zion NP, but without all the people. For many locals, this is how they see Zion, by riding into the wilderness surrounding it.

There is one other minor but very cool feature of this park. It has an extensive collection of sand from all over the world. Each little jar is labeled with the sand's location. The collection, which takes up an entire wall in the visitor center, started as a ranger's hobby, but has grown considerably as tourists have sent in their local samples. It is quite possibly the largest collection of sand in the world and is worth checking out.

## Hiking in Coral Pink Sand Dunes State Park

### Coral Pink Sand Dunes Arch

Easy – (0.2 mi / 0.3 km), round trip, allow 15 minutes elev. Δ: 50 ft / 15 m, trailhead on Hancock Road

This is by no means the grandest arch you will see, but is a welcome surprise for a park whose primary feature is a set of

*Coral Pink Sand Dunes After a Rain Shower*

sand dunes. Getting to this arch is easy. At the turnoff from Hancock Road from Highway 89, mark your trip meter and drive 0.8 miles. Drive off the road on your right for about 150 yards, heading towards the sole obvious hoodoo. From here, get out and walk past this hoodoo using the ATV trail on the left and look for two rock outcroppings. Here you will find a small but definite arch.

## Coral Pink Sand Dunes

Easy – (1.0 mi / 1.6 km), round trip, allow 1 - 2 hours, elev. Δ: a00 ft / 30 m, trailhead at campground

The dunes are in easy sight as you pull up and the trailhead is easy enough to find, however it is recommended to keep along the established route so as not to disturb the fragile flora. Like all dunes, walking in sand can be more tiring than the same distance on hard ground. Also, hiking to the tallest dune, at a 300 feet elevation gain from its base, will add to the time. Look for insect and animal tracks, as well as areas of "plant art", where tall grasses have left their marks in the sand by the prevailing winds.

The one caution with the dunes is that the area is shared with ATV's. Keep an eye out for fast moving visitors. The ATV's can be a bit loud, but they are also fun to watch from the tall dunes.

## South Fork Indian Canyon

Easy – (1.0 mi / 1.6 km), round trip, allow 30 minutes, elev. Δ: 150 ft / 46 m, trailhead at end of South Fork Indian Canyon Road off Sand Spring Road

This trail leads to some truly amazing pictographs. Formed around 1200 BCE, this rock art was created using natural pigments versus a petroglyph, which are formed by actually carving into the rock. The pictographs are quite rare and sit behind a protective fence. Bring a zoom lens if you want great pictures. This trail requires a 4WD vehicle that can handle the aptly named Sand Spring Road.

Take Sand Spring Road from Hancock for about a mile through the edge of the dunes and then a little less than two miles up South Fork Indian Canyon to the obvious parking lot for the pictographs. In many ways, this is the gem of the park and not the only one of its kind (See Hell Dive Canyon below)

## Hell Dive Canyon

Moderate – (6.6 mi / 10.6 km), round trip, allow 4 – 5 hours, elev. Δ: 580 ft / 177 m, trailhead on 4WD road west of Water Canyon

This is another set of pictographs that are farther to get to and not protected. Please do not touch these very fragile pieces of

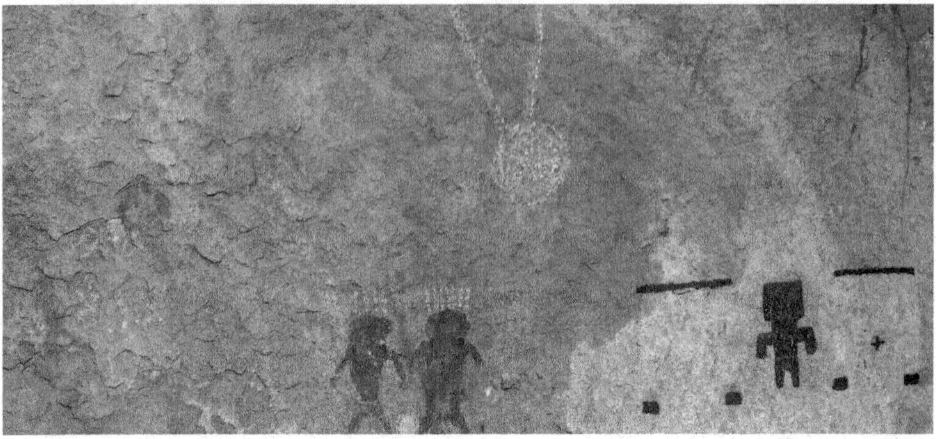

*Pictographs at South Fork Indian Canyon*

*Still Life with Sand*

history. Any contact with them can do permanent harm. To get here, head to the South Fork Indian Canyon road on Sand Spring Road and upon reaching it, stay right for about 0.8 miles, continuing on Sand Spring Road. At a fork in the road, head left and continue another 0.75 miles stopping when the road gets too rough for vehicles.

After parking, continue hiking down this road. The road becomes more trail and winds down to the bottom of Water Canyon and then climbs up a ridge to another intersection. Turn left here and continue in a southerly direction. Don't fret, as the trail veers to the northeast for a couple of miles, just make sure you don't take any right turns and you'll end up at Hell Dive Canyon. Continue into the alcove, where the pictographs can be found. Again, please be respectful in this area and don't touch the art.

## Peek-a-Boo Slot Canyon

Easy – (0.7 mi / 1.1 km), round trip, allow 1 hour, trailhead described below

Peek-a-Boo or Red Canyon is not that long and is a very easy walk through a narrow red rock walled slot canyon with plenty of twists and turns (hence the nickname). While the trail itself isn't that long, the primary reason is the journey itself. It takes about 3 hours to get to the trailhead along deep sandy 4WD roads or optional ATV routes. The scenery along the way and the adventure getting there makes the slot canyon itself icing on the cake.

This canyon isn't in the park boundaries itself, but is very popular for ATV enthusiasts staying in Coral Pink Sand Dunes SP. From the park, head back to Highway 89 via Hancock Road and turn south. Look for the Best Friends Animal Society and make a left towards it. Total distance from the park to the sanctuary is 16 miles. Now on road 102M, make a left just before the animal sanctuary and continue on this deep sandy path for the canyon. Stay right at the first juncture where 102M splits for road 102. Continue on road 102 unless you can navigate very deep sand and want a bit more adventure, then take 102L, which is slightly shorter but has a nice steep hill to navigate. The slot canyon is at the end of the road.

# Snow Canyon State Park

## Quick Facts

**Official Park Website:** http://stateparks.utah.gov/parks/snow-canyon/

**Visitor Center:** (435) 628-2255

**Park Accessibility:**

- Okay for 2WD and RVs
- Day and Overnight Use

**Experience Level:**

- Family Friendly to Experienced Hiker

**Camping in Park:**

- Snow Canyon Campground: 31 T/RV, drinking water, flush toilets, showers, hookups, dump station, some pull thru sites, call visitor center for reservations

**Lodging and Dining in Park:**

- None

**Nearest Town with Amenities:**

- Ivins, UT is 4 mi / 6 km from park

**Getting There:**

- From St George, UT: Take UT-18 North to Snow Canyon Drive. Total distance is 13 mi / 21 km to park

*Sweeping views and fantastic trails at Snow Canyon State Park*

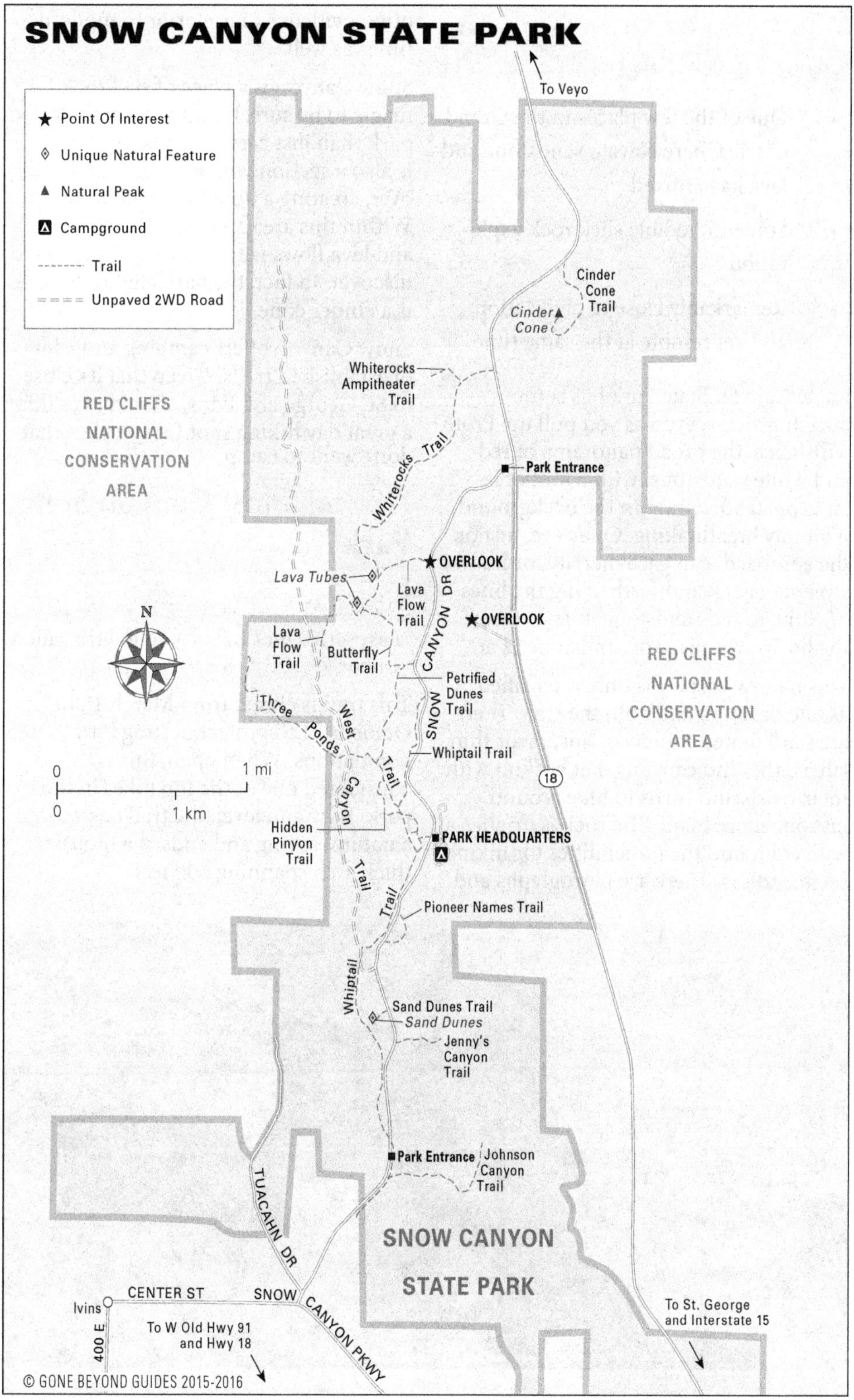
SNOW CANYON STATE PARK
Point Of Interest
Unique Natural Feature
Natural Peak
Campground
Trail
Unpaved 2WD Road
To Veyo
Cinder Cone Trail
Cinder Cone
Whiterocks Ampitheater Trail
Whiterocks Trail
RED CLIFFS NATIONAL CONSERVATION AREA
Park Entrance
OVERLOOK
Lava Tubes
Lava Flow Trail
OVERLOOK
SNOW CANYON DR
Butterfly Trail
Petrified Dunes Trail
Three Ponds
West Canyon Trail
Whiptail Trail
18
0
1 mi
0
1 km
Hidden Pinyon Trail
PARK HEADQUARTERS
Trail
Pioneer Names Trail
Whiptail
Sand Dunes Trail
Sand Dunes
Jenny's Canyon Trail
Park Entrance
Johnson Canyon Trail
TUACAHN DR
SNOW CANYON STATE PARK
CENTER ST
SNOW
CANYON PKWY
Ivins
400 E
To W Old Hwy 91 and Hwy 18
To St. George and Interstate 15
© GONE BEYOND GUIDES 2015-2016

## What Makes Snow Canyon State Park Special

- One of the few places in the Grand Circle where Navajo sandstone and lava have mixed
- Some incredible slick rock exploration
- Remarkably close to civilization and yet remote at the same time

Snow Canyon State Park has some amazing views, even as you pull up. From a distance, the broad panorama of red and white sandstone, with a hint of lava-capped adventure in the background, is simply breathtaking. One's eye, just on the approach, can gaze merrily for hours, sweeping back and forth along the lines of white to red sandstone. It is, even on the horizon, a place of sandstone as art.

This natural display is only intensified as one draws in and onto the trail. There are sand dunes, hoodoos, fins, razor thin labyrinths, and canyons that beckon with their twists and turns to hike around just one more bend. The rock is bright with color and the possibilities for hiking seem endless. There are petroglyphs and other evidence of use prior to modern times as well.

Snow Canyon is a place of slickrock magic to be sure, but there is more to the park than just carved sandstone. There is also a section where lava has covered over, creating a different exploration. Within this area are lava tubes, caves, and lava flows with some cool features to discover. In fact, the park's tallest feature is a cinder cone.

Snow Canyon offers camping and a lot of established trails. Given that it's close to St. George and Ivins, Utah makes this a great day hiking spot for travelers that don't want to camp.

## Hiking Snow Canyon State Park

### Johnson Canyon

Easy – (2.0 mi / 3.2 km), round trip, allow 1 hour

This trail is closed from March 15 to October 31 to protect nesting bird populations. When open, this is considered one of the top hikes in the park. Easy and level, the trail passes by a natural spring and ends at a monster thick arch spanning 200 feet.

## Whiptail Trail

Easy – (6.0 mi / 9.7 km), round trip, allow 3 hours

Whiptail is a paved there and back route popular with the locals. There are plenty of bikers, joggers, and walkers on this trail. The trail sits at the base of Snow Canyon's red (and white) rocks, giving a nice backdrop for all users. There is a small elevation gain but the trail is wheelchair accessible. This is a popular hike, especially on weekends.

## Jenny's Canyon

Easy – (0.5 mi / 0.8 km), round trip, allow 30 minutes

This trail is closed from March 15 to June 1 to protect nesting bird populations. A short level hike that ends at an interesting slot canyon. Jenny's Canyon Trail is great for kids.

## Sand Dunes

Easy – (0.5 mi / 0.8 km), round trip, allow 30 minutes

A quick an easy jaunt to a small set of sand dunes. This is a great family hike with fabulous scenery from every angle. If you have small children, this is a perfect place for playing in the dunes.

## Pioneer Names Trail

Easy – (0.5 mi / 0.8 km), round trip, allow 30 minutes

Pioneer Names Trail takes a somewhat sandy but otherwise ambling and quick path to a red rock alcove. Within it are the names of several Mormon pioneers from 1881. Getting to the alcove and up close to the pioneer graffiti requires a short but steep climb up slick rock at the end. The surroundings are a pleasing mix of red sandstone and the green of the desert pinyon juniper woodlands.

## West Canyon Trail

Moderate – (8.0 mi / 12.9 km), round trip, allow 4 hours

This trail is an old dirt road that leads up into the main canyon in the park. The hike itself is level for the most part and offers great views into all of the side washes, sand stone hills, and cliff faces. This is a great place to go on an adventure, with plenty of slickrock to explore. The canyon is wide and inviting, traveling much of the time through grasslands. Stay on the trail whenever possible and avoid walking on undisturbed soil.

*Snow Canyon*

## Hidden Pinyon

Moderate – (1.5 mi / 2.4 km), round trip, allow 1 hour

Stunning views are to be found on this hike. Great hike to capture the essence of the park in a short amount of time. This is an interpretative trail that describes the geologic features and native flora in the park.

## Three Ponds

Moderate – (3.5 mi / 5.6 km), round trip, allow 2 hours

This is for the most part a hike through a sandy wash with some slick rock. The trail follows through a twisty wash with deep "slog worthy" sand to the mouth of a large canyon. The trail ends at the first of three potholes that seasonally fill with water. There are two other pools further on. While hiking to murky stagnant water may not be for everyone, the surroundings along the way are very nice and sure to please.

## Petrified Dunes Trail

Moderate – (1.0 mi / 1.6 km), round trip, allow 45 minutes

Here is another trail taking the hiker to "sand dunes frozen in time". Geologically speaking, much of the Grand Circle was a vast sand dune, so in effect, all the redrock you see falls under this moniker. That said, this is one of the nicest hikes in the park. The sandstone here is unique, odd, and beautiful, all at the same time.

## Butterfly Trail

Moderate – (2.0 mi / 3.2 km), round trip, allow 1 hour

This trail is a continuation of Petrified Dunes Trail giving similar awesome scenery. Connects with West Canyon Overlook and the Lava Flow Trail. Some steep sections.

## Lava Flow Trail

Moderate – (2.5 mi / 4.0 km), round trip, allow 1 - 2 hours

This is an easy to follow trail with some caves near the trailhead. Bring your headlamps. The trail itself is uneven throughout as it heads up into an ancient lava field. This trail can be very hot in the summer, but does show a different side of the park.

## Whiterocks Amphitheater

Moderate – (4.0 mi / 6.4 km), round trip, allow 2 hours

This is a straightforward trail into the main white sandstone area of Snow Canyon. The trail starts out in moderately deep sand, but quickly hits the slickrock for an ascent of about 100 feet. The trail officially ends at a bowl of white rock, surrounding the hiker in amphitheater fashion, on three sides. It is possible to continue on in scramble mode to the top for better views. Some parts require Class 3 level scrambling. At the top, the hiker is rewarded with some fantastic views of the park.

There is a shorter trail of about one mile in length located north of the junction of Snow Canyon Drive and SR18 (north of the junction 0.5 miles).

## Cinder Cone Trail

Strenuous – (1.5 mi / 2.4 km), round trip, allow 1 - 2 hours

Hiking up cinder cones can feel like you are going nowhere fast, but the trail does reach the top. The trail corkscrews up with an elevation gain of 500 feet. Once at the top, you will be greeted with a view of the crater and the park's gorgeous views.

# Gunlock State Park

*The Picturesque Waterfalls at Gunlock State Park*

**Official Park Website:** http://stateparks.utah.gov/parks/gunlock//

**Visitor Center:** (435) 680-0715

**Park Accessibility:**

- Okay for 2WD and RVs
- Day and Overnight Use

**Camping in Park:**

- Gunlock Campground: 5 T/RV, no water, vault toilets, first come-first served

**Getting There:**

- From St George, UT: Take Old US Hwy 91 East. Total distance is 20 mi / 32 km to park

## What Makes Gunlock State Park Special

- A very unique and fun set of waterfalls and pools to play in
- Boating and fishing, but read below
- Close to St. George, Utah

Although Sand Hollow is very close to Quail Creek State Park and despite both Gunlock is a small 266-acre park that protects a reservoir of the same name. The park is mainly a day use area for boating and fishing, though there is a campground for overnighters.

One of the nicest part of Gunlock Park is a beautiful set of waterfalls at the south end of the park. Referred to as the Gunlock Falls and Pools, this area of cascading waterfalls over angled and red slickrock is a favorite amongst locals.

Recently, the park has closed for day use due to the drought. As of this writing, the park is open through September. Check the website before going to see current conditions. They do update the water level stats frequently.

# Frontier Homestead State Park Museum

*Frontier Homestead State Park Museum*

**Official Park Website:** http://stateparks.utah.gov/parks/frontier-homestead//

**Visitor Center:** (435) 586-9290

**Nearest Town with Amenities:**

- The park is located in the town of Cedar City, UT

**Getting There:**

- From St George, UT: Take I-15 North. Total distance is 54 mi / 87 km to park

One of the best places to see Mormon pioneering history and artifacts, plus, some iron mining history, all in a clean mid-sized American town.

Frontier Homestead State Park Museum is located on Main Street in the pleasant town of Cedar, Utah. Cedar is one of those towns that started out through a defined purpose, in this case mining for iron. When the primary reason to be there ran dry, enough people stuck around anyway and figured out how to keep the town thriving. Today, Cedar is one of the larger towns in Utah and home to Southern Utah University and the Utah Shakespeare Festival.

Within the clean and well-organized society of Cedar is a museum holding a healthy amount of Mormon pioneer artifacts. The museum doesn't just hold little stuff; this place is large enough to showcase stagecoaches and horse buggies as well as the expected assortment of pioneer and ancestral inhabitant artifacts. The museum also tells the story of iron mining in the area under the direction of Brigham Young. Occasionally, the park holds frontier days, where folks dress up in period costumes and take part in pioneer tasks such as washing clothes by hand and roping cattle.

## Quick Facts

**Official Park Website:** http://www.nps.gov/cebr

**Visitor Center:** (435) 586-0787 ext. 4022

**Park Accessibility:**

- Okay for 2WD and RVs
- The park is open all year, however the road to park, UT-148, is closed after the first snowfall, usually in mid-November. The visitor center and campground are closed, but the park itself remains open during this time.

**Experience Level:**

- Family Friendly to Experienced Hiker

**Camping in Park:**

- Point Supreme Campground: 25 T/RV, drinking water, showers, restrooms, no hookups

**Lodging and Dining in Park:**

- None

**Nearest Town with Amenities:**

- Cedar City, UT is 27 mi / 43 km from park

**Getting There:**

- From St. George, UT: Take I-15 North to UT-14 East to UT-148. Total distance is 75 mi / 121 km to park entrance.

*Sun beam on Cedar Breaks*

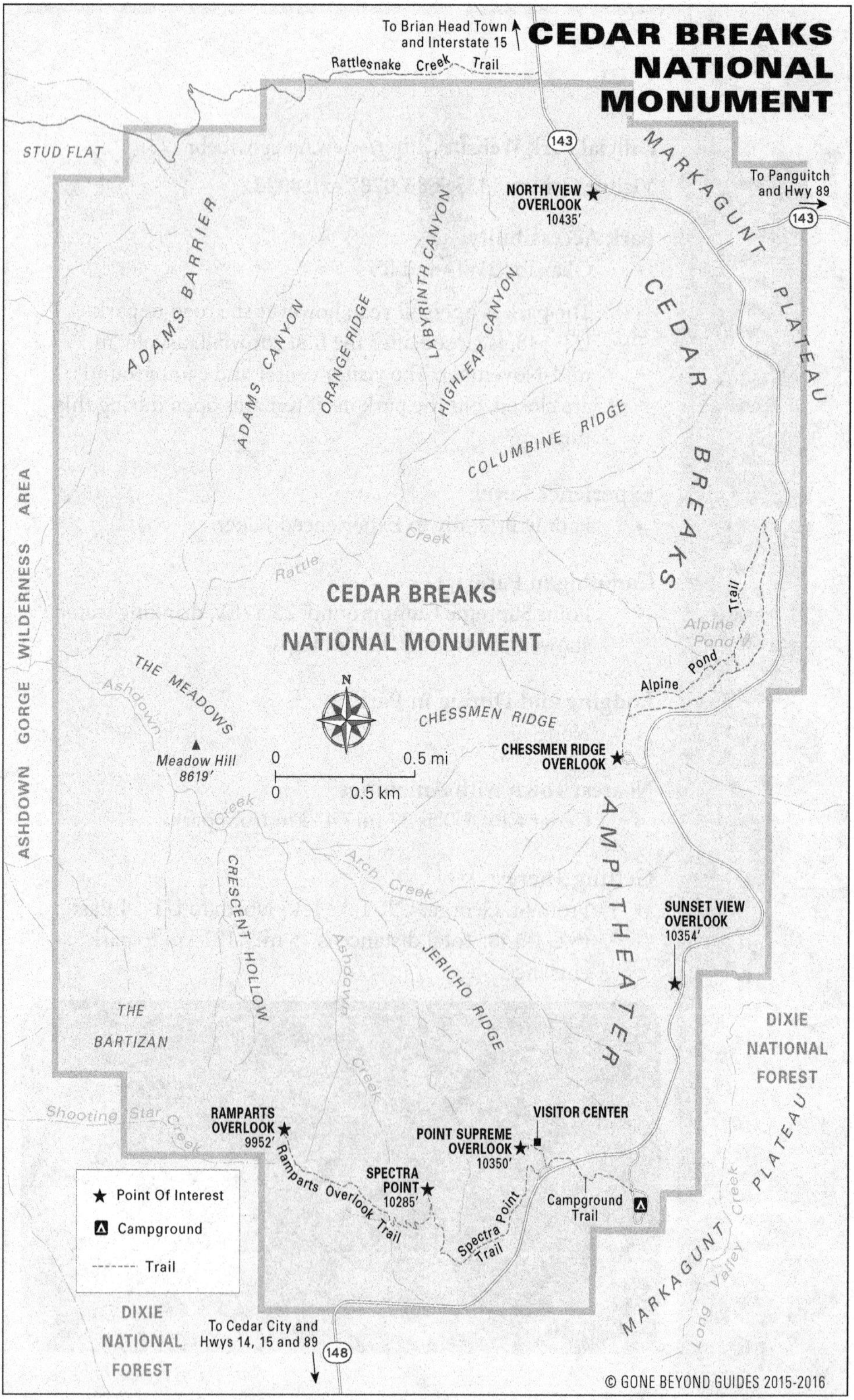
CEDAR BREAKS NATIONAL MONUMENT
To Brian Head Town and Interstate 15
Rattlesnake Creek Trail
143
STUD FLAT
MARKAGUNT PLATEAU
To Panguitch and Hwy 89
NORTH VIEW OVERLOOK 10435′
ADAMS BARRIER
ADAMS CANYON
ORANGE RIDGE
LABYRINTH CANYON
HIGHLEAP CANYON
CEDAR BREAKS
COLUMBINE RIDGE
Rattle Creek
CEDAR BREAKS NATIONAL MONUMENT
ASHDOWN GORGE WILDERNESS AREA
Trail
Alpine Pond
Alpine Pond
THE MEADOWS
Ashdown
Meadow Hill 8619′
N
0 0.5 mi
0 0.5 km
CHESSMEN RIDGE
CHESSMEN RIDGE OVERLOOK
AMPHITHEATER
Creek
Arch Creek
CRESCENT HOLLOW
Ashdown Creek
JERICHO RIDGE
SUNSET VIEW OVERLOOK 10354′
THE BARTIZAN
DIXIE NATIONAL FOREST
Shooting Star Creek
RAMPARTS OVERLOOK 9952′
VISITOR CENTER
POINT SUPREME OVERLOOK 10350′
SPECTRA POINT 10285′
Ramparts Overlook Trail
Spectra Point Trail
Campground Trail
Point Of Interest
Campground
Trail
MARKAGUNT PLATEAU
Long Valley Creek
DIXIE NATIONAL FOREST
To Cedar City and Hwys 14, 15 and 89
148
© GONE BEYOND GUIDES 2015-2016

*Panoramic View of Cedar Breaks National Monument*

## What Makes Cedar Breaks Special

Cedar Breaks is kind of like the Pluto of the national monuments within the Grand Circle. At only 6,000 acres, it is debatable as to whether it is big enough to be a national monument, for one. Plus, it's kind of out of the way for folks doing the typical Grand Circle circuit. However, the biggest similarity is that upon closer inspection, the park is full of greatness and features you wouldn't expect to see.

Cedar Breaks is a natural amphitheater, similar to what you would expect to see at Bryce Canyon, but with colors that are darker and richer. The tones are deeper and more subdued at Cedar Breaks, something akin to Bryce Canyon's older, but wiser, fun-sized brother.

At 6,150 acres, the park is easily covered. There are only a handful of trails but most folks just come to lean up against the overlook and gaze out at "the breaks". For those that do stay at the campground and hike around, the reward is an intimate experience in the park coupled with a satisfying feeling you were able to "see it all".

## Hiking in Cedar Breaks National Monument

The one constant for all of these hikes is the altitude. The elevation here is 10,000 plus feet, which can cause shortness of breath and will make an easy hike feel more strenuous. Also, there is less sun protection at this altitude, so make sure you lather up with sunscreen, and wear a hat and sunglasses. This is high enough in the mountains where odd parts get burned, such as the tips of your ears or the top of one's head for the hair challenged. Be prepared and as always, bring plenty of water and some clothing layers.

### Campground Trail

Easy – (1.0 mi / 1.6 km), round trip, allow 30 minutes

This is a partially ADA compliant one mile walk that provide views of the amphitheater. The trail starts at the campground and ends at the visitor center. A great walk for kids wanting to get their junior badge programs or just to stretch the legs. The trail is dog friendly, as long as there is a leash involved.

### Spectra Point & Ramparts Overlook Trail

Moderate – (4.0 mi / 6.4 km), round trip, allow 2 hours

This is the best hike to take for views of the Cedar Breaks amphitheater. The hike to Spectra Point Overlook is just one mile, which gives a more face on view of the amphitheater. If you do continue on the second mile of this there and back hike, you'll be treated by some ancient bristlecone pines.

## Alpine Pond Nature Trail

Easy – (2.0 mi / 3.2 km), round trip, allow 1 hour

This is a great double loop through the high alpine woodlands of the Dixie National Forest. There are great views of the Cedar Breaks amphitheater, but often, sprays of native wildflowers will do a good job of trying to steal the show. There is also a small strand of ancient bristlecone pines to be seen along the way. The trail passes by the small Alpine Pond and is picked up from Chessman Ridge Overlook. To cut the hiking time in half, simply do not take the upper loop.

## Rattlesnake Creek Trail

Strenuous – (19.6 mi / 31.5 km), round trip, full day hike or overnight backpacking trip

Tucked away at the northern entrance to the park is a really incredible hike. Here you are hiking at times amongst some of the same strata that formed the lower elevation red rock features, such as Zion NP, but at a much higher elevation. The result is a more forested, lush environment wrapping around the familiar rock layers of the other parks. The other upsides here are pleasant summer weather and the sounds of the forest, such as the leaves of an Aspen grove. The one downside is the need for bug spray.

Most of the trail is managed by the U.S. Forest Service and is not maintained. There are spots where the trail is ill defined and will require some navigational and map reading skills. Bring a compass and a topo of the area if taking this trail. This trail has no easy exit and is essentially deep within the Dixie National Forest. Make sure you plan ahead and come prepared.

Rattlesnake Creek Trail drops a whopping 2,500 feet over four miles where it meets up with Ashdown Creek. From Ashdown Creek, you can either follow it upstream back into the canyons that make up the foot of the Cedar Breaks amphitheater or head downstream into the Ashdown Gorge Wilderness Area. Either direction is amazing; it is hard to make a recommendation of one over the other. Note that there is a fair amount of travel across privately owned land. Leave no trace and pass through with respect.

*Thems the Breaks*

# South Central Utah

Bryce Canyon National Park ....... 55
Grand Staircase-Escalante National Monument ....... 62
Escalante Petrified Forest State Park ....... 76
Kodachrome Basin State Park ....... 77
Anasazi State Park Museum ....... 79
Capitol Reef National Park ....... 80
Glen Canyon National Recreation Area ....... 93
Rainbow Bridge National Monument ....... 100


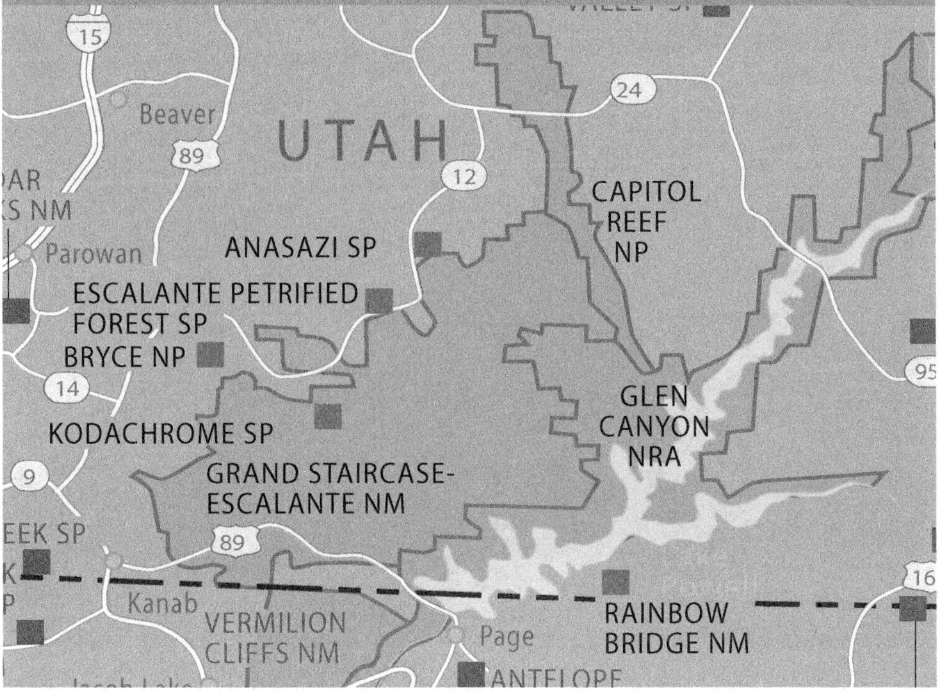

*Zig-zagging down Navajo Trail in Bryce Canyon NP*

# Bryce Canyon National Park

*Sunrise at Bryce Canyon*

## Quick Facts

**Official Park Website:** www.nps.gov/brca

**Visitor Center:** (435) 834-5322

**Park Accessibility:**

- Okay for 2WD and RVs
- Day and Overnight Use

**Experience Level:**

- Family Friendly to Experienced Hiker

**Camping in Park:**

- North Campground: 102 T/RV, drinking water, vault toilets, some pull thru sites, no hookups, dump station in summer, some sites reservable. Reserve at http://www.recreation.gov/
- Sunset Campground: 101 T/RV, drinking water, showers, vault toilets, no hookups, closed in winter, some sites reservable. Reserve at http://www.recreation.gov/

**Lodging in Park:**

- Bryce Canyon Lodge, Phone: (435) 834-8700

**Dining in Park:**

- Bryce Canyon Lodge offers breakfast, lunch and dinner. There is also a general store.

**Nearest Town with Amenities:**

- Bryce, UT is 1.5 mi / 2.4 km from park

**Getting There:**

- From St. George, UT: Take I-15N to UT-9 East, US-89 North and UT-12 East to UT-63 South 125 mi / 201 km to park entrance

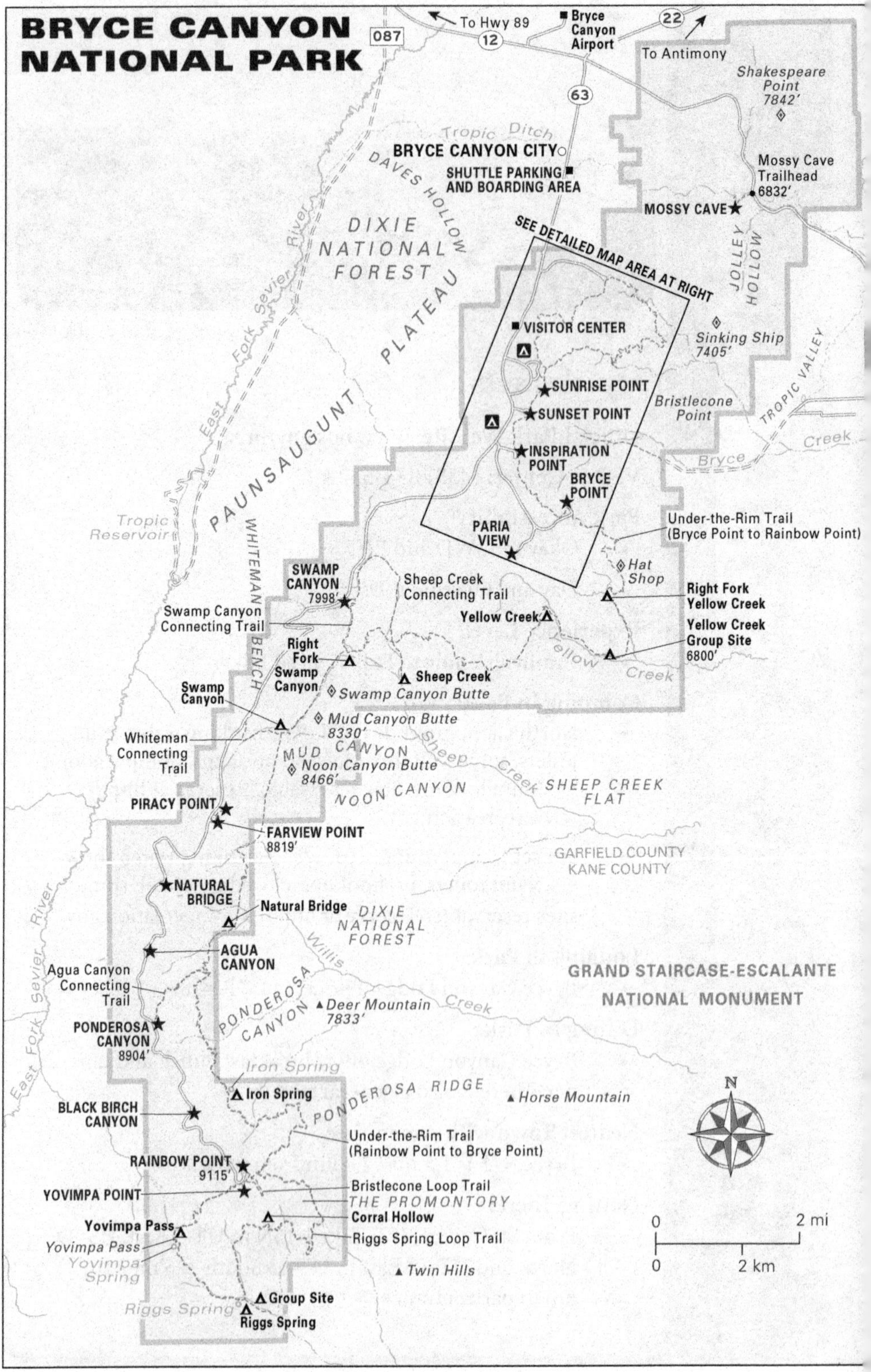
BRYCE CANYON NATIONAL PARK
To Hwy 89
087
12
22
Bryce Canyon Airport
To Antimony
63
Shakespeare Point 7842′
Tropic Ditch
BRYCE CANYON CITY
SHUTTLE PARKING AND BOARDING AREA
DAVES HOLLOW
Mossy Cave Trailhead 6832′
MOSSY CAVE
DIXIE NATIONAL FOREST
SEE DETAILED MAP AREA AT RIGHT
JOLLEY HOLLOW
East Fork Sevier River
PLATEAU
VISITOR CENTER
Sinking Ship 7405′
SUNRISE POINT
TROPIC VALLEY
SUNSET POINT
Bristlecone Point
PAUNSAUGUNT
Creek
Bryce
INSPIRATION POINT
BRYCE POINT
Tropic Reservoir
WHITEMAN BENCH
PARIA VIEW
Under-the-Rim Trail (Bryce Point to Rainbow Point)
Hat Shop
SWAMP CANYON 7998′
Sheep Creek Connecting Trail
Right Fork Yellow Creek
Swamp Canyon Connecting Trail
Yellow Creek
Yellow Creek Group Site 6800′
Right Fork Swamp Canyon
Sheep Creek
Yellow Creek
Swamp Canyon
Swamp Canyon Butte
Mud Canyon Butte 8330′
Whiteman Connecting Trail
MUD CANYON
Sheep Creek
Noon Canyon Butte 8466′
SHEEP CREEK FLAT
NOON CANYON
PIRACY POINT
FARVIEW POINT 8819′
GARFIELD COUNTY
KANE COUNTY
NATURAL BRIDGE
Natural Bridge
DIXIE NATIONAL FOREST
Willis
AGUA CANYON
GRAND STAIRCASE-ESCALANTE NATIONAL MONUMENT
Agua Canyon Connecting Trail
East Fork Sevier River
PONDEROSA CANYON
Deer Mountain 7833′
Creek
PONDEROSA CANYON 8904′
Iron Spring
Iron Spring
PONDEROSA RIDGE
Horse Mountain
N
BLACK BIRCH CANYON
Under-the-Rim Trail (Rainbow Point to Bryce Point)
RAINBOW POINT 9115′
YOVIMPA POINT
Bristlecone Loop Trail
THE PROMONTORY
Corral Hollow
0
2 mi
Yovimpa Pass
Yovimpa Pass
Riggs Spring Loop Trail
Yovimpa Spring
0
2 km
Twin Hills
Group Site
Riggs Spring
Riggs Spring

REFER TO MAP AREA AT LEFT

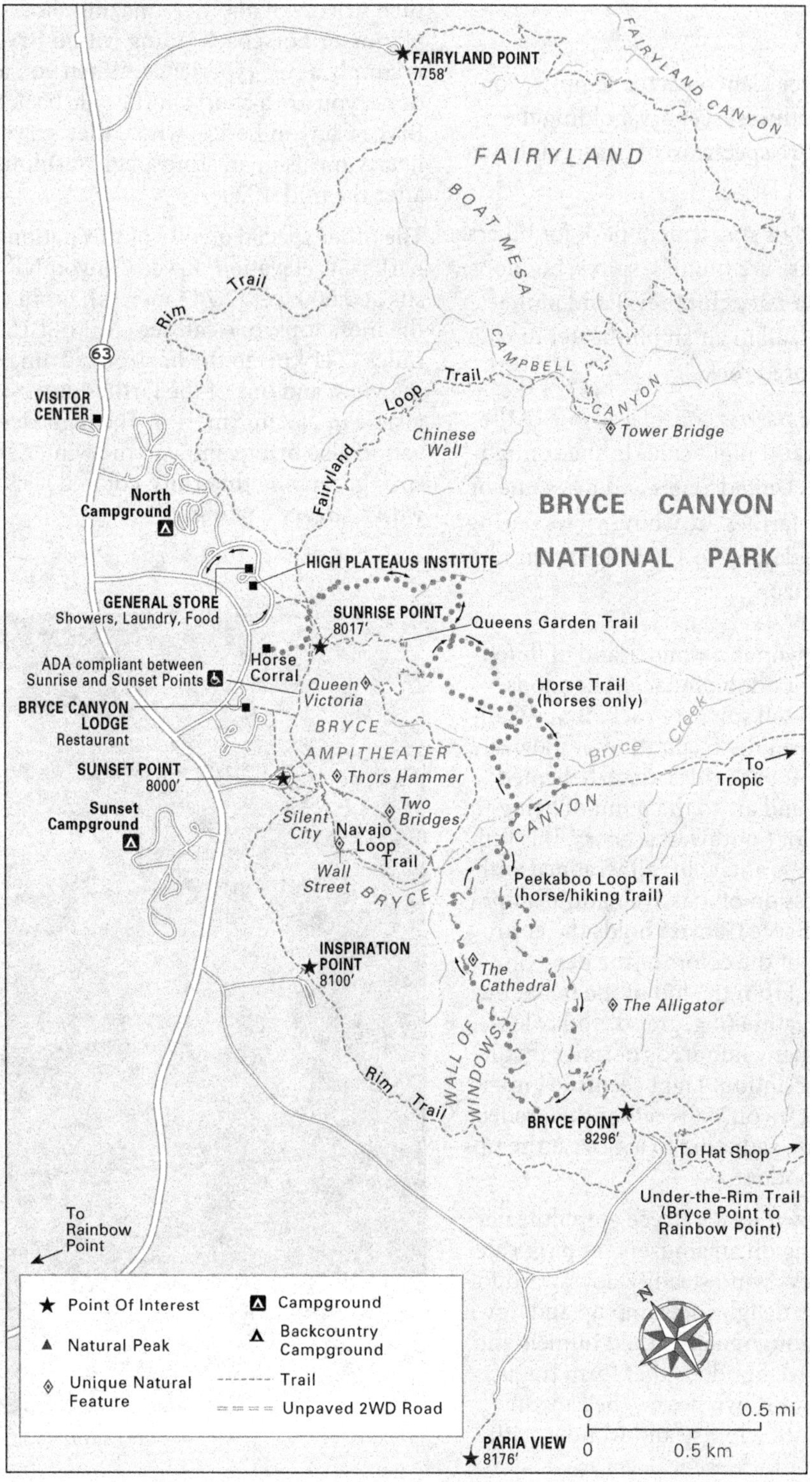
FAIRYLAND POINT
7758′
FAIRYLAND CANYON
FAIRYLAND
BOAT MESA
Rim Trail
63
CAMPBELL CANYON
Fairyland Loop Trail
VISITOR CENTER
Chinese Wall
Tower Bridge
North Campground
BRYCE CANYON NATIONAL PARK
HIGH PLATEAUS INSTITUTE
GENERAL STORE
Showers, Laundry, Food
SUNRISE POINT
8017′
Queens Garden Trail
Horse Corral
ADA compliant between Sunrise and Sunset Points
Queen Victoria
Horse Trail (horses only)
BRYCE CANYON LODGE
Restaurant
BRYCE AMPITHEATER
Bryce Creek
To Tropic
SUNSET POINT
8000′
Thors Hammer
Sunset Campground
Silent City
Two Bridges
CANYON
Navajo Loop Trail
Wall Street
BRYCE
Peekaboo Loop Trail (horse/hiking trail)
INSPIRATION POINT
8100′
The Cathedral
The Alligator
WALL OF WINDOWS
Rim Trail
BRYCE POINT
8296′
To Hat Shop
Under-the-Rim Trail (Bryce Point to Rainbow Point)
To Rainbow Point
Point Of Interest
Campground
Natural Peak
Backcountry Campground
Unique Natural Feature
Trail
Unpaved 2WD Road
N
0 0.5 mi
0 0.5 km
PARIA VIEW
8176′

## What Makes Bryce Canyon Special

- Bryce Canyon is the template for Southwest scenery, holding the entire spectrum of desert colors in one place.
- It is an amusement park for hikers. There are tunnels, spires, hoodoos, (aka fairy chimneys) and pinnacles, all in an amphitheater of fruit colored rock.
- The park is considered one of the darkest night skies in the contiguous United States and has some of the farthest-reaching views during the day, up to 150 miles to the horizon.

Bryce Canyon is a wonderland of fluted rock and hoodoo pinnacles; hoodoos being thin tall spires of rock. Bryce Canyon has been the inspiration of movies, amusement park rides, desert-themed musicals, and art to the point of being the template for Southwest scenery. It is full of grandness and color all wrapped within a succession of massive natural amphitheaters. Bryce Canyon holds the entire spectrum of the colors of the desert in one place. From the top of the mesa, the view is breathtaking, grand, and colorful in so many hundreds of tones that it defies description. Light seems to emit from the canyon walls rather than reflect off of them, radiating to a glow at the tips of each hoodoo.

Hiking down inside Bryce amphitheater is like going on an amusement park ride. All journeys wind steadily downward followed by a delightful tramp up and down knolls, through man-carved tunnels and past massive hoodoos that form fragile spires. Once down below, the canyon floor is more whimsy and wonder with pines growing as tall as the spires, each turn worthy of another amazing shot. Hiking or horseback riding within Bryce is simply a fun experience. When you are done, you are a short shuttle ride back to Bryce Canyon Lodge, where they serve hearty meals in an atmosphere fashioned after the mid-1920s.

The other special quality of this national park is its elevation. Bryce Canyon NP sits at 9,000 feet (2,743 meters). From the mesa tops, one can see clear out 150 miles (241 km) to the horizon, an amazing view, and one of the farthest horizons visible in North America. The high elevation also brings snow in the winter and spring, capping the fruity-colored rocks with a sugary coating.

*Douglas firs within the hoodoos*

# Hiking in Bryce Canyon NP

## Mossy Cave

Easy – (0.8 mi / 1.3 km), round trip, allow 30 minutes, elev. Δ: 300 ft / 91 m, trailhead on Highway 12, 4 mi east of SR 63

A short hike that follows along a stream created by a man made diversion during the late 1800's by Mormon Pioneers. There are two spurs to this hike. The left spur ends at Mossy Cave, a large rocky overhang with a small waterfall that creates a nice mossy environment for plants. During the winter, look for icicle sheets created by the dripping waters, which are very cool and unusual. The right spur leads to a good-sized waterfall that also has been known to freeze completely during the winter.

## Rim Trail

Easy – (0.9 mi / 1.5 km), one way, allow 1 hour, elev. Δ: 1,235 ft / 376 m, multiple trailheads along rim of Bryce Canyon

The Rim Trail from Sunrise Point to Sunset Point is flat and offers a leisurely way to take in the park. Pick up the trail from either point and follow the well-marked path. The Rim Trail does continue south from Sunset Point for a total of 5.5 miles (9.2km) one-way, but the trail from here has a lot of ups and downs and is considered strenuous.

## Fairyland Loop

Strenuous – (8.0 mi /12.9 km), round trip, allow 5 hours, elev. Δ: 2,309 ft / 704 m, trailheads at Sunrise and Fairyland Points

Fairyland Loop is similar to Peekaboo but as it is a little longer, offers even more to the hiker. There is plenty to see on the trail, including China Wall, an impressively long wall of rock. You can also see a double arch with unique monolithic sentinels called Tower Bridge. Fairyland Loop is the least crowded trail of the popular trails at Bryce Canyon and is well worth it if you want to do a longer hike. Pick up the trail at Fairyland Point. The trail uses the Rim Trail to create a full loop.

## Tower Bridge

Moderate – (3.0 mi / 4.8 km), round trip, allow 2 – 3 hours, elev. Δ: 950 ft / 290 m, trailhead at Sunrise Point

See Fairyland Loop for additional details. The trail starts at Sunrise Point and follows Fairlyland Loop partially down until a juncture to a short spur trail to view Tower Bridge. Tower Bridge is a formation of two colorful hoodoos connected by a fragile layer of rock midway down the "towers". There is another natural bridge that can be seen in the same view. Head back up the same way you came down or continue onwards on the longer Fairyland Loop.

## Queen's Garden Trail

Easy – (1.8 mi / 2.9 km), round trip, allow 2 hours, elev. Δ: 320 ft / 98 m, trailhead at Sunrise Point

Queen's Garden is 0.9 miles (1.4 km) down and the same distance back up. The trail is the least strenuous in terms of steepness compared to the other trails that head into the canyon, but it is by no means a flat trail. Picking up the Queen's Garden trail from Sunrise Point, hike down and wind your way through tunnels to the hoodoo called Queen Victoria and the surrounding rock formations that make up her garden. You can follow the trail back to the top, though many folks opt to combine this trail with the Navajo Trail to create a loop.

## Peekaboo Trail

Strenuous – (5.5 mi / 8.8 km), round trip, allow 3 – 4 hours, elev. Δ: 1,555 ft / 473 m, trailhead at Bryce Point

Peekaboo is one of the best trails in Bryce Canyon. The loop is picked up from either Bryce Point or Sunset via the Navajo Trail. The trail gives the hiker a sense of

remoteness and a personal experience as you walk up and down gullies and past goblins, fins and rows of hoodoos. Every bend rewards the hiker with a different view of often-unimaginable rock shapes. You will find yourself a ways from the rim, in the heart of the amphitheater, which gives a better sense of grandness of Bryce Canyon. The loop can be done on its own or combined with Navajo or Queen's Garden Trails. Peekaboo is not terribly crowded, though it does get a fair amount of horse traffic.

## Hat Shop Trail

Moderate – (4.0 mi /6.4 km), round trip, allow 2 - 3 hours, elev. Δ: 1,436 ft / 438 m, trailhead at Bryce Point

From the trailhead, descend via the Under the Rim Trail for 2 miles to a set of thin spired hoodoos with delicately balanced capstones defying gravity. The hike is a down and up, there and back hike. There are ample other Bryce Canyon type features along the way to the final destination.

## Swamp Canyon

Moderate – (4.3 mi / 7.2 km), round trip, allow 2 - 3 hours, elev. Δ: 800 ft / 244 m, trailhead at Swamp Canyon Overlook

Swamp Canyon Trail starts at about the mid-point in the park, further south of the main amphitheaters. This loop trail offers a mixture of denser forest and the famous hoodoos. Unlike the endless stream of hikers coming down Navajo Trail, Swamp Canyon is definitely more intimate and may be a better option on crowded days.

## Bristlecone Loop

Easy – (1.0 mi / 1.6 km), round trip, allow 30 minutes, elev. Δ: 195 ft / 59 m, trailhead at Rainbow Point, southern end of park

While most of the attention in Bryce is near the entrance of the park, the southern section of the park receives lets attention. Here the area contains more of a pleasant evergreen forest offering. Bristlecone Loop is a short hike in the southern section, displaying expansive views from 9,100 feet across a forested and green part of the state. As the trail name suggests, there are examples of the bristlecone pine, a gnarled and aged tree that can grow to 1,800 years here.

*Bryce Canyon in early spring*

The hike is pleasant and as the highest trail in the park, can be a little breathtaking for many reasons.

## Riggs Spring Loop

Strenuous – (8.5 mi / 13.7 km), round trip, allow 4 – 5 hours, elev. Δ: 2,248 ft / 685 m, trailhead at Yovimpa Point

A very different side of Bryce, Riggs Spring is an ambling pleasant hike through fir, spruce, quaking aspens, and even ancient bristlecone pines. The hike is the southernmost trail in the park. As the trail's title suggests, there is a little spring in a shady setting. Do treat the water before using. This is a popular trail for overnight campers.

*Along the floor of Bryce Canyon*

# Grand Staircase-Escalante National Monument

## Quick Facts

**Official Park Website:** www.blm.gov/ut/st/en/fo/grand_staircase-escalante.html

**Visitor Center:**

None in park, contact: BLM Kanab Headquarters, 669 South Highway 89A, Kanab, Utah 84741, Phone: (435) 644-1200

**Park Accessibility:**

- 2WD, 4WD recommended for most roads
- Day and Overnight Use

**Experience Level:**

- Primarily Experienced Hiker – Backcountry Hiker,
- Some trails Family Friendly - Casual Hiker

**Camping in Park:**

- No developed campground, backcountry camping okay with permit

**Lodging and Dining in Park:**

- None

**Nearest Town with Amenities:**

- Tropic, UT is 5 mi / 8 km from park

**Getting There:**

- From St. George, UT: Take UT-59 South and AZ-389 East 81 mi / 130 km to park entrance
- From Page, AZ: Take US-89 North 17 mi / 27 km to park entrance

*Wahweap Hoodoo*

## What Makes Grand Staircase-Escalante Special

- Being nearly 1.9 million acres of pristine, diverse and multifaceted Utah desert, knowing you are hiking in the heart of the Colorado Plateau
- A remarkable and vast array of all manner of rarely seen arches, petroglyphs, hoodoos, canyons, slot canyons, lush riparian folds cut deep into rock walls and well, anything and everything that can be found in the Utah desert
- Roughly the size of three Rhode Islands and only two paved roads

A connection can be made with Glen Canyon National Recreation Area and the Grand Staircase-Escalante National Monument. The most obvious is that they are two very large parks siting right next to each other. Glen Canyon NRA protects a substantial portion of the Escalante River and its watershed, so they both share the last river to be named in the continental US. They both cover land that has been little disturbed, primarily because it is so rugged a country as to make it hard for the toils of man to penetrate. This is in fact why nearby Glen Canyon was filled with water, because there were no roads or towns to move. From the lens of the Bureau of Reclamation, there was nothing there.

It was only after the deed was done that folks realized there was something there after all, that this was a land worth protecting. Perhaps then, this is the deepest connection between the two parks. Within the profound disappointment by many of burying Glen Canyon with water, there was an acknowledgment that more must be done for those lands around it that are similar in spirit. To that, using the Antiquities Act, President Bill Clinton created Grand Staircase-Escalante National Monument in 1996. It is the largest land area of all the US National Monuments.

While this act was applauded by environmentalists and can be seen as a sentiment in the right direction over what was done with Glen Canyon, it was not seen as positive by many of the residents of Utah. Clinton barely gave 24-hour notice to the Utah governor and state congress, giving them no time to react. The designation was attacked from many different angles and remains a sore subject with Utah residents.

Politics aside, Grand Staircase-Escalante is a massive, rugged, and pristine world. Entering it requires preparation, topo maps, and backcountry skills and for all of this preparation, its rewards are many. It is in many ways, the last frontier within the contiguous United States, where the meter of a person is on equal ground with the land.

## Hiking Grand Staircase-Escalante NM

All of these hikes have dozens of variants. The routes described below are the most commonly traveled routes.

### Lower Calf Creek Falls

Moderate – (5.9 mi / 9.5 km), round trip, allow 3 hours, elev. Δ: 250 ft / 76 m, trailhead at Calf Creek Campground

The trail starts by acknowledging the soft sand underneath your feet on a trail that seems nearly surreal in its beauty. The line of the trail cuts into a tree-lined oasis as the canyon floor meets with massive blocks of darkly streaked walls of Navajo Sandstone that tower above on each side. The hike up has to be seen to be believed. Look for numerous cliff dwelling ruins tucked into alcoves as well as alien looking humanoid petroglyphs.

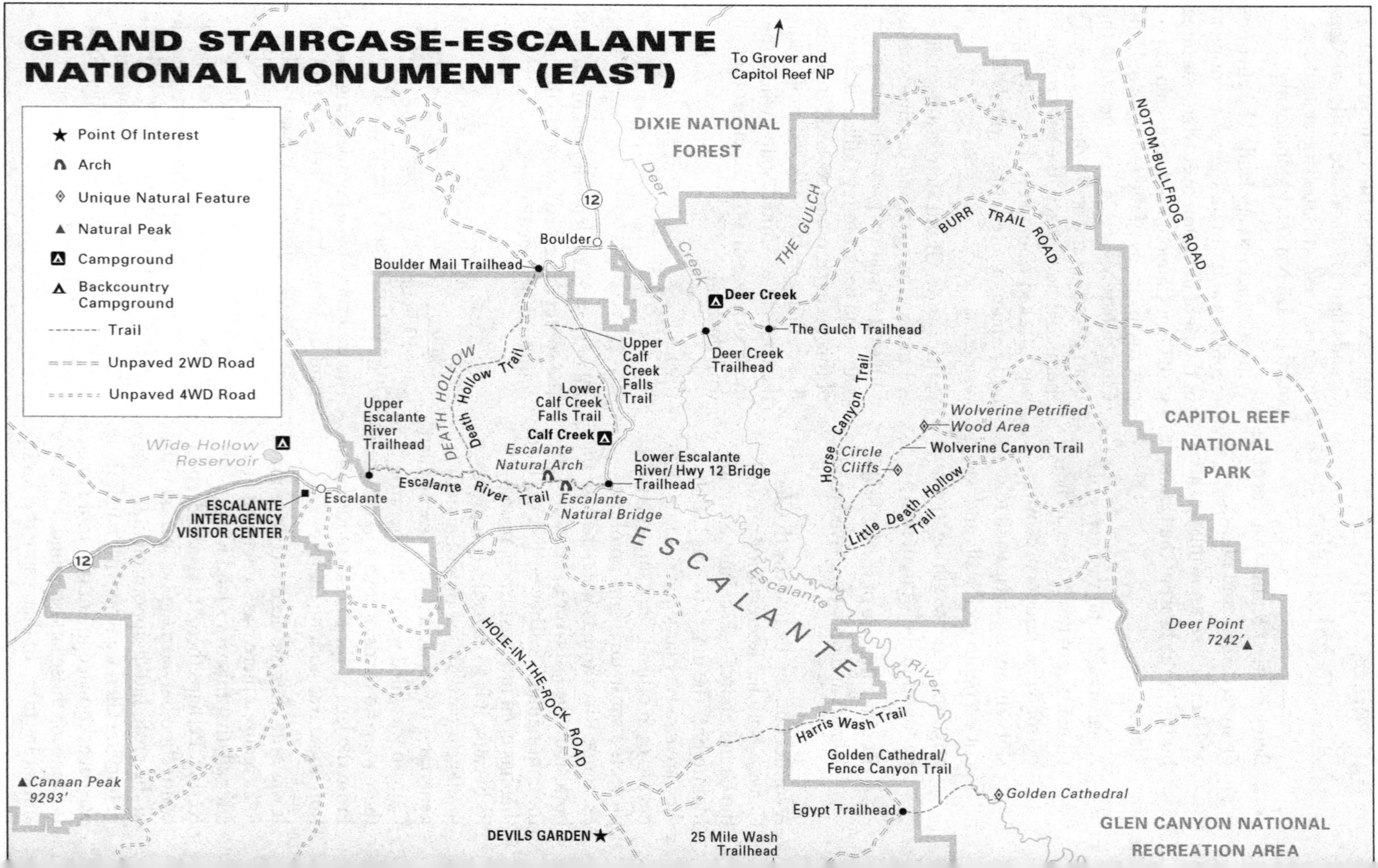
GRAND STAIRCASE-ESCALANTE NATIONAL MONUMENT (EAST)
Point Of Interest
Arch
Unique Natural Feature
Natural Peak
Campground
Backcountry Campground
Trail
Unpaved 2WD Road
Unpaved 4WD Road
To Grover and Capitol Reef NP
DIXIE NATIONAL FOREST
Deer Creek
THE GULCH
BURR TRAIL ROAD
NOTOM-BULLFROG ROAD
CAPITOL REEF NATIONAL PARK
12
Boulder
Boulder Mail Trailhead
Deer Creek
The Gulch Trailhead
Deer Creek Trailhead
Upper Calf Creek Falls Trail
DEATH HOLLOW
Death Hollow Trail
Lower Calf Creek Falls Trail
Calf Creek
Escalante Natural Arch
Upper Escalante River Trailhead
Wide Hollow Reservoir
Escalante
ESCALANTE INTERAGENCY VISITOR CENTER
Escalante River Trail
Escalante Natural Bridge
Lower Escalante River/ Hwy 12 Bridge Trailhead
Horse Canyon Trail
Circle Cliffs
Wolverine Petrified Wood Area
Wolverine Canyon Trail
Little Death Hollow Trail
ESCALANTE
Escalante River
Deer Point 7242'
HOLE-IN-THE-ROCK ROAD
Harris Wash Trail
Golden Cathedral/ Fence Canyon Trail
Golden Cathedral
Egypt Trailhead
Canaan Peak 9293'
DEVILS GARDEN
25 Mile Wash Trailhead
GLEN CANYON NATIONAL RECREATION AREA

# Grand Staircase-Escalante

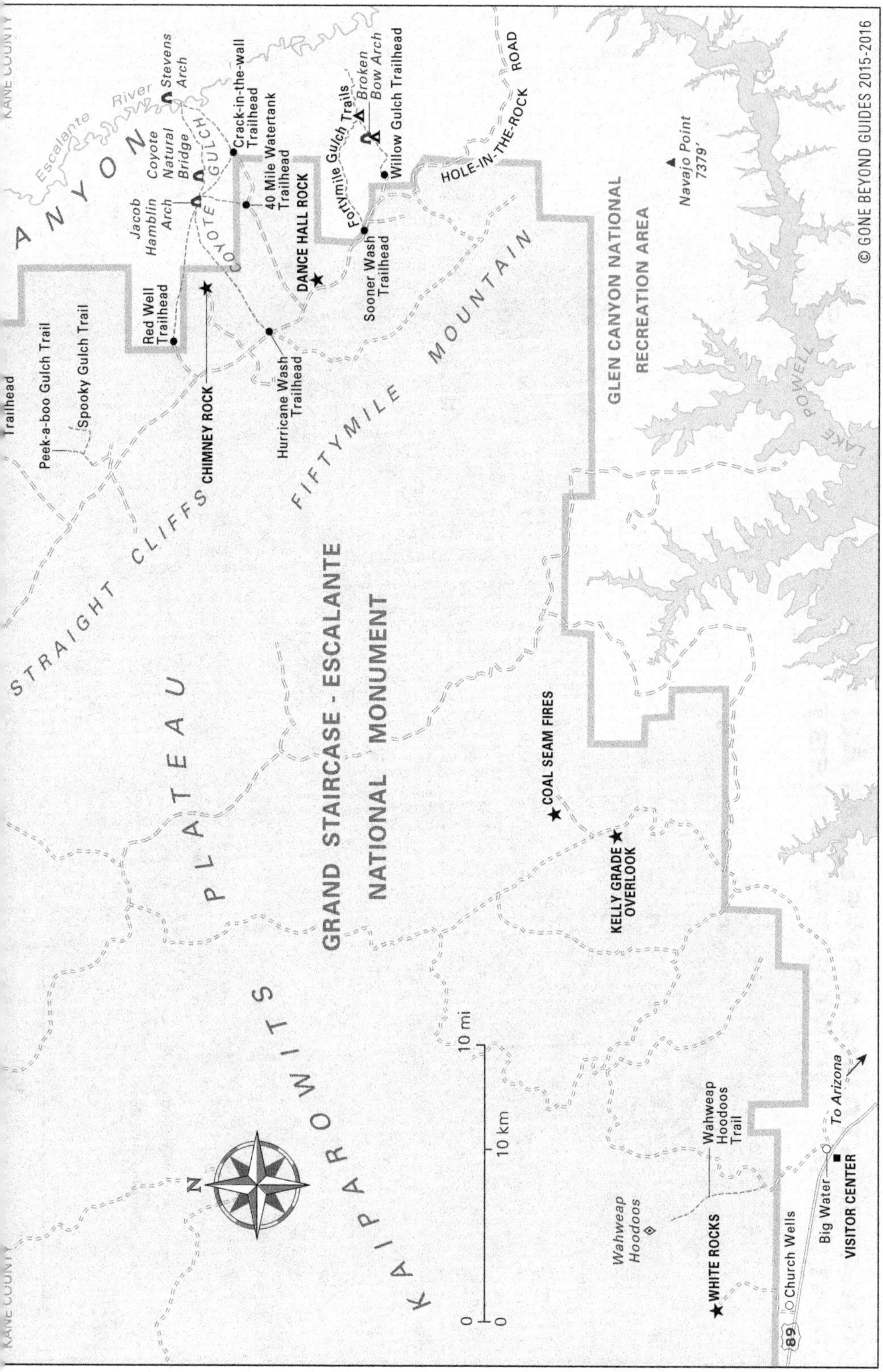

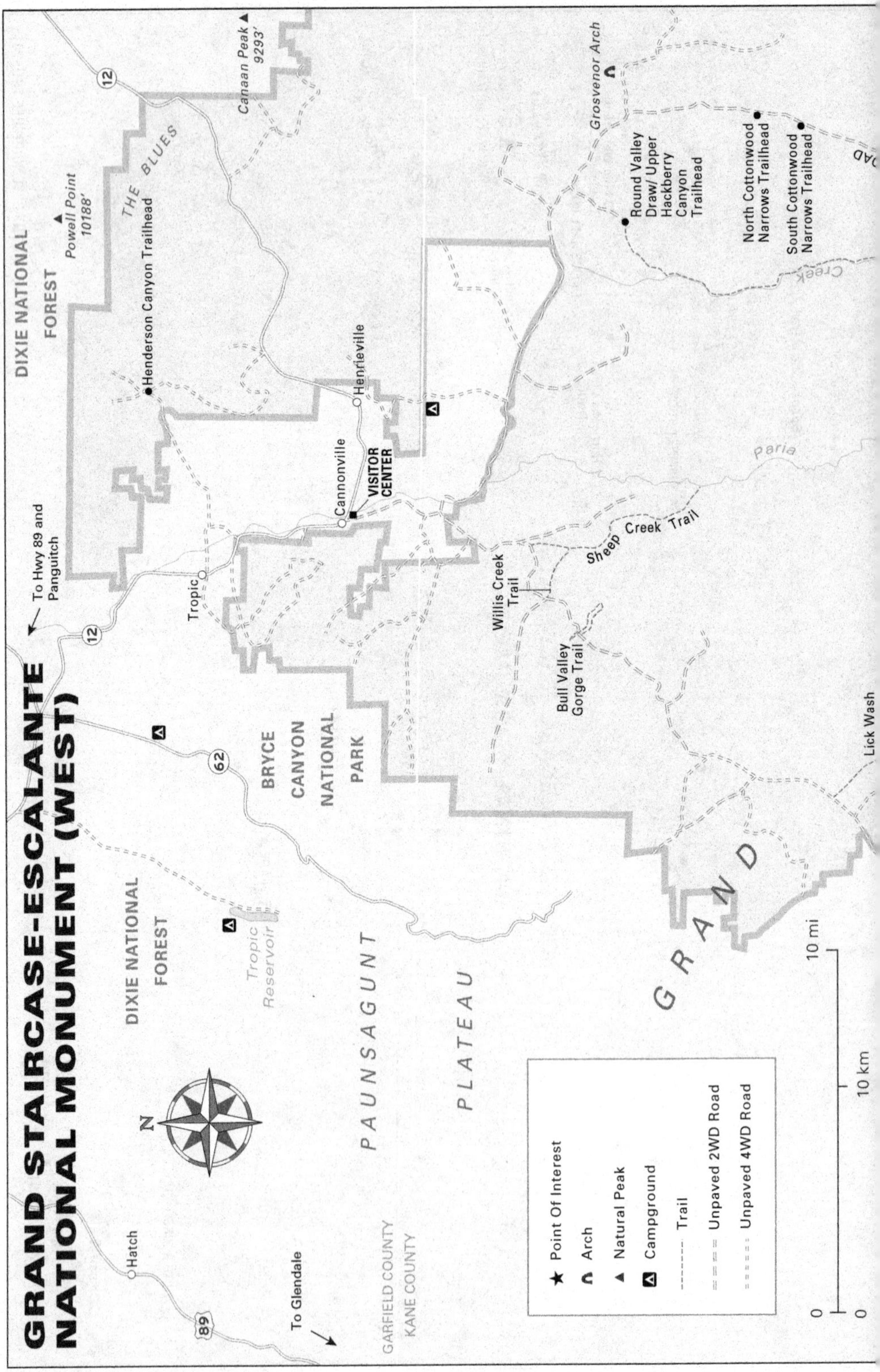
GRAND STAIRCASE-ESCALANTE NATIONAL MONUMENT (WEST)
DIXIE NATIONAL FOREST
DIXIE NATIONAL FOREST
Powell Point 10188'
Canaan Peak 9293'
THE BLUES
Henderson Canyon Trailhead
Henrieville
Cannonville
VISITOR CENTER
Tropic
To Hwy 89 and Panguitch
12
62
89
Hatch
To Glendale
Tropic Reservoir
BRYCE CANYON NATIONAL PARK
PAUNSAGUNT
PLATEAU
GARFIELD COUNTY
KANE COUNTY
N
Grosvenor Arch
Round Valley Draw/ Upper Hackberry Canyon Trailhead
North Cottonwood Narrows Trailhead
South Cottonwood Narrows Trailhead
Creek
Paria
Sheep Creek Trail
Willis Creek Trail
Bull Valley Gorge Trail
Lick Wash
GRAND
Point Of Interest
Arch
Natural Peak
Campground
Trail
Unpaved 2WD Road
Unpaved 4WD Road
0
10 mi
0
10 km

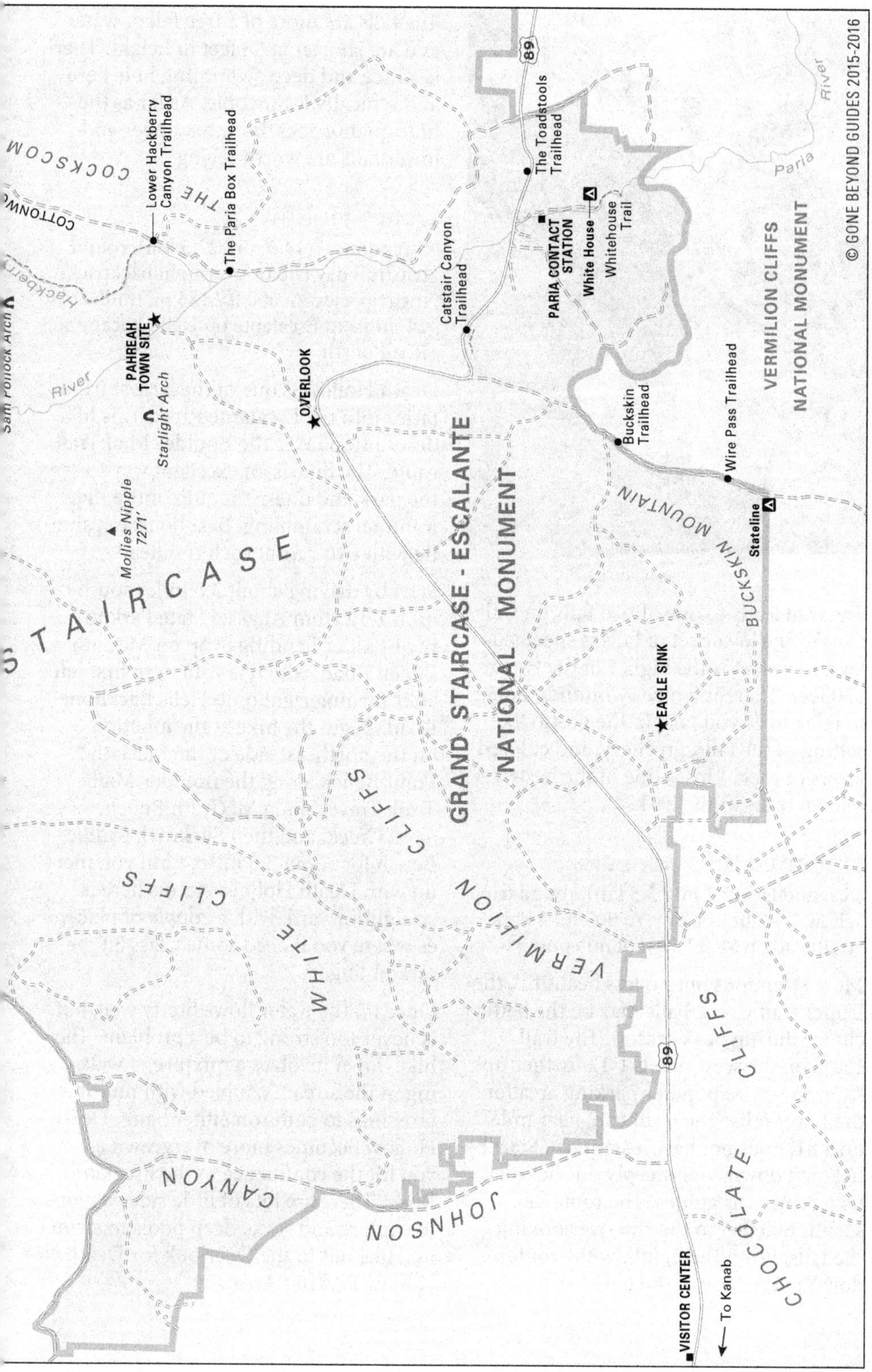

GRAND STAIRCASE - ESCALANTE
NATIONAL MONUMENT
VERMILION CLIFFS
NATIONAL MONUMENT
STAIRCASE
WHITE CLIFFS
VERMILION CLIFFS
CHOCOLATE CLIFFS
JOHNSON CANYON
BUCKSKIN MOUNTAIN
THE COCKSCOMB
Lower Hackberry Canyon Trailhead
The Paria Box Trailhead
PAHREAH TOWN SITE
Starlight Arch
Mollies Nipple 7271'
OVERLOOK
Catstair Canyon Trailhead
The Toadstools Trailhead
PARIA CONTACT STATION
White House
Whitehouse Trail
Buckskin Trailhead
Wire Pass Trailhead
Stateline
EAGLE SINK
VISITOR CENTER
To Kanab
89
Paria River
River
© GONE BEYOND GUIDES 2015-2016

Grand Staircase-Escalante

SOUTH CENTRAL UTAH

*Lower Calf Creek Falls*

The trail leads to one of two falls on Calf Creek. The lower set of falls is spectacular and in fact is the higher of the two at 130 feet. There is a nice swimming hole to relax in as you take in the grotto like setting of the falls, greenery, and colored layers of rock. This is one of the best-known trails in the park.

## Upper Calf Creek Falls

Strenuous – (2.2 mi / 3.5 km), round trip, allow 1 – 2 hours, elev. Δ: 505 ft / 154 m, trailhead on SR 12, east of milepost 81

More strenuous but no less beautiful, the Upper Calf Creek Falls may be the better choice during peak season. The trail starts on the west side UT 12 further up from the more popular parking area for the lower falls. The trailhead, near milepost 81, does not have a signpost. Start by heading downslope steeply on slickrock, using cairns as guides. The route descends 600 feet to the rim overlooking the falls. From there, follow the route down to the base of the falls.

The falls are more of a free fall of water and are shorter at 88 feet in height. There is a nice and deep swimming hole here and typically less people. As far as the hike quality goes, both the upper and lower falls are worth seeing.

## Death Hollow

Strenuous – (14.0 mi / 22.5 km), round trip, full day trip or overnight backpacking trip, elev. Δ: 600 ft / 183 m, trailhead 24 mi from Escalante on Hell's Backbone Road north

Death Hollow is one of the largest tributaries into the Escalante River. This hike description takes the Boulder Mail Trail route. The hike is an excellent way to see the park and doesn't require more than minimal scrambling. Best done as a shuttle with two cars at each trailhead.

Start by driving about 3.8 miles south on UT 12 from Anasazi State Park to the Boulder Landing Strip on McGath Bench Road, which is your very first left after turning right onto Hells Backbone Road. Begin the hike at the junction on the northeast side of the McGath Point Bench along the Boulder Mail Trail. Travel along McGrath Bench, Sand Creek, and then Slickrock Saddle Bench for about 3.5 miles until you meet up with Death Hollow. Access here is straightforward, with a couple of places where you'll need some Class 3 type scrambling.

Once in, the water flows pretty well, but is never too strong to be a problem. The hike down involves a mixture of walking in the stream coupled with multiple crossings to paths on either bank. Death Hollow becomes more overgrown as you hit the confluence to the Escalante River. There are lots of little side canyons to explore and some deep pools to swim in. Hike out to the Overlook for Death Hollow Parking Area.

## Upper Escalante River

Moderate to Strenuous – (13.0 mi / 20.9 km), one-way, elev. Δ: 500 ft / 152 m, trailhead along river at Escalante, UT

There aren't many hikes in the world where you can literally close the door to your hotel room and just take a long walk down a river canyon and when you are done, get picked up with ease right from the highway. This hike exists and it is one of the gems of the Southwest in terms of beauty. It meanders gently downstream and passes arches and natural bridges, thick wonderful canyon walls, and even some swimming holes.

First off, for hikers, this description can be followed during the dry season when the river is low enough to wade down. During the wet season, the route is more suitable for river rafting, inner tubing, and kayaking.

The hike starts just about anywhere within the town of Escalante where you can access the river. If you want to reduce the amount of river wading whilst in town, find your way to the Pine Creek Escalante River Confluence at the northeast end of town. Not much in the way of parking here, but you'll soon be in the thick of the riparian desert wilderness from here.

Once inside the canyon, the river meanders almost as a rule, snaking along one bend after the other, giving to the curious the wonder of what could be around the next bend. The meanders allow for constantly changing views as well. One of the first notable formations to see is the Escalante Natural Arch, which sits high up on the south wall and is super easy to miss. Look for it after the confluence with Sand Creek. Less than 0.5 miles further on is Escalante Natural Bridge, a humbling and beautiful sight as well as the largest formation in the park. The bridge also marks the home stretch of the hike. Look for the UT 12 Bridge and your ride to home base back in Escalante. Your ride will pass by the Kiva Koffeehouse, which serves espressos seasonally from April to October in a very nice rustic building with great views.

## Escalante Natural Bridge

Easy – (3.5 mi / 5.6 km), round trip, allow 2 hours, elev. Δ: 100 ft / 30 m, trailhead at Highway 12 bridge over Escalante River

For those that don't have the time to hike downstream from the town of Escalante, it is possible to see the Escalante Natural Bridge and do a bit of river trail hiking coming from the UT 12 Bridge that crosses over the Escalante River. Look for signs that indicate Escalante River trailhead access about 14 miles from the town of Escalante, heading south. The Escalante Natural Arch is about 0.5 miles further upstream (add 1.0 mile to your round trip distance).

## Fortymile and Willow Gulch Loop

Moderate – (11.0 mi / 17.7 km), round trip, allow 6 hours, elev. Δ: 540 ft / 165 m, trailhead at Sooner Wash Trailhead off Hole in the Rock Road

Narrow canyons, bold rock faces, and a maze of seemingly endless hiking possibilities, this is Fortymile and Willow Gulch. There are many ways to explore this area, but in this description, the route starts at Sooner Wash Trailhead. Folks can start out at the adjacent Dance Hall Rock Campsite and check out the cool looking Sooner Rocks. The trailhead and the campsite are off Hole in the Rock Road. Note that this hike has spots where you will need to wade through waterholes and depending on water levels, may even require some swimming to get past the water obstacles.

From Sooner Wash Trailhead hike for 1.5 miles into the confluence of Sooner Wash and Fortymile Gulch. This portion will have some areas that require wading through canyon water pockets.

Continue for several miles to the Willow Gulch confluence. Here you can keep going down Fortymile Gulch as it meets up with Lake Powell, however the going is muddier. This description heads up Willow Gulch, which avoids the mucky bits and takes the hiker to Broken Bow Arch, which is about 0.5 miles up Willow Gulch from the confluence.

*Devils Garden at night*

Willow Gulch is definitely the more pristine of the two choices at the juncture. To exit, hike up any of the three main streams that feed the tributary. The northernmost stream is the most convenient of the three as it passes by a parking area near Hole in the Rock Road. Either hike back to your car from here or be thankful you brought two cars and parked one at the exit site. If you do have a second car, the total trip is 8.2 miles.

## Hole in the Rock Trail

Strenuous – (1.0 mi / 1.6 km), round trip, allow 1 hour, elev. Δ: 600 ft / 182 m, trailhead on Highway 12 , just southeast of Escalante

Early Mormon pioneers used this steep but marginally passable draw as the route down to the Colorado River. The first thing one thinks when coming to the rim of the steep and narrow gully is something along the lines of, "They took their wagons and animals down that??" The pioneers blasted the crevice to make it wide enough for wagons.

Today, this old supply route can be hiked down to what is now Lake Powell. It's very steep and very rocky, but fortunately only about a half mile. The trail has a plaque at the bottom commemorating the tenacity of these early settlers.

## Devils Garden

Easy – (0.5 mi / 0.8 km), round trip, allow 30 – 60 minutes, elev. Δ: 10 ft / 3 m, trailhead on Hole in the Rock Road

This is a great family trail just off the Hole in the Rock Road. Here there be hoodoos and arches, of all manner of shapes and sizes, oddly misshapen things, every last one of them. To get to this garden of the devil himself, simply head east five miles on UT 12 from Escalante to the unpaved Hole in the Rock Road, which is suitable for 2WD vehicles in dry weather. Another 13 miles on Hole in the Rock takes you to a signed turnoff to Devils Garden. Park and roam around. There are picnic tables, BBQ grills and a pit toilet here, making this a nice lunch spot. This is a great place to make a deal.

## Golden Cathedral

Moderate – (9.5 mi / 15.3 km), round trip, allow 5 - 6 hours, elev. Δ: 1,260 ft / 384 m, trailhead in Egypt area off Hole in the Rock Road

Golden Cathedral is a strikingly beautiful and unworldly set of three arches. Together they form a line of holes that resemble a massive rock spine. There is great light play here, that helps give the formation its name. The hike requires some decent navigational skill, winding down Fence Canyon into the confluence of Neon Canyon and the Escalante River.

Take Hole in the Rock Road to Egypt Bench Road and follow it for 9.9 miles. High clearance vehicles recommended here, as there are several washes to cross. At 2.9 miles, you will pass the trailhead for Twentyfive Mile Wash. At 6.4 miles, the road will turn sharply right into a wash and one mile later, you will need to navigate up a short but rocky and steep incline. Take the fork at 9.3 miles and turn right, parking the car at the Egypt trailhead after 9.9 miles.

From here, while there isn't much in the way of official trail, there are plenty of cairns to follow. You are at the highest point in the hike and will now drop down into Fence Canyon. Keep to the left of Fence Canyon as you come to it in order to head down into the wash and the confluence of the Escalante River and Fence Canyon. Also, be sure to note the route as you head down so you can find it on your way back.

From here, pull out your water shoes and follow the Escalante River downstream one-mile south from the confluence with Fence Canyon to Neon Canyon, which is the first side canyon on your left.

Head up Neon Canyon for another 0.9 miles to Golden Cathedral. This last stretch and the triptych of arches is serene and majestic and worth the trek to get there. Heading further up Neon Canyon requires ropes and technical skills.

## Peek-a-Boo Gulch

Moderate – (2.0 mi / 3.2 km), round trip, allow 1 – 2 hours, elev. Δ: 100 ft / 30 m, trailhead at Dry Fork area off Hole in the Rock Road

Peek-a-Boo is a really fun little slot canyon. The trailhead is 26 miles northeast on Hole in the Rock Road and then take Dry Fork Turnoff, staying left. Take the short hike from Dry Fork Overlook to the bottom of Dry Fork. Peek-a-Boo is just ahead to the north. Dry Fork Road is barely passable by 2WD vehicles, but is better for high clearance rigs.

What makes this slot canyon fun is all of the little scramble puzzles that need to be figured out. Lots of little dry falls and chockstones. Finding the right route

*In Coyote Gulch*

up the dry fall or figuring out whether to go under the big rock in the way or climb over it makes this a fun canyon to solve. A great hike for kids as none of the scrambling is that technical, though smaller children may need the occasional boost up.

The slot canyon is very narrow, though Spooky Gulch, which is typically combined with a hike through Peek-a-Boo, makes this gulch seem wide and spacious by comparison. Most folks scramble up Peek-a-Boo and then cross over and head into Spooky Gulch.

To combine the two slot canyons and make it a loop hike, scramble up Peek-a-Boo and then head overland through sandy red open terrain to the wide dry wash of Spooky Gulch. From there, head through Spooky back to Dry Fork and your car. This loop is 3.5 miles total.

## Spooky Gulch

Moderate – (3.2 mi / 5.1 km), round trip, allow 2 -3 hours, elev. Δ: 100 ft / 30 m, trailhead at Dry Fork area off Hole in the Rock Road

Spooky Gulch is another short slot canyon that can be done alone or by combining with Peek-a-Boo Gulch. To get to Spooky Gulch, take the same route as to Peek-a-Boo from the Dry Fork Road.

Spooky Gulch is very different from Peek-a-Boo, though they are right next to each other. Whereas Peek-a-Boo is essentially a fun series of scramble puzzles to solve, Spooky is an extremely thin and deep slot canyon. It is so narrow that in some places there is only room for one person at time to pass. The canyon can make it feel like you are being compressed by the walls and some folks hit the narrow section at first thinking that it is too narrow to enter. You can and it does go all the way through, but it is definitely more of a spooky slot canyon than a soulful one. Those that are claustrophobic might want to take a pass on this one.

## Coyote Gulch

Strenuous – (11.5 mi / 18.5 km), round trip, allow 5 - 6 hours or two-night backpacking trip, elev. Δ: 970 ft / 296 m, trailhead, see below

Coyote Gulch offers incredible scenery and some unique formations along the way. The trek is strenuous and it is recommended to make this a two-day jaunt. There is one section, Crack-in-the-Wall, that makes an argument for the day hike option if you don't have two days to spare, simply because it such an amazing and cool way to get down a cliff face.

The hike starts at some water tanks located 4.4 miles up Fortymile Ridge Road after coming from Hole-in-the-Rock Road in Escalante. The trail climbs up to Crack-in-the-Wall (or Crack-in-the-Rock), which is the first obstacle to surmount. The crack in question is a massive section of sandstone cliff that has broken off from the main section and moved outwards just enough for a grown person to shimmy in between. For the uninitiated, this may sound terrifying but it is easier than it may sound. Start by following the cairns to the very edge of the cliff and head right and down to what looks like the end of the cliff. Here you will find a crack that you shimmy in between to work to the canyon floor. There are two areas of exposure, but for the most part, the crack is safe and is an exhilarating means of getting down to the river and upstream from there. If you are backpacking, it is recommended to lower your packs down by rope.

The scenery is amazing throughout and Coyote Gulch itself does not disappoint. Here one can fine one of the largest arches in the United States, Stevens Arch, standing 160 feet tall and spanning 225 feet. This is a hulk of an arch, simply massive. Then there is Coyote Bridge, a very picturesque natural bridge with water flowing underneath it year round.

Finally, there is Jacob Hamblin Arch, which marks the exit point for the hike. This is for some the hardest part of the hike. Hikers must be able to navigate up a 100-foot section of very steep slickrock to exit onto Fortymile Ridge. If you have anyone in the group that has doubts about this section, have the leader ascend and drop a rope down to aid in the climb up. This section is very exposed and at 45 degrees, is very steep. Once at the top of the ridge, head back to the water tanks and your vehicle.

## Little Death Hollow

Easy – (16.0 mi / 25.7 km), round trip, full day or backpacking trip, elev. Δ: 600 ft / 183 m, trailhead: see description below

Grand Staircase has not one but two areas named Death Hollow. This hike refers to the beautiful slot canyon of Little Death Hollow. No one is sure what the relationship is between the Hollows, father and son perhaps? Whatever the connection, you can discuss this as you travel through this remote canyon. Little Death Hollow is popular for its long and narrow slot canyon, which is for the most part, obstacle free. The hike heads into the canyon and slot canyon further up with a turnaround point at the confluence with Horse Canyon. As with all hikes that involve narrow slot canyons,

*Little Death Hollow Slot Canyon*

be well aware of the weather to avoid being caught in a flash flood.

Little Death Hollow is in a more remote and generally less accessible part of the park, east of UT 12. To get there drive 19 miles east from Boulder, UT along Burr Trail Road and then turn right and head south on the unpaved Wolverine Loop Road. From this junction you will see a signpost indicating that the trailhead for Little Death Hollow is 12 miles on. This road is recommended for high clearance vehicles and even then, is impassable when wet. The main problem areas are at the two streambed crossings, Horse Canyon and Wolverine Creek. It will look level and inviting at the junction, but the road has some steep and sandy parts that are designed by nature to get 2WD cars stuck.

Once the turnoff for Wolverine Loop Road is found, take the right junction, heading counter-clockwise around the loop. This will allow for checking out the Wolverine Petrified Wood Natural Area, which is as amazing as Petrified Forest National Park, but without the crowds. Be courteous to all of the generations ahead of you and refrain from picking up any pieces. From the petrified wood area, continue on the loop. It will cut east and then south into a valley before the entrance to Little Death Hollow. As remote as this is, there is a trail register and official trailhead. If you gotten this far, "Woot!" Let the hiking begin.

The canyon of Little Death Hollow starts out wide at first with cattle tracks paralleling the trail at first. The canyon continues to narrow and at some point, you realize you are in the slot canyon. In some sections, the canyon is just two feet wide and the water cut sandstone produces multiple lines horizontal to the ground. Depending on the season, there are pools of standing water that need to be crossed. These can be more like quicksand at times, especially after a rainstorm, so be careful.

The route ends at the confluence with Horse Canyon. From here, you can continue downstream to the Escalante River (about 3 miles further on) or head upstream to Wolverine Creek. If you take the upstream route, you can head up Wolverine Creek and hike the length of it to the head of the canyon, which sits just below the Wolverine Petrified Wood Natural Area. This adds another 1.5 miles to the hike, but gives a completely different view on the way back. Wolverine Creek is the first canyon on the right as you head up Horse Canyon. There is one junction as you head up Wolverine, stay to the right to exit closer to the Little Death Hollow Trailhead.

## Cottonwood Canyon Road

Easy to Strenuous – Distance Varies

Cottonwood Road loosely follows the Paria River through Grand Staircase-Escalante NM from Highway 89 to Cannonville 46 miles to the north. The road offers incredible scenery, with views of

*Cottonwood Canyon Road*

river canyons, fins, and barren alien lands that look as if not of this planet. The road is impassable when wet, but is otherwise a great way to see a decent cross section of the park. Along the stretch are seemingly endless hiking opportunities. Sites to explore include Hackberry Canyon, Yellow Mountain, Cottonwood Canyon Narrows, the Cockscomb, and Grosvenor Arch.

The road also leads to Kodachrome State Park. Cottonwood Canyon Road can be picked up near milepost 18 on Highway 89 or from Kodachrome State Park Road.

## Round Valley Draw

Moderate – (4.3 mi / 6.9 km), round trip, allow 2 -3 hours, elev. Δ: 400 ft / 122 m, trailhead is 1.5 miles on Rush Beds Road

Off Cottonwood Canyon Road and close to Grosvenor Arch is another slot canyon called Round Valley Draw. This slot canyon has some beautiful striations and in some areas is covered by suspended rock fall held in place above by the canyon walls.

From the north end of Cottonwood Canyon Road, drive south, then east for 14 miles. There is a signed spur road that heads south and winds up the Round Valley Wash to the mouth of the slot canyon. Off roaders can take the creek bed right up to the mouth, use good judgment on when to get out and start hiking otherwise.

From here, descend into the slot from the mesa top. There is a tree stump at the initial descent point to help navigate down into the slot. The total elevation down is about 15 feet. When the canyon opens up again, climb out back onto the mesa and hike out the way you came. For a longer journey, continue down the draw to Hackberry Creek. Round trip from Hackberry Creek is 5.5 miles.

Note that this slot canyon has contained obstacles that are best navigated with canyoneering skill and equipment (a good length of rope). There is one boulder that can sometimes be navigated by going under while at other times, the 15-foot obstacle requires a rope or good free climbing skills.

## Paria Rimrocks Trail

Moderate – (1.5 mi / 2.4 km), round trip, allow 30 minutes, elev. Δ: 100 ft / 30 m, trailhead: see description below

Some of the coolest rock features in the area; Paria Rimrocks has to be seen to be believed. The trail follows a wash and then cairns to a goblin and hoodoo garden. The area is laden with hoodoos and toadstools, including one known as ET

*Paria Rimrocks - Toadstool Trail*

(aka Red Toadstool). Bring your camera; this is one of the more amazing hikes in the area.

Paria Rimrocks are near Highway 89 near mile marker 19. If driving north from Glen Canyon Dam, there will be a dirt parking area on the right just past the marker. There are maps available at the Grand Staircase-Escalante NM Visitor Center.

## Harris Wash

Moderate – (21.2 mi / 34.1 km), round trip, full day or backpacking trip, elev. Δ: 700 ft / 213 m, trailhead is 4.5 mi south of Escalante on Hole-in-the-Rock Road

Harris Wash is one of the more accessible areas of Grand Staircase-Escalante NM and is also one of the most rewarding. It is the longest tributary of the Escalante River and can be done in full to the river as an overnight backpacking trip or as a day hike, going as far one's spirit of adventure takes them. There are many tributaries to explore, including Zebra and Tunnel Slot canyons, making this one of those hikes where there is seemingly something new around every bend.

Upper Harris Wash offers little in terms of scenery. The beginning of the route is as a small child, shy at first and not showing its true self until deeper into the draw. Big Horn Canyon joins from the north about 1.8 miles in and holds many interesting branches and narrow sections to explore.

At 4.3 miles one reaches Zebra Slot canyon, known for its orange sandstone layers striped with thin bands of white. This tributary is well worth exploring. There are some dryfall obstacles to overcome as well as water filled pools, especially in wet weather.

Going downstream in Harris Wash another mile from Zebra Slot canyon leads to Tunnel Slot canyon. This is a short and cave like section, that follows for about 50 yards with high cliff walls surrounding a narrow passage. One typically will need to wade or even swim through a deep pool at start. The canyon then opens up to a scene of riparian brush and trees. The tunnel is just a few minutes from the main canyon.

There is another tributary about a half mile further downstream, containing serene vistas, several small springs and a simply pleasant vibe all around. Further down is Red Breaks, a seldom explored side canyon with deep passages and some shallow slot canyons. Opposite Red Breaks is the Harris Wash trailhead, used as a short cut to Escalante River from Halfway Hollow. It is possible to take Halfway Hollow back to Hole-in-the-Rock Road and north 3.5 miles to your car.

*Harris Wash*

# Escalante Petrified Forest State Park

**Official Park Website:** http://stateparks.utah.gov/parks/escalante-petrified-forest/

**Visitor Center:** (435) 826-4466

*Petrified Wood Cove Trail specimen*

**Park Accessibility:**

- Okay for 2WD and RVs
- Day and Overnight Use

**Experience Level:**

- Family Friendly to Casual Hiker

**Camping in Park:**

- Lake View and Wide Hollow Campgrounds: 22 T/RV, 1 group site, drinking water, showers, restrooms, partial hookups, some pull through sites, reservable at www.reserveamerica.com/

**Lodging and Dining in Park:**

- None

**Nearest Town with Amenities:**

- Escalante, UT is 1.0 mi / 1.6 km from park

**Getting There:**

- From Escalante, UT: Take West Main Street (UT 12) to N 300 W to Pine Creek Lane

## What Makes Escalante Petrified Forest State Park Special

Located just outside the town of Escalante, this park protects 1,350 acres of petrified logs and fossilized dinosaur bones. The agate logs are full of color and one log on display is 50 feet in length.

Besides the campground and the stocked Wide Hollow Reservoir, there are three trails for visitors. The Petrified Forest Trail winds from the campground to the top of a ridge. This one-mile round trip loop takes about 45-60 minutes. The steeper Sleeping Rainbows Trail comes off the Petrified Forest Trail and is 0.75 miles. Sleeping Rainbows Trail contains some excellent examples of petrified logs but is steep and requires some scrambling. Finally, the short (0.1 mi) and wheelchair accessible Petrified Wood Cove Trail offers quick access to specimens and flora near the Wide Hollow Reservoir.

# Kodachrome Basin State Park



## Quick Facts

**Official Park Website:** http://stateparks.utah.gov/parks/kodachrome-basin/

**Visitor Center:** (435) 679-8562

*Sand pipe at Kodachrome Basin State Park*

**Park Accessibility:**

- Okay for 2WD and RVs
- Day and Overnight Use

**Experience Level:**

- Family Friendly to Casual Hiker

**Camping in Park:** For reservations, call the visitor center

- Basin Campgrounds: 37 T/RV, mix of reservable and first come-first served, some sites allow generators, flush toilets, showers, restrooms
- Bryce View Campground: 11 T/RV, all reservable, vault toilets, drinking water, no hookups

**Lodging and Dining in Park:**

- There are cabins at the park, but currently no concessionaire to run them as of this writing. Check the site for current information on lodging

**Nearest Town with Amenities:**

- Kodachrome Basin State Park is in Cannonville, UT. As well, Tropic, UT is 5 mi / 8 km from park.

**Getting There:**

- From St George, UT: Take I-15 North to UT-20 East to US-89 South to UT-12 East to Kodachrome Road in Cannonville, UT. Total distance is 151 mi / 243 km to park.

## What Makes Kodachrome Basin Special

- Seeing some 67 tall stone circular monoliths set in a backdrop of wonderfully bright and colorful rocks
- Figuring out from an old timer what Kodachrome means
- Stargazing with little interference from light pollution

Kodachrome Basin State Park holds one of the most unique features in all of the Grand Circle, the sand pipe or chimney. The sand pipes are similar in shape to sandstone towers but the process of formation is radically different. In fact, they are so different that geologists don't exactly know how these things were created.

There are 67 recorded sand pipes in the park, ranging from six feet to 170 feet high. They stand as vertical round chimneys of rock. There are two theories on how they were formed. One is that there were once geysers here and the vents eventually filled up with sediment and solidified. The strata around these sediment pipes then eroded, leaving the sand pipes. The other theory is that there was a tectonic force that essentially liquefied the strata and forced the "liquid rock" into the surrounding strata, essentially an extrusion into rock. All of this occurred beneath the surface and again, the surrounding strata eroded away, leaving the spires.

Beyond the spires, the park itself is worth seeing in its own right. Located within the Grand Staircase-Escalante NM, the area is full of great views. There are plenty of trails in this small park as well, making this one of the top places to visit for its uniqueness and beauty.

## Hiking in Kodachrome Basin State Park

### Shakespeare Arch Trail

Easy – (0.5 mi / 0.8 km), round trip, allow 15 minutes

To hike or not to hike this trail, that is the question. Pick up a guide pamphlet at the trailhead and follow this trail to a small arch named after Shakespeare (or "Willy the Shake" to his hip hop friends).

### Sentinel Trail

Easy – (1.0 mi / 1.6 km), round trip, allow 30 -45 minutes

This trail starts near the Shakespeare Arch Trail to create an extension that takes one to an overlook about 100 feet above. Sweeping panoramic views.

### Grand Parade Trail

Easy – (1.5 mi / 2.4 km), round trip, allow 45 minutes

Good family friendly loop hike that passes by a handful of the famous Kodachrome sand pipes and into and out of two box canyons. The box canyons are picturesque, making this a great hike for all.

### Panorama Trail

Moderate – (5.3 mi / 8.5 km), round trip, allow 3- 4 hours

The best bang for the buck trail in the park. The hike covers a number of different sand pipes, as well as incredible panoramic views. It is possible to see to Bryce Canyon and overall is an absolutely breathtaking hike. Along the way is Cool Cave, a cove with a slot canyon look. There are many side trips that one can take to see all of the different sand pipes.

## Angels Palace Trail

Easy – (1.3 mi / 2.1 km), round trip, allow 30 minutes

Angel's Palace Trail offers unique rock formations along a trail up a small canyon. Great views of the surrounding area and an excellent location for late afternoon photography.

## Nature Trail

Easy – (0.5 mi / 0.8 km), round trip, allow 15 minutes

This is a kid friendly paved interpretative trail that showcases a sand pipe and the pinyon juniper forest setting of the park.

## Eagle's View Trail

Moderate to Strenuous – (0.5 mi / 0.8 km), round trip, allow 30 minutes

Eagle's View is a short but steep climb to a viewpoint that allows for exceptional views of the park and surrounding area.



# Anasazi State Park Museum

**Official Park Website:** http://stateparks.utah.gov/parks/anasazi/

**Visitor Center:** (435) 335-7308

**Park Accessibility:**

- Okay for 2WD and RVs
- Day Use Only

**Experience Level:**

- Family Friendly

**Nearest Town with Amenities:**

- The park is located in the town of Boulder, UT

**Getting There:**

- From St George, UT: Take UT-12 West to Boulder, UT. Total distance is 37 mi / 60 km to park

## What Makes Anasazi State Park Museum Special

Anasazi State Park Museum is a small 6-acre park within the town of Boulder, Utah. The park holds a visitor center, museum, and a guided tour of the Coombs Village Site, a reconstruction of ruins of the Ancestral Puebloan. Visitors can walk through the ruins and piece together the past using interpretive signs along the way.

For reference, Anasazi is an outdated term. The word is from the Navajo language and means "ancestors of the enemies". The term Ancestral Puebloan is the more commonly used term for the people of this period. The term Anasazi was put into use in 1927 by archaeologist Linda Cordell and the name stuck. Anasazi was widely used through the park's creation in 1960 and began to fall out of favor in the late 1990's to early 2000's.

Since we are here, the term "American Indian" is right out baffling to most who are referred to by this term. It's easy to see why, seeing as the term defines a people that are neither from India or ever called themselves American prior to the Europeans coming over. Most just prefer to be referred to by their nation's name, such as Navajo, Hopi, Ute, etc.

# Capitol Reef National Park

## Quick Facts

**Official Park Website:** http://www.nps.gov/care

**Visitor Center:** (435) 425-3791

**Park Accessibility:**

- Okay for 2WD and RVs
- 4WD recommended in some areas
- Day and Overnight Use

**Experience Level:**

- Family Friendly to Backcountry Hiker

**Camping in Park:**

- Fruita: 71 T/RV, drinking water, restrooms, dump station, no hookups, first come-first served

**Lodging and Dining in Park:**

- Gifford's Pie Shop, serves fresh baked pie, ice cream, snacks

**Nearest Town with Amenities:**

- Torrey, UT is 11 mi / 18 km from park

**Getting There:**

- From Moab, UT: Take US-191 North, I-70 West-and UT-24 West 146 mi / 235 km to park entrance
- From St. George, UT: Take 1-15 North, UT-20 East, US-89 North and UT-24 East 215 mi / 346 km to park entrance

*Capitol Reef NP is a mix of moonscape and magic*

## What Makes Capitol Reef Special

- The Waterpocket fold, the single largest monocline in the world. We are talking a 150-mile stretch of vastly different rock layers a full mile and half thick, titled at an angle and exposed in dramatic fashion
- Fruita, a once Mormon communal homestead turned to peaceful campground that serves pie and ice cream against the backdrop of the Fremont River
- Cathedral Valley, which sets a new standard in stunning during the day and the darkest skies you will likely ever see at night

The park gets its name because pioneers were faced with one cliff "reef" after the other as they headed westward. Given the Waterpocket Fold stretches for some 150 miles from north to south, it was just as tough to go around. The vast monocline represented a daunting challenge to pioneers, but this same ruggedness is what makes Capitol Reef NP so special. There is nothing else out this way except for a couple of towns and a couple of roads. Plus, this means that the night skies of Capitol Reef are top notch. In some areas, there are no soft glows of distant towns, let alone any other man made light. It is just you and the night sky.

## Hiking in the Fruita Historic District

### Chimney Rock Loop

Strenuous – (3.6 mi / 5.8 km), round trip, allow 2 -3 hours, elev. Δ: 800 ft / 244 m, trailhead on Highway 24, 3 mi west of visitor center

Chimney Rock Loop, located near the park's western boarder along Highway 24, offers some great views of Chimney Rock and the surrounding landscape.

*Gifford Barn near Fruita Campground*

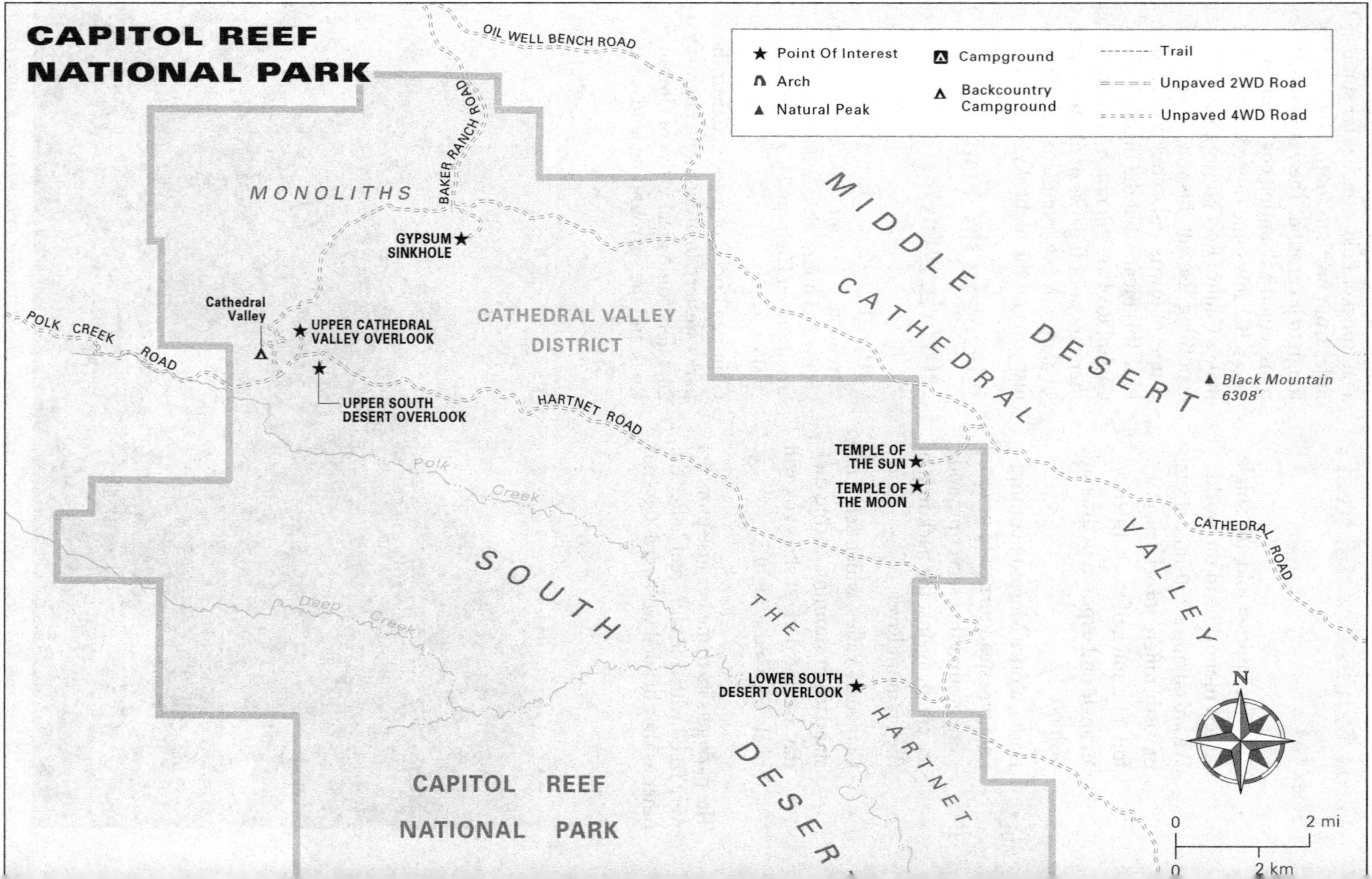
CAPITOL REEF
NATIONAL PARK
Point Of Interest
Arch
Natural Peak
Campground
Backcountry Campground
Trail
Unpaved 2WD Road
Unpaved 4WD Road
OIL WELL BENCH ROAD
BAKER RANCH ROAD
MONOLITHS
GYPSUM SINKHOLE
Cathedral Valley
UPPER CATHEDRAL VALLEY OVERLOOK
UPPER SOUTH DESERT OVERLOOK
POLK CREEK ROAD
CATHEDRAL VALLEY DISTRICT
HARTNET ROAD
MIDDLE DESERT
CATHEDRAL
Black Mountain 6308′
TEMPLE OF THE SUN
TEMPLE OF THE MOON
CATHEDRAL VALLEY
CATHEDRAL ROAD
Polk Creek
Deep Creek
SOUTH
THE
DESER
HARTNET
LOWER SOUTH DESERT OVERLOOK
CAPITOL REEF NATIONAL PARK
N
0
2 mi
0
2 km

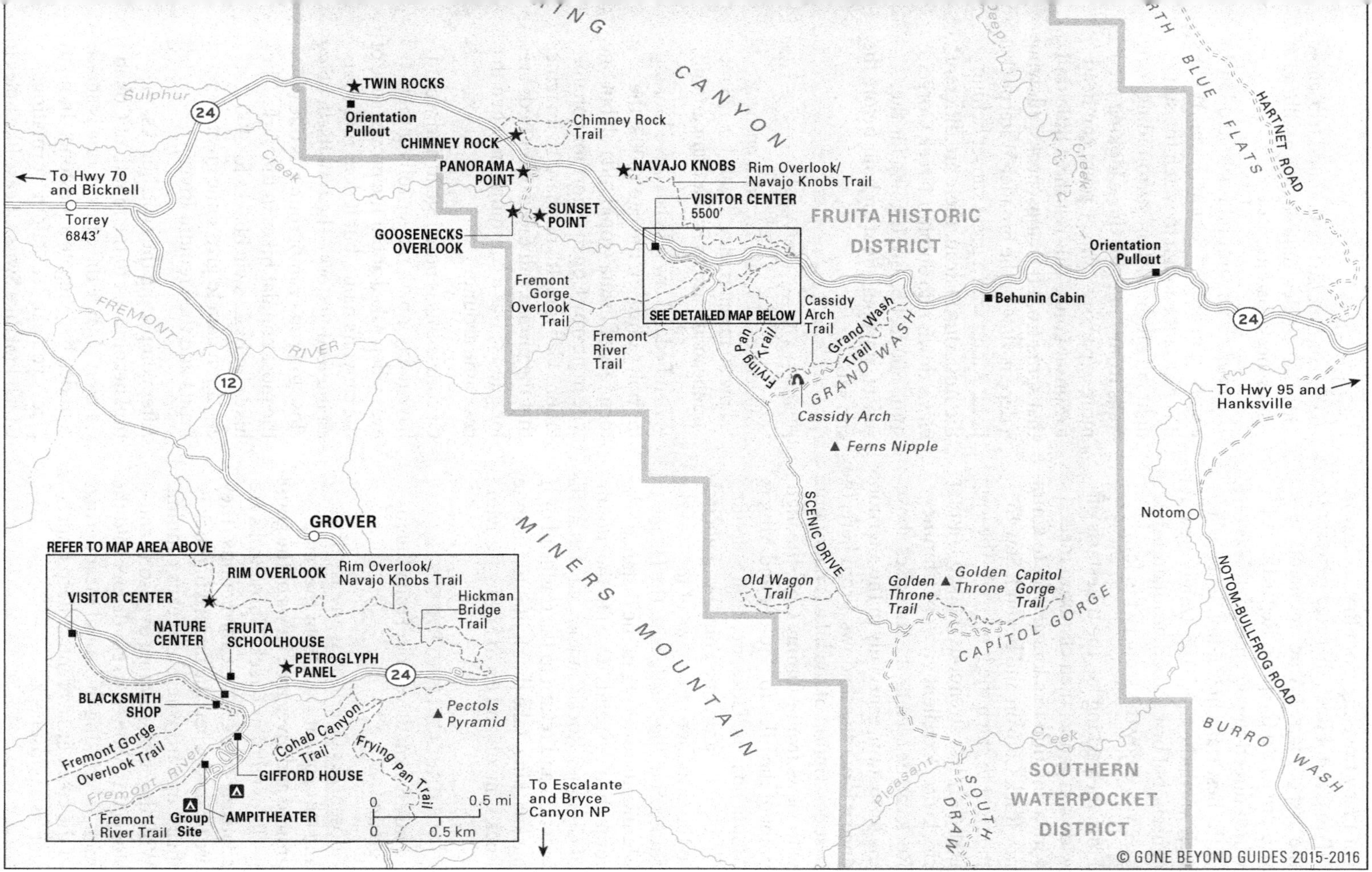
TWIN ROCKS
Orientation Pullout
CHIMNEY ROCK
Chimney Rock Trail
PANORAMA POINT
SUNSET POINT
GOOSENECKS OVERLOOK
NAVAJO KNOBS
Rim Overlook/ Navajo Knobs Trail
VISITOR CENTER 5500'
FRUITA HISTORIC DISTRICT
Orientation Pullout
Behunin Cabin
CANYON
BLUE FLATS
HARTNET ROAD
Sulphur
Creek
To Hwy 70 and Bicknell
Torrey 6843'
24
12
FREMONT RIVER
Fremont Gorge Overlook Trail
Fremont River Trail
SEE DETAILED MAP BELOW
Cassidy Arch Trail
Grand Wash Trail
GRAND WASH
Frying Pan Trail
Cassidy Arch
Ferns Nipple
To Hwy 95 and Hanksville
Notom
NOTOM-BULLFROG ROAD
SCENIC DRIVE
GROVER
MINERS MOUNTAIN
Old Wagon Trail
Golden Throne Trail
Golden Throne
Capitol Gorge Trail
CAPITOL GORGE
BURRO WASH
Pleasant Creek
SOUTH DRAW
SOUTHERN WATERPOCKET DISTRICT
To Escalante and Bryce Canyon NP
REFER TO MAP AREA ABOVE
RIM OVERLOOK
Rim Overlook/ Navajo Knobs Trail
Hickman Bridge Trail
VISITOR CENTER
NATURE CENTER
FRUITA SCHOOLHOUSE
PETROGLYPH PANEL
BLACKSMITH SHOP
Pectols Pyramid
Cohab Canyon Trail
Frying Pan Trail
Fremont Gorge Overlook Trail
Fremont River
GIFFORD HOUSE
AMPITHEATER
Fremont River Trail
Group Site
0 0.5 mi
0 0.5 km
© GONE BEYOND GUIDES 2015-2016

Capitol Reef

For many traveling from Bryce Canyon NP to Capitol Reef, this area represents the first of many "Wow" moments as you drive into the park. Regardless of which direction you entered, this is one of the best trails in Capitol Reef and is well worth the time. This trail is great for sunsets, but bring good headlamps just in case you enjoy the scenery too long.

From the parking lot, the trail starts off wide and gentle, then climbs to meet with a junction to a longer hike to Chimney Rock Canyon and beyond. Stay to the right to catch the loop trail. The loop is slightly less strenuous if taken counterclockwise. Excellent views of Chimney Rock can be seen as the trail rises above the formation, especially in the afternoon once it is out the shadows. From here, the best description of the hike is panoramic, with views from Mummy Cliff, the high point of the hike, to Boulder and Miners Mountains, the Goosenecks of Sulphur Creek and Panorama Point. As you circle to the east, there are views of the Navajo Knobs and The Castle with the Henry Mountains towering in the distance. The route then descends down to the mouth of Chimney Rock Canyon. Stay left at the junction and return to the trailhead or if backpacking, take the right into Chimney Rock Canyon and on to Spring Canyon.

## Goosenecks Overlook

4 mi / 6.4 km drive from Fruita Campground

Goosenecks Overlook is an easy drive and subsequent walk from the campground and gives nice views of the goosenecks of Sulphur Creek. Goosenecks are relatively rare geologic formations. They are formed when the underlying rock is thrust upward where a creek is running. With the creek running over soft sandstone, it is allowed to cut deeper into the rock, imprinting the initial meanderings of the creek or river into a deep impression as a gooseneck.

## Sunset Point

Easy – (0.7 mi / 1.1 km), round trip, allow 30 minutes, elev. Δ: negligible, trailhead at Goosenecks parking area

The Fruita campground is situated low in a canyon near the Fremont River. While it is pleasant enough to watch the sun light fall off the distant surrounding rock walls from camp, for those looking for a more expansive vantage point can head to Sunset Point. This is a short little trail that spurs from the Goosenecks, allowing a decent view of the broader Waterpocket Fold. Along with a great sunset behind the Aquarius Plateau, there are different views down into Sulphur Creek Gorge, some 600 feet below. If going for the sunset, start out about an hour before the sun sets.

## Cohab Canyon Trail

Moderate– (1.7 mi / 2.7 km), one way, allow 90 minutes, elev. Δ: 402 ft / 123 m, trailhead just across Fruita Campground

When Federal law officials were looking for polygamists in the late 1800's, the men folk of Fruita would hide all but one wife in nearby Cohab (short for cohabitation) Canyon. It's not hard to imagine that the phrase, "all those other beds are for guests", was a common one when the law came around.

Of course this is pure legend and would have many a park ranger rolling their eyes when asked about the provenance of the canyon's name, but it does make for an interesting story. The trail itself, being close to Fruita campground, is one of the most popular hikes in the park. The hike climbs 22 switchbacks for 400 feet elevation gain to give some great views of Fruita and the Fremont River.

After completing the switchbacks, the trail become flat to the mouth of Cohab Canyon. Inside the canyon, one is surrounded by Wingate Sandstone. In many places you can see "tafoni" formations, which look like Swiss Cheese like holes in the rock walls. Tafoni are formed when the calcium carbonate holding the sand together into sandstone dissolves, leaving a sponge like system of holes.

Inside Cohab Canyon are several side canyons worth exploring, locally referred to as the "Wives". In the main canyon, look for the Cohab Arch and some solitary hoodoos. If you want to add a little more to the hike, take the spur trail from the Cohab Arch to the Fruita Overlooks. This side trip is well worth taking, providing some excellent views of the Fremont River Canyon and Walker Peak. There are two overlooks, named North and South respectively. The spur trails add an additional 1.2 miles and an hour to the hike.

Back on the main trail, continue heading up Cohab Canyon. Along the way, the trail passes Frying Pan Trail and onwards to Highway 24 a little more than a half mile further on. This final leg gives some great views of the Fremont River Canyon and Capitol Dome off in the distance. Hikers can opt to get picked up from here, head on to Hickman Bridge or turn around and head back.

## Hickman Bridge

Moderate – (0.9 mi / 1.4 km), round trip, allow 1 – 2 hours, elev. Δ: 379 ft / 116 m, trailhead on Highway 24, 2 mi east of visitor center

This is a great little hike and a comfortable add on to the Cohab Canyon trail. It is one of the most hiked trails in the park and for good reason, as it offers great views along the way to a 133-foot natural bridge. The trail starts at Highway 24 or from Fruita Campground via Cohab Canyon. The lighting in this hike can be exceptional in the morning, plus getting an early start will also ensure a parking space during peak season. The trail starts along the Fremont River for a small stretch before climbing a series of switchbacks. Elevation gain here is about 100 feet, coming out onto a small grassy shelf. At this point, look for an informal looking spur trail that quickly ends at the remains of a pit house built by the Fremont people somewhere between 600-1300 AD.

After a very short distance, the trail meets with the junction to the Rim Overlook and Navajo Knobs. Stick to the left and climb again, passing the cone shaped Navajo Dome to the north. Capitol Dome is to the east and is where the park gets half of its name. The trail then descends through pinyon juniper forests, giving a good feel of immersion into the wilds of the park. After a short distance, the trail passes a small bridge in a wash, known as Nels Johnson Bridge. The trail ends at a 1/3-mile loop that passes under and around Hickman Bridge.

A couple of things about Hickman Bridge, it is pretty tough to photograph since it is surrounded by cliff walls. It is 125 feet high and 133 feet long. Arches and bridges both have water as one of the erosional elements that help create them.

*Hickman Bridge*

Bridges are distinguished from arches in that they are created from the direct result of free flowing water. Arches on the other hand are caused by the indirect effects of water, wind, and time on sandstone fins.

## Rim Overlook / Navajo Knobs Trail

Strenuous – (4.6 mi / 7.4 km), round trip for Rim Overlook, (9.4 mi / 15.2 km), round trip for Navajo Knobs), elev. Δ: 540 ft / 165 m to Rim Overlook, trailhead at Hickman Bridge trailhead

The Rim Overlook starts from the Hickman Bridge trail. The full hike is strenuous due to elevation gains. The Rim Overlook is 4.5 miles (7.2 km) round trip, climbs 1,110 feet and gives great views of Fruita and the surrounding valley. The Navajo Knobs trail extends from the Rim Overlook trail. The Knobs are a collection of Navajo sandstone hills that are uniquely formed. The trail leads to one of the smaller knobs, though it is possible for a skilled scrambler to scale the other formations as well. The Navajo Knobs give 360-degree views as the reward for climbing an additional 500 feet over 2.5 miles (4.0 km).

## Frying Pan

Strenuous – (2.9 mi / 4.7 km), one way, allow 1 – 2 hours, elev. Δ: 810 ft / 247 m, trailhead at Grand Wash Trailhead

Frying Pan Trail is a connector trail linking Cohab Canyon and Cassidy Arch Trails and beyond to the Grand Wash Trail. The trail travels along high and scenic ridgetops offering great and expansive views. There is a spur trail into Frying Pan Canyon, which starts about 2.2 miles in from Cassidy Arch Trail junction. This little canyon is fun to explore, with water pockets and high walls at the end of the canyon. Add another mile to the trip if going into the Frying Pan (Canyon, that is).

## Fremont Gorge Overlook

Strenuous – (4.6 mi / 7.4 km), round trip, allow 3 - 4 hours, elev. Δ: 1,090 ft / 332 m, trailhead on Scenic Drive

This is a great hike. There is a short ascent of about 1/3 of a mile that puts the hiker on a wonderful mesa trail. If you enjoy being on a lone single track within a mesa top of desert brush, high up with the blue sky yet above you, the grassy shrubs below and thick red rock cliffs looming grand in the front, this is the hike for you. Look for rounded and varnished volcanic black boulders along the way.

After the gentle stroll across the mesa, the trail ascends steeply to Fremont Gorge Overlook. This last stretch is strenuous at times leading to a solitary formation of Moenkopi rock. Once past this formation, the trail juts left to the rim of Fremont Gorge. The overlook gives spectacular views down into the deep gorge. From here, enjoy a snack and head on back the way you came.

## Fremont River

Easy to Moderate – (2.6 mi / 4.2 km), round trip, allow 1.5 – 2 hours, elev. Δ: 400 ft / 122 m, trailhead near Fruita Campground, loop B

As the name of this trail suggests, this little path follows along the Fremont River. The first stretch is flat and open to dogs and bikes and is ADA accessible. After about 0.4 miles, the trail switches into more of a rugged single track, with a gated passage that asks that all but hikers turn back. From here, the trail climbs steadily, ending at absolutely stunning views of the Fremont Gorge and river as well as the Waterpocket Fold. At trails end, it is possible to wander around the area. Look for Fern's Nipple, a cone shaped formation that stands out in the southeast.

## Cassidy Arch

Strenuous – (3.4 mi / 5.5 km), round trip, allow 2 -3 hours, elev. Δ: 670 ft / 204 m, trailhead at Grand Wash trailhead

The arch is named after none other than Butch Cassidy, the leader of an infamous band of thieves known as the "Wild Bunch" in the 1890's. It is reputed that Butch had dinner at the cabin of area pioneer Elijah Cutler Behunin along the Fremont River and that the group frequented the area. For a hike through land good enough for outlaws to an arch worthy of Butch Cassidy himself, look no further than Cassidy Arch trail.

*Cassidy Arch*

The hike begins at the end of Grand Wash Road and immediately starts into a 600-foot ascent. Along the climb, the ledges of Kayenta sandstone are quite evident. As elevation is gained, the ecology of the trail changes to more densely packed pinyon juniper forest with stunning views of the surrounding sandstone. At the juncture to Frying Pan Trail, Cassidy Arch Trail juts to the left, down a gradual grade of slickrock to the canyon's rim and Cassidy Arch.

Once at your destination, look for the western themed Starbucks served by the great-great grandson of Butch Cassidy himself at the apex of the arch. As one hiker put it, "It was a delightful end to the hike", while another hiker has been quoted as saying, "The apex of the arch? Seriously? The author has clearly been out in the desert too long." Anyway, you get back to me with *your* experience.

## Grand Wash

Easy – (4.8 mi / 7.7 km), round trip, allow 2 hours, elev. Δ: 200 ft / 61 m, trailhead on Scenic Drive, 4.7 mi from visitor center

This there and back trail is one of the flattest hikes in the park. It's a great walk for children (even small kids part way) and can be accessed from either the Scenic Drive or Highway 24. One of the highlights is the Narrows, which is found about 0.7 miles in from the Highway 24 trailhead. This half-mile narrow stretch is banded by sheer walls of Navajo red sandstone, towering 500 feet on either side, with dark stains of desert varnish running down the cliffs. Farther into the hike, the canyon widens, allowing the hiker to take in the views at a leisurely pace. This section also contains more plant life than the regularly scoured sections of the Narrows.

## Old Wagon Trail

Strenuous – (3.8 mi / 6.1 km), round trip, allow 2 -3 hours, elev. Δ: 1,080 ft / 329 m, trailhead on Scenic Drive, 6.5 mi from visitor center

Perhaps the best part of this hike is its closeness to the Fruita Campground yet relatively unused aspect of the trail. While most of the trails along Scenic Drive take the hiker into the canyons and washes, Old Wagon Trail heads west away from them. This dishes up a hike that is more pinyon juniper in terrain. The trail is as persistent as it is straight as it climbs the 1,000 feet upwards, but does reward with some great views once elevation is reached. The Old Wagon Trail is not Capitol Reef's darling, sometimes the views are obscured by forest and the elevation gain can feel more like a dull march up alluvium, but it does offer unique views and hikers will likely have the entire journey to themselves.

### Golden Throne Trail

Strenuous – (4.0 mi / 6.4 km), round trip, allow 2 - 3 hours, elev. Δ: 1,100 ft / 335 m, trailhead at Capitol Gorge parking area off Scenic Drive

*Golden Throne*

Golden Throne trail is a short but steep trail that winds through the backcountry of the Waterpocket Fold. It takes the viewer to the base of a large monolith known as the Golden Throne. This up-then-down hike gets the hiker up in elevation quickly, climbing 800 feet and following a series of well-marked switchbacks. This is a great hike to climb up into the higher realms of the backcountry in short order and still leave time to take in the amazing views.

### Capitol Gorge

Easy – (2.0 mi / 3.2 km), round trip, allow 1 hour, elev. Δ: 100 ft / 30 m, trailhead at Capitol Gorge parking area off Scenic Drive

Until 1962, this was the only road that passed through the Waterpocket Fold. The road passes through a high cliff-walled gorge that displays pleasant shadows in the late afternoon. For those up for a short hike, continue to the Pioneer Register, which contains the names of early Mormon pioneers etched into the side of the canyon. Across the wall where the pioneers "signed in," and all over, one can find petroglyphs as well. Also visible are the remains of old telephone lines. The trail officially ends at "The Tanks", a set of water pockets set in a row above the canyon floor. The natural curvature of these pools makes for a great resting spot. Those with more time can continue through Capitol Gorge to the eastern boundary of the park.

## Hiking in Cathedral Valley District

Getting to all of the hikes in the Cathedral Valley area requires traveling on the unpaved 28 mile Hartnet Road as part of a 59-mile loop. Much of the road is okay for most cars; however, there are a couple of spots, including a river crossing, which bumps up the need for a high clearance vehicle. This northern section of the park is very different than the rest of the park, being cooler, more densely forested in pinyon juniper and with the fluted monolithic spires collectively referred to as the Cathedrals.

### Upper South Desert Overlook

Easy – (0.4 mi / 0.6 km), round trip, allow 15 minutes, elev. Δ: 80 ft / 24 m, trailhead is 39 mi NW of visitor center on Hartnet Road to South Desert trailhead

This overlook provides wide expansive views of the Upper South Desert, a region dominated by a wide expansive valley of grasslands banded by sloping sandstone and some volcanic intrusion. Off in the distance, the Henry Mountains, the last mountain range in the contiguous United States to be mapped, lie as a centerpiece to this natural diorama. To the northwest lie the Thousand Lake Mountains, a wholly different world of Aspen trees, rambling creeks and even a bit of snow.

*Upper Cathedral Valley*



Take the obvious trail from the parking area and take the short hike to the overlook. The last portion does have a very short but steep ascent to the final viewing area.

## Cathedral Valley Overlook

Easy – (0.2 mi / 0.3 km), round trip, allow 15 minutes, elev. Δ: 50 ft / 15 m, trailhead on Hartnet Road

The Cathedral Valley is special. Within it are 400-foot sheets of monolithic rock, distinctly orange in color, standing vertical right to their pointed tips. They look like curtains of rock, being a juxtaposition of fluidity and motion standing against an impression of eternal stillness. The Cathedral Valley Overlook is a little hike that gives one of the best views of this valley. Standing at the end of a rock peninsula, as high as the monoliths themselves, the overlook gives one of the most majestic views in the entire park.

There are picnic tables with some shade at the start of the trail. From the picnic area, follow the obvious trail through some trees down to the end of the peninsula. Note that the trail becomes a narrower route towards the end, with very steep drop-offs on either side. Use caution here.

## Cathedrals Trail

Moderate – (2.2 mi / 3.5 km), round trip, allow 90 minutes, elev. Δ: 375 ft / 114 m, trailhead on Hartnet Road

Given the amount of time needed to undertake the 59-mile loop through Cathedral Valley, this trail often is overlooked. That said, what a wonderful little hike this is, hiking through arguably the heart of the Cathedrals, with some elevation gain to help give proper perspective to these unique and magical spires of Entrada Sandstone.

The trail starts in the Upper Cathedral Valley a couple miles prior to making the climb up to the primitive Cathedral Valley Campground (or down from the campground, depending). As the road climbs a small hill look for a sign that says, "Cathedral Trail Trails End 1.1". Park near the sign and head out on the trail, which starts to climb at a descent rate. As you round a corner past some trees, look for Needle Mountain and other Cathedrals. It will be easy to spot Cathedral Mountain, the largest of the monoliths. The trail levels out from here, giving up pleasant hiking and great views, and then climbs steeply to the final viewpoint at the end. If one looks closely, the Morrell Cabin can be seen along the trail.

### Morrell Cabin Trail

Easy – (0.4 mi / 0.6 km), round trip, allow 30 minutes, elev. Δ: negligible, trailhead on Hartnet Road

This little cabin still contains a few artifacts just laying around to examine. They are still around because folks leave them be, so please keep with the sentiment of past hikers. The cabin is part of a ranch owned by a cattle rancher by the name of Lesley Morrell in the 1930's. For many, it became a way station for ranchers looking for a place to bed down for the night until the 70's, when it was placed into a preservation mode by the park. The little one room cabin is now listed on National Register of Historic Places

For those that make it out to Cathedral Valley, this becomes one of the must do hikes along the way as it hard to justify coming all this way and NOT seeing the cabin. The hike itself is straightforward with no real elevation gain and is accessed along a very well maintained path. It is possible to go inside the cabin, where there are tons of old relics found around the area. The views along the way are impressive and peaceful to the eye. Wildlife is often spotted along the trail.

## Hiking in the Southern Waterpocket District

This is the least visited section of the park and as such, the trails are often more rugged and unmaintained. For most that make it out here, the Waterpocket District offers a more immersive experience, where the route taken is defined only by one's skill. The section below outlines the various trails in this region of the park. Consult with a ranger at the visitor center for more detail on any of these hikes.

*Old Ford at Fruita*

### Burro Wash

Strenuous – (3.4 mi / 5.5 km), round trip, allow 3 -4 hours, elev. Δ: 350 ft / 107 m, trailhead is 9 mi south on Notom-Bullfrog Road

The "stubbornest" of the three slot canyons in this area. Expect many chockstone obstacles and two sets of narrows that confine the hiker to shoulder width. It is not unheard of in some places to climb out of the slot canyon briefly to reengage it at wider spot or to navigate a chockstone.

### Cottonwood Wash

Strenuous – (3.3 mi / 5.3 km), round trip, allow 3 -5 hours, elev. Δ: 350 ft / 107 m, trailhead is 9 mi south on Notom-Bullfrog Road

This is the most obstacle laden and wettest of the slot canyons in this area. Start by scrambling up and over or around a set of large chockstones as the canyon narrows. Continue to a thin lens of water that must be waded through to continue. If you decide to continue (first off congrats, most folks turn around here), you will be rewarded with yet more chockstones that need to negotiated often and even more pools of water. Finally, gaze upon an impassable 35-foot dry fall and either turn around or get out the ropes and continue deeper into the canyon for more. After all this hard work, just think how good dinner will taste when you get back to your camp!

## Sheets Gulch

Strenuous – (6.7 mi / 10.8 km), round trip, allow 5-7 hours, elev. Δ: 500 ft / 152 m, trailhead is 13 mi south on Notom-Bullfrog Road

A rough around the edges slot canyon in three sections. Plenty of chockstone and waterpocket pool obstacles to navigate, making this a nice scramble puzzle, and potentially wet fun.

## Red Canyon Trail

Moderate – (4.5 mi / 7.2 km), round trip, allow 2 - 3 hours, elev. Δ: 400 ft / 122 m, trailhead is 21 mi south on Notom-Bullfrog Road

This hike offers wide-open expanses to slot canyons; Red Canyon Trail showcases the varied aspects of Capitol Reef National Park.

## Upper Muley Twist Canyon

Strenuous – (9.0 mi / 14.5 km), round trip, hard day hike or 2-3 day backpacking trip, elev. Δ: 800 ft / 244 m, trailhead is 2.9 mi south on Strike Valley Road

Freedom, surprise, and possibly even a little wonder combine in this multi-faceted citadel of red rock, white rock, arches, double arches, and even narrows. Some of the best views of the Waterpocket Fold to be seen are on this trail.

## Strike Valley Overlook

Moderate – (0.8 mi / 1.3 km), round trip, allow 30 minutes, elev. Δ: 100 ft / 30 m, trailhead is 2.9 mi south on Strike Valley Road

A great hike for those looking for that picture perfect view of the Waterpocket Fold. This is a short hike but gives views of the classic picture of the monocline that is seen in brochures.

## Lower Muley Twist Canyon

Easy – (8.0 mi / 12.9 km), round trip, allow 4 -5 hours, elev. Δ: 600 ft / 183 m, trailhead at Burr Trail, 2 mi west of Notom-Bullfrog Road junction

For this description, the trail starts at the Lower Muley Twist Canyon and ends at the Post Cut Off Junction. A great canyon hike, more wonder and scenic charm

*The Waterpocket Fold from Strike Valley Overlook*

than slotted narrows, but well worth the effort. Lots of red rock in all its varieties to be seen along the way.

## Surprise Canyon

Easy – (2.0 mi / 3.2 km), round trip, allow 90 minutes, elev. Δ: 240 ft / 73 m, trailhead is 34 mi south on Notom-Bullfrog Road

Surprise Canyon is the next-door neighbor to Headquarters Canyon. The biggest difference between the two canyons is Surprise opens up wide at the end versus Headquarters, which remains narrow throughout.

## Headquarters Canyon

Easy – (3.4 mi / 5.5 km), round trip, allow 2 hours, elev. Δ: 400 ft / 122 m, trailhead is 35 mi south on Notom-Bullfrog Road

Headquarters Canyon is a narrow slot canyon with a sandy floor and tan water

*Upper Muley Twist*

carved walls. This is a good hike for families, though be sure to check the weather before entering.

## Oak Creek Canyon Trail

Moderate – (5.0 mi / 8.0 km), round trip, allow 2 -3 hours, elev. Δ: 200 ft / 61 m, trailhead is 4 mi east on Oak Creek access road

Waterfalls, diversions, dams, and scenic expanses can all be found on this hike with only 200 feet in elevation gain. Pleasant and peaceful, with a little alcove at the end to stop and have a snack while peering out into the canyon. A very worthwhile hike.

## Lower Muley Twist Canyon and Hamburger Rocks

Strenuous – (17.0 mi / 27.4 km), round trip, hard day hike or 2-3 day backpacking trip, elev. Δ: 900 ft / 274 m, trailhead at Post Corral off Notom-Bullfrog Road

A dreamland of rock with unreal curvatures, heights, colors, and form. Akin to hiking in a museum of art for the day, where even the corridors to the next gallery are impressive. One highlight is the Hamburger Rocks, a study in erosion creating a series of logic defying toadstool like formations that just have to be seen to be believed. Allow another 3 hours to take the spur trail to these rocks.

## Halls Creek Narrows

Strenuous – (22.4 mi / 36.0 km), round trip, hard day hike or 2-3 day backpacking trip, elev. Δ: 1,000 ft / 304 m, trailhead is 3.6 mi south of Halls Creek Overlook on airport road

The hike is like combining the Narrows of Zion with the purity of Capitol Reef. Towering rock walls bend and turn on the whims of the watercourse that created this slot canyon, all coming together to create one of the best-kept secrets in the entire park.

# Glen Canyon National Recreation Area

## Quick Facts

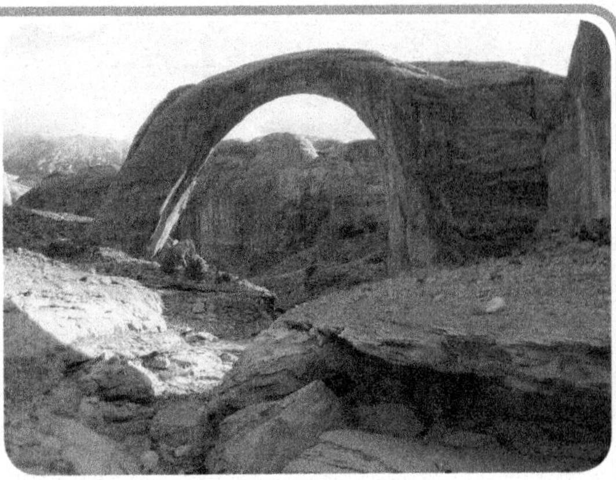
*Rainbow Bridge within Glen Canyon*

**Official Park Website:** http://www.nps.gov/glca

**Visitor Center:** (928) 608-6200

**Park Accessibility:**

- Okay for 2WD and RVs
- Day and Overnight Use

**Experience Level:**

- Family Friendly to Backcountry Hiker

**Camping in Park:**
There are several campgrounds within the Glen Canyon NRA. Some are operated by the National Park Service, while others are operated by private concessionaires. There is also primitive camping allowed on the Lake Powell shoreline. Go here for a full list of camping opportunities within the park: http://www.nps.gov/glca/planyourvisit/camping.htm

**Lodging in Park:**

- There are two lodges within the park operated privately. Go here for details and reservations: http://www.lakepowell.com/

**Dining in Park:**
Numerous options, go here for details: http://www.nps.gov/glca/planyourvisit/restaurants.htm

**Nearest Town with Amenities:**
Bullfrog, Antelope Point, and Halls Crossing are the closest areas within the park with amenities. Page, AZ is closest town to the southern section of the park.

**Getting There:**

- From Flagstaff, AZ: Take US-89A North 135 miles / 217 km to park entrance

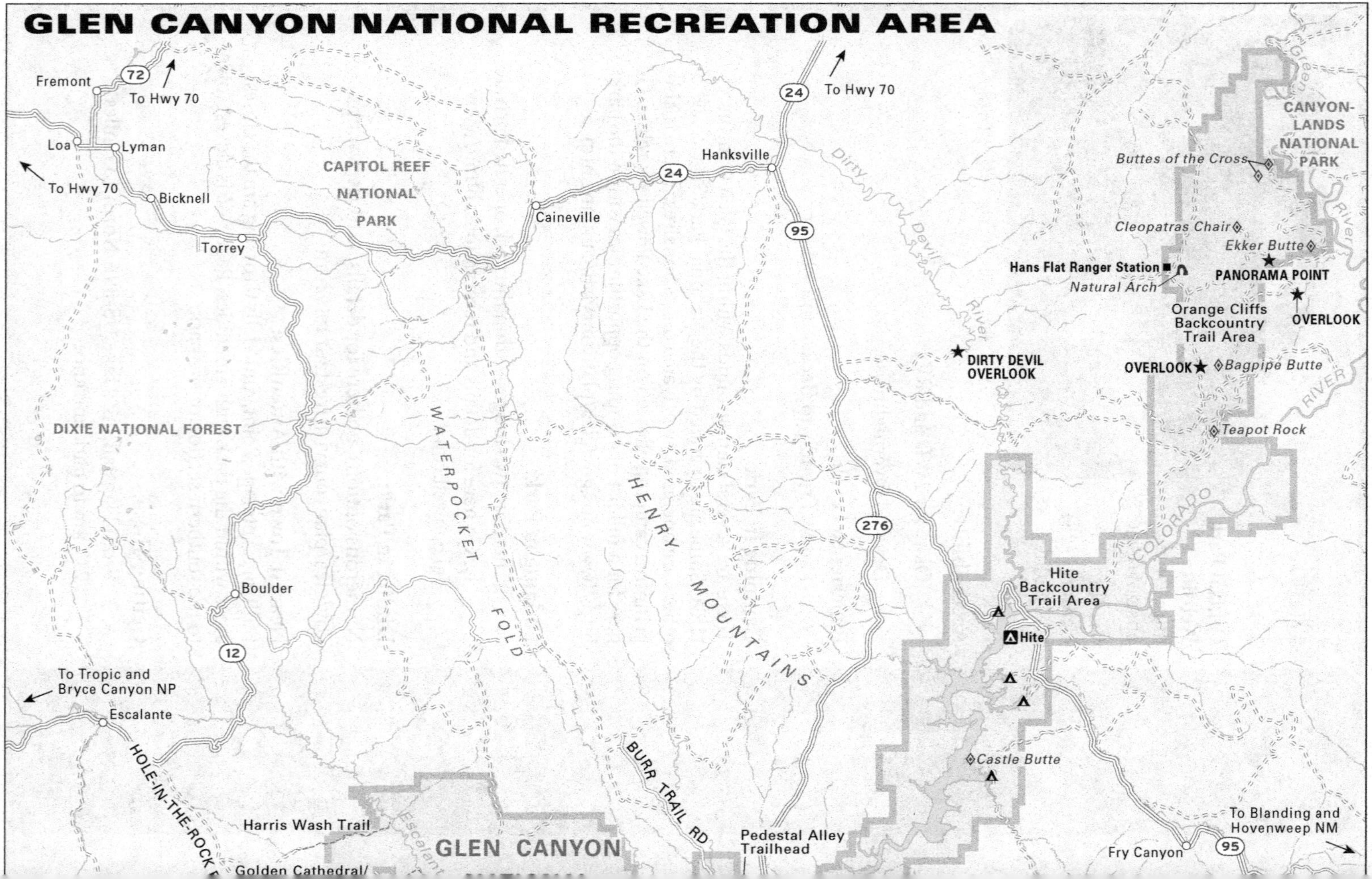
GLEN CANYON NATIONAL RECREATION AREA
Fremont
72
To Hwy 70
Loa
Lyman
To Hwy 70
Bicknell
Torrey
CAPITOL REEF NATIONAL PARK
Caineville
24
Hanksville
24
To Hwy 70
Dirty Devil River
95
DIRTY DEVIL OVERLOOK
CANYON-LANDS NATIONAL PARK
Green River
Buttes of the Cross
Cleopatras Chair
Ekker Butte
Hans Flat Ranger Station
Natural Arch
PANORAMA POINT
OVERLOOK
Orange Cliffs Backcountry Trail Area
OVERLOOK
Bagpipe Butte
RIVER
Teapot Rock
COLORADO
DIXIE NATIONAL FOREST
WATERPOCKET FOLD
HENRY MOUNTAINS
276
Hite Backcountry Trail Area
Hite
Castle Butte
Boulder
12
To Tropic and Bryce Canyon NP
Escalante
HOLE-IN-THE-ROCK
Harris Wash Trail
Escalante
Golden Cathedral/
GLEN CANYON
BURR TRAIL RD
Pedestal Alley Trailhead
Fry Canyon
95
To Blanding and Hovenweep NM

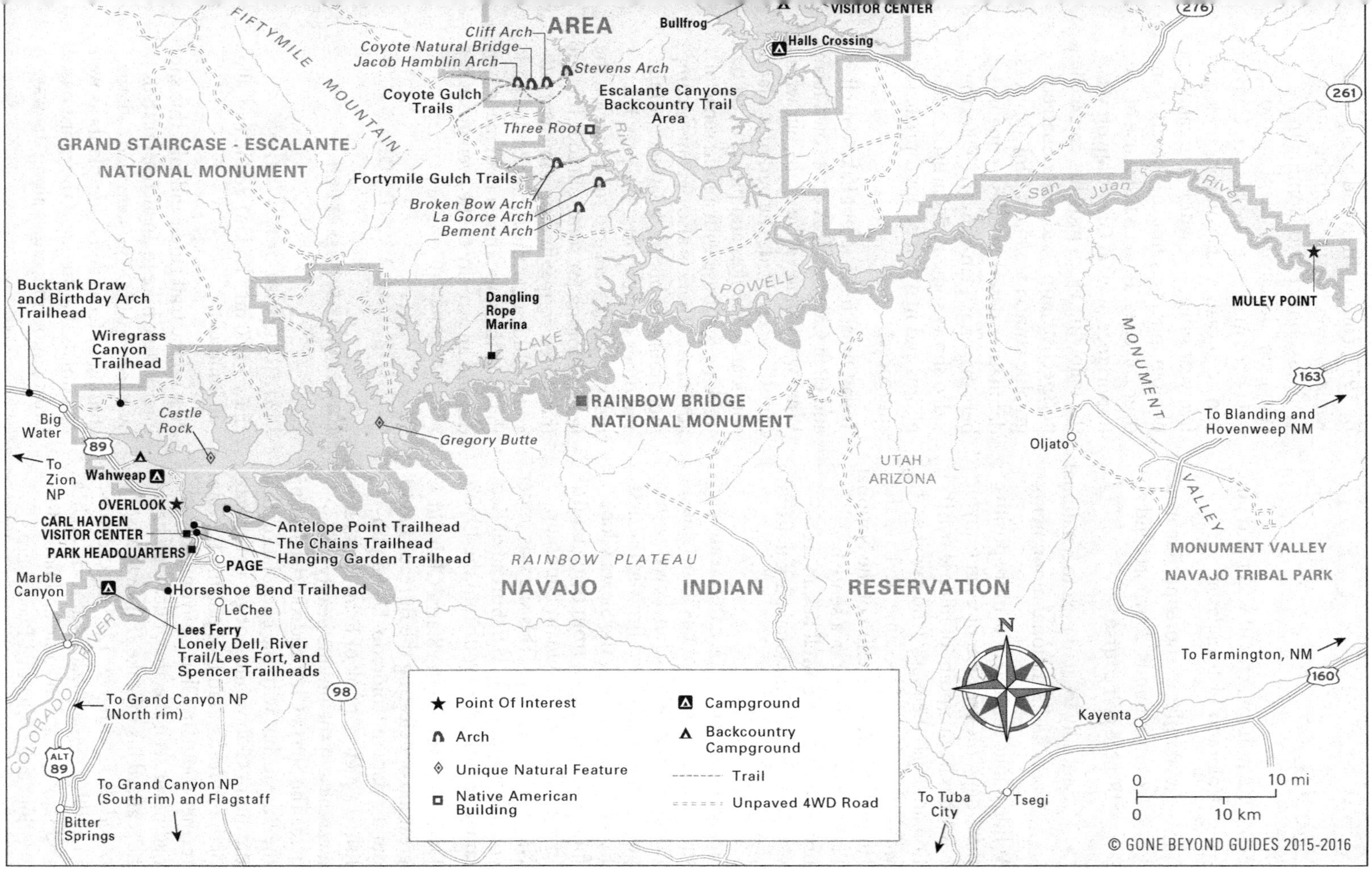
VISITOR CENTER
AREA
Bullfrog
Halls Crossing
Cliff Arch
Coyote Natural Bridge
Jacob Hamblin Arch
Stevens Arch
Coyote Gulch Trails
Escalante Canyons Backcountry Trail Area
FIFTYMILE MOUNTAIN
GRAND STAIRCASE - ESCALANTE NATIONAL MONUMENT
Three Roof
Fortymile Gulch Trails
Broken Bow Arch
La Gorce Arch
Bement Arch
San Juan River
MULEY POINT
POWELL
LAKE
Dangling Rope Marina
Bucktank Draw and Birthday Arch Trailhead
Wiregrass Canyon Trailhead
Castle Rock
Gregory Butte
RAINBOW BRIDGE NATIONAL MONUMENT
MONUMENT VALLEY
To Blanding and Hovenweep NM
Oljato
Big Water
To Zion NP
Wahweap
OVERLOOK
CARL HAYDEN VISITOR CENTER
PARK HEADQUARTERS
PAGE
Antelope Point Trailhead
The Chains Trailhead
Hanging Garden Trailhead
UTAH
ARIZONA
RAINBOW PLATEAU
NAVAJO INDIAN RESERVATION
MONUMENT VALLEY NAVAJO TRIBAL PARK
Marble Canyon
Horseshoe Bend Trailhead
LeChee
Lees Ferry
Lonely Dell, River Trail/Lees Fort, and Spencer Trailheads
COLORADO RIVER
To Grand Canyon NP (North rim)
To Grand Canyon NP (South rim) and Flagstaff
Bitter Springs
To Farmington, NM
Kayenta
Tsegi
To Tuba City
N
Point Of Interest
Arch
Unique Natural Feature
Native American Building
Campground
Backcountry Campground
Trail
Unpaved 4WD Road
0
10 mi
0
10 km
© GONE BEYOND GUIDES 2015-2016

Glen Canyon

## What Makes Glen Canyon Special

- 1.2 million acres of water and pure Colorado Plateau desert
- 2,000 miles of shoreline, 5 marinas, 4 campgrounds, 2 airports and an 18-hole golf course
- Centrally located next to 3 national parks and 3 national monuments

While public sentiment is more positive these days, the creation of Glen Canyon NRA has been a point of intense frustration amongst the many who saw it as it was before the waters came. To have the land under the protection of the National Park Service is ironic in a sense because underneath Lake Powell lies an area worthy of being a national park in its own right.

In another twist of irony, the creation of the Glen Canyon Dam has its originations with the Sierra Club. Paved with good intentions, David Brower, the first Executive Director of the Sierra Club, fought to keep a dam from being built in Echo Park, Colorado, in Dinosaur National Monument. This site was under consideration by the U.S. Bureau of Reclamation from the 1940's into the 1950's.

David Brower and the Sierra Club did a great job of defeating the Bureau's bid to build a dam in Colorado. David published a picture book of Echo Park raising awareness of the unique beauty of the area. The Sierra Club ended up defeating the Bureau, but with the consolation that the Sierra Club would not get in the way of the Bureau's Plan B of putting the dam further south, in Glen Canyon. Brower had never seen the area, but when he did, he realized his mistake. This was a world of red rock, with over 125 side canyons, incredible amphitheaters of rock, arches, and lands sacred to some and home to the flora and fauna that lived there.

By 1957, construction had begun and while Brower tried to stop the Bureau Commissioner Floyd Dominy from changing "the environment for the benefit of man", the fate of Glen Canyon had been cast. Archaeologists took on a five-year salvage expedition to catalogue, photograph, and remove artifacts from over 250 sites. To get a full sense of the importance of what Glen Canyon was, the following video provides an excellent perspective. http://video.nationalgeographic.com/video/short-film-showcase/damnation-desert-goddess-remembers-arizonas-glen-canyon (Note: the video shows some B&W artistic nude photos and may not be appropriate for all audiences).

Today, most folks accept Lake Powell and Glen Canyon NRA on its own terms. What was will never be again, but what is, can still be enjoyed. The park has a large abundance of hikes and plenty of off trail trekking for those with a solid sense of adventure. There is also of course, camping, mountain biking, boating, fishing, and other water sports. The park is a mecca for the weekend road warrior, the family looking for some outdoor fun and the retired couple finding some warmth and solitude near the shores of this park that is at the same time a man made wonder and an atrocity to the even greater wonders of nature.

## Hiking Glen Canyon NRA

### Page/Wahweap Area

#### Hanging Garden Trail

Easy – (1.0 mi / 1.6 km), round trip, allow 30 minutes

Pick up the trail guide and take this short interpretive hike to an alcove created by a seep spring. The seep feeds a large amount of ferns and other plants as well as animals that frequent the moist oasis. Great panoramic views along the way.

*Horseshoe Bend*

## Horseshoe Bend Trail

Easy – (1.5 mi / 2.4 km), round trip, allow 30 minutes

If you are looking for the most iconic and picture perfect gooseneck ever to grace a southwest themed calendar, this is the hike you want to take. This is a short and straightforward hike to the overlook of Horseshoe Bend. Once you get to the overlook and gaze over, the image should be immediately recognizable. Watching the rafters float into sight, around the bend and out of sight is a peaceful thing to watch, akin to leaves floating down a stream.

## Antelope Point

Easy to Moderate – Distance Varies

Antelope Point Marina is a good launching point for a walk along the red rock shores of Lake Powell. There are no trails here, but easy enough to just park and walk around. Hiking here is a pleasant activity after a lunch at the marina. Great scenery with excellent spots for a swim in the lake, plus an added bonus of watching the boats come and go.

## The Chains

Easy to Moderate – Distance Varies

The Chains is the name of a popular lakeshore access spot. The lake is calm and deep with some steep sections getting down to it. This spot is a favorite and is well known. This place can be a bit of a party spot, mind the broken glass, and boom boxes if you go here.

# Hwy 89 North

## Bucktank Draw and Birthday Arch

Moderate – (6.0 mi / 9.7 km), round trip, allow 4 hours

Located just west of Big Water on Highway 89 is a trail to Birthday Arch and a small slot canyon. Drive towards Big Water from Carl Hayden Visitor Center to mile marker 9, hit your trip meter and drive another 0.75 miles to a pull off big enough for 3-4 cars and the trailhead.

The trail follows up a sandy wash with two small dryfalls to navigate. At about 1.8 miles look for the trail that breaks out of the wash towards the arch. There are typically some cairns to mark this exit point, but nothing official from the BLM. The arch is not easy to see and there are a lot of false trails created by those that have come before. Head west uphill over a sandy incline. The arch is not seen until you are nearly right under it. It is possible to stand directly underneath the arch, though doing so will require Class 3 scrambling and a good eye for the correct route.

From the arch, if you look across the valley you will see a very narrow short slot canyon. Heading back to the wash and up it will get you to this canyon or you can scramble down in more of a straight line to the same destination. Look for cairns to lead you out of the wash to the slot canyon. There is a petroglyph and some apparently ancient notches that looked like handholds to climb up the chute. The mouth of this slot canyon is overgrown, but not impassable.

### Wiregrass Canyon Route

Moderate – (6.0 mi / 9.7 km), round trip, allow

This trail uses a wash as the route to a natural bridge with other small arches, side canyons, and balanced rocks to be seen along the way. This is a fun and easy "off trail" hike that doesn't require a huge amount of experience but allows for the feeling you are heading into the wilderness. There are a few dry falls to navigate, but all can be detoured by walking briefly out of the wash and around them. This trail is very exposed in the summer.

### Pahreah Townsite

Easy – (1.0 mi / 1.6 km), round trip, allow 30 minutes

This is the movie location for Clint Eastwood's Outlaw of Josie Wales and many others. Take Paria River Valley Road five miles from milepost 31 on Highway 89. Panoramic views along the way via this dirt road that also passes the Paria Cemetery and Pahreah Townsite across the Paria River from the cemetery. Most of the area has been returned to the area's natural state due to natural flooding that has occurred. There is not much left of the Client Eastwood movie site but the area is still very recognizable if you are fan. See Starlight Canyon below for a hike that starts from the Pahreah Townsite.

### Starlight Canyon

Easy – (5.8 mi / 9.3 km), round trip, allow 3 – 4 hours

Starlight Canyon is a fun little slot canyon that is a tributary of the Paria River. Continue from the Pahreah Townsite another six miles (when dry, impassable when wet) to the canyon. The hike in the canyon is short but deep and narrow. There are lots of side canyons and camping spots available at the end the road.

## Lees Ferry Area

### Lonely Dell

Easy – (1.0 mi / 1.6 km), round trip, allow 30 minutes

This hike is a flat and easy walk to the Lonely Dell Ranch site. The ranch was built by John D. Lee (of Lees Ferry fame). Poor John D. Lee was convicted of the Mountains Meadow Massacre and sentenced to death for this crime in 1877, the only Mormon to be convicted. Two years later, the LDS Church purchased the rights to Lee's Ferry from his widowed wife Emma. Brigham Young married John and Emma back in 1858 and the church was well aware of the importance of this river crossing as a link between settlements in Utah and Arizona.

It is possible to continue up the canyon as a day hike extension or a multi-day backpacking trip. The Paria Canyon continues for another 45 miles one way. A permit is required for overnight trips.

## River Trail/Lees Fort

Easy – (2.0 mi / 3.2 km), round trip, allow 1 hour

This sandy but otherwise easy trail follows the shores of the Colorado to Lees Fort. Construction for this fort began in 1874 due to mounting tensions between the Navajo and the Mormons.

## Spencer Trail

Strenuous – (2.2 mi / 3.5 km), round trip, allow 1 -2 hours

This trail starts from the end of River Trail (see above) near Lees Ferry. Spencer trail climbs steadily to the top of the Vermilion Cliffs for an absolutely stunning panoramic view of the Colorado River, Lake Powell, and surrounding area. Be advised of numerous switchbacks and steep inclines going up on this there and back trail, but the top of the world views are worth the ascent.

# Bullfrog

## Pedestal Alley

Easy – (3.0 mi / 4.8 km), round trip, allow 2 – 3 hours

One of the best hikes in the Bullfrog area. Starts up a sandy wash for about one mile then travels across slick rock via well-established cairns for another half mile to an area of eroded hoodoos balanced precariously for the time being.

# Escalante Canyon

A good portion of Glen Canyon NRA protects the watershed of the Escalante River. Here, not only is the river itself within the park's boundaries, but also a very large portion of land surrounding the river. In fact, this area is so large as to make up nearly half of the park. Factoring in that this already large segment of the Colorado Plateau is surrounding by the even larger Grand Staircase-Escalante NM means one thing; a vast area that is remote, rugged and pristine.

The Escalante River was the last river to be named in the continuous United States. There was little development prior to its protection meaning much of this land is as it was 10,000 years ago. A trip to this area of the Southwest is to see what few have seen and large enough that return trips can be to and new area with each visit.

This area is jointly managed by the National Park Service, Bureau of Land Management, and the Dixie National Forest Service. All travel into the Escalante Canyons section requires a backcountry permit. These can be picked up at the Escalante Visitor Center within the Grand Staircase-Escalante NM. The hikes below are backcountry trips and are more routes than trails. This is an area where desert-backpacking experience is a must. This includes knowing how to read topo maps and a compass. Most of these trips are done after a lot of planning and typically done as multiday trips. This is some of the most remote land in the United States, venture into it with this in mind.

There is an excellent 32-page brochure on many of the hikes in this area. The brochure describes everything needed to have an enjoyable trip in the Escalante Canyon area. http://www.nps.gov/glca/planyourvisit/upload/Canyons%20of%20the%20Escalante.pdf

# Orange Cliffs

The Orange Cliffs make up the most northern section of Glen Canyon NRA and border The Maze District of Canyonlands NP. This is remote, rugged country. Overnight camping requires a backcountry permit and a campground reservation to visit. Requests are only handled via email. Go here for more information: http://www.nps.gov/cany/planyourvisit/backcountrypermits.htm.

## Hite

The northern reaches of Glen Canyon NRA contain a remote ranger station called Hite. The area is named after the former town and the man who founded it, Cass Hite. Cass came to the area in 1883 looking for gold. He built a cabin near one of the easiest natural crossings of the Colorado River, then named Dandy Crossing.

Hite City came and went before the land became part of Glen Canyon NRA. Today, there is a limited amount of developed area with camping, a ranger station, a gas station, and boat launches. The boat launches are closed currently due to the drought. In fact, the lake is down completely here, leaving a lonely boat ramp leading to a dry shore with the Colorado River in the distance. Some good backcountry exploration. Those who visit the backcountry tend to have the place to themselves.

# Rainbow Bridge National Monument

**Official Park Website:** www.nps.gov/rabr

**Visitor Center:** (719) 378-6399

**Park Accessibility:**

- Park can be accessed primarily by boat and on foot via permit. Boating tour information can be found here: http://www.lakepowell.com/

**Experience Level:**

- Family Friendly – Casual Hiker

Rainbow Bridge is a bit of an oddity. To some it is an incredible feat of nature, protected by President Taft in 1910 with the words that this is an "extraordinary natural bridge". For others, the area has long been held sacred to the original inhabitants and their descendants, to a point of reverence such that even walking on and under the bridge is seen as disrespectful. For others still, it is something to do while boating on Lake Powell, a cool must see for those that are able.

The oddity here is that the bridge tries to be many things to many people. On the one hand, it truly is a place held sacred, to the point of lawsuits and continual mediation between the NPS and the five tribes that hold it as such. Yet it is also a tourist destination, amazing all the same, but often for very different reasons. The reason this is pointed out is if you do go, visit with respect. If there is one thing requested by the five tribes that hold Rainbow Bridge as deeply sacred is simply enjoy it from the viewing area, don't walk underneath it and don't try to climb it.

The bridge itself is 290 feet high and spans 275 feet across the river. What truly makes this natural bridge impressive is in its girth and rounded rainbow like shape. The top of the arch is an impressive 42 feet thick and 33 feet wide.

Most everyone gets to the bridge via a tour boat or via private boat. There is a courtesy dock for temporary boat parking. From the dock, it is a 2-mile hike to the viewing area. In the summer, temperatures can get to an excess of 100 degrees, so plan accordingly with water and sun protection.

It is possible to backpack to the bridge; however, a permit is needed directly from the Navajo Nation. Write to Navajo Nation, Parks and Recreation Department, Box 9000, Window Rock, Arizona 86515.

# Southeast Utah

Goblin Valley State Park .......... 103
Canyonlands National Park - Island in the Sky District .......... 106
Canyonlands National Park - Needles District .......... 114
Canyonlands National Park - Maze District .......... 121
Dead Horse Point State Park .......... 123
Arches National Park .......... 126
Goosenecks State Park .......... 134
Edge of the Cedars State Park .......... 136
Natural Bridges National Monument .......... 137
Hovenweep National Monument .......... 142
Four Corners Monument .......... 145


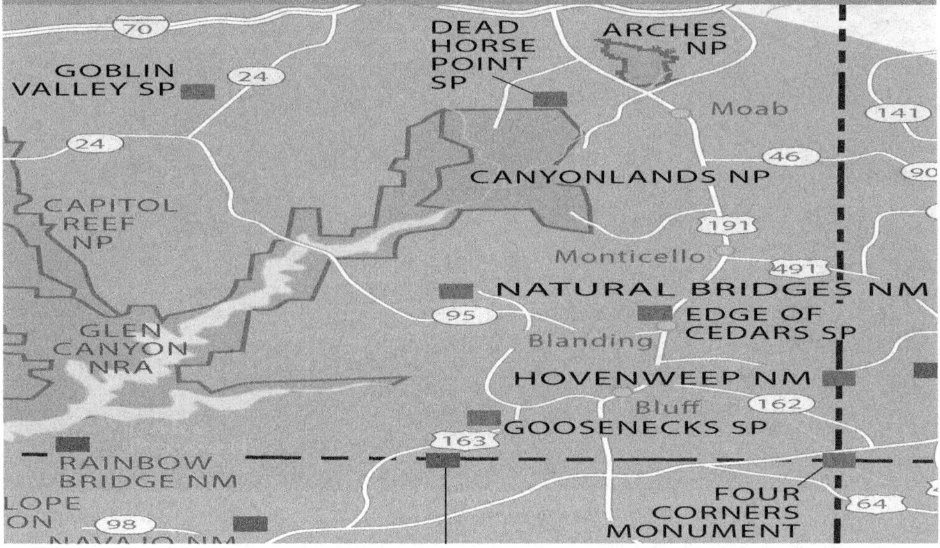

*A great place to take it all in, Beehive Arch, Maze District, Canyonlands NP*

Goblin Valley State Park



## Quick Facts

**Official Park Website:** http://stateparks.utah.gov/parks/goblin-valley/

**Visitor Center:** (435) 275-4584

**Park Accessibility:**

- Okay for 2WD and RVs
- Day and Overnight Use

**Experience Level:**

- Family Friendly to Casual Hiker

**Camping in Park:**

- Goblin Valley Campground: 10 T/15 RV + 2 yurts, drinking water, showers, flush toilets, 4 first come-first served, rest are reservable through Reserve America: (800) 322-3770 or at www.reserveamerica.com

**Lodging and Dining in Park:**

- None

**Nearest Town with Amenities:**

- Hanksville, UT is 32 mi / 51 km from park

**Getting There:**

- From Moab, UT: Take US-191 North to I-70 West to UT-24 West. Total distance is 101 mi / 162 km to park

*Three gregarious goblins graciously greeting guests*

## What Makes Goblin Valley Special

- Thousands of red-orange mushroom shaped hoodoos of varying shapes and sizes
- The nearby slot canyon within the Little Wild Horse Canyon
- Feeling like you are in the middle of nowhere on the Molly's Castle Overlook Trail

Goblin Valley is a unique place in terms of geologic formations. Here is an area that contains thousands of hoodoos. However, this is not your typical hoodoo formation. They are short and stubby toadstool shaped things, each with a unique personality. Whether you call them hoodoos or goblins, this is a fun little place.

The way these goblins were formed is even more amazing. There is evidence that the area of the park was once at the edge of a sea, where the tide ebbed and flowed. The rounded heads of the toadstools are where, for the most part, that part of the formations stayed above tidal waters while the stalks were worn down just a bit by the tidal currents.

Now for a little segment called, "name them and shame them". In October 2013, Glenn Tuck Taylor pushed over one of these ancient marvels, as his buddy and fellow Boy Scout leader, David Benjamin Hall, filmed the vandalism and then posted it on Facebook. For some reason they thought this was the right thing to do. They were stripped of their leadership roles almost immediately and then asked to leave the Boy Scouts altogether shortly thereafter. They were prosecuted and the two goblin topplers received one year of probation each. The life lesson here is don't vandalize parks. To see the actual vandalism caught on tape and more, go here: https://www.youtube.com/watch?v=3GtbSd-biCE.

## Hiking Goblin Valley State Park

### Valley of Goblins

Easy – distance and time varies

Most visitors just walk off the rim from the overlook and wander among the goblins. If you do come to this park, at least do this. It is cool to see these formations up close and there are some unique rock formations that you can only experience by getting down among them.

## Curtis Bench Trail

Easy – (2.1 mi / 3.4 km), round trip, allow 1 hour

This is an easy trail to the Curtis Bench, which gives a nice panoramic view of the Henry Mountains and the goblins in their valley below. There are also views of Molly's Castle, Three Sisters, and Wild Horse Butte.

## Entrada Canyon Trail

Easy – (2.4 mi / 3.9 km), round trip, allow 30 minutes

Another easy trail suitable for small children leading into red rock badlands. Unique and somewhat unnatural looking hoodoos in a setting that seems like you are walking in a gigantic dried mud patch.

## Carmel Canyon Trail

Easy – (1.6 mi / 2.6 km), round trip, allow 1 hour

A fun and short hike that walks past Goblin Valley and into the badlands and the very short Carmel slot canyon. The trail also includes a trip to Molly's Castle Overlook. This is another good hike for kids. The slot canyon does get narrow but is never very intimating.

## Little Wild Horse Canyon

Strenuous – (8.0 mi / 12.9 km), round trip, allow 4 – 5 hours

This is a great hike just outside of Goblin Valley State Park. Little Wild Horse Canyon is one of the most accessible slot canyons in the entire Grand Circle. In fact, it's so accessible, you cross the entrance to Little Wild Horse Canyon on the way into the park. The visitor center at Goblin Valley has a brochure on the hike that is worth picking up. Pick up the trailhead by backtracking about 0.25 miles from the visitor center to a maintained dirt road with a sign for Little Wild Horse Canyon. The trailhead with restrooms and a trail register is another 5.3 miles down this road.

The hike starts along a seasonal wash and after 0.3 mile heads into the spectacular slot canyon of Little Wild Horse Canyon and then left onto a connector road into the slightly wider Bell Canyon for the return. Little Wild Horse is 3.6 miles, 1.6 for the connector road and 1.8 for Bell Canyon. There are signposts marking the way but these can be hard to read and even find. Little Wild Horse is suitable for most hikers while Bell Canyon has some Class 3 scrambles to negotiate. If in doubt, return via Little Wild Horse Canyon.

*There are lots of goblins at Goblin Valley State Park*

# Canyonlands National Park - Island in the Sky District

## Quick Facts

**Official Park Website:** www.nps.gov/cany

**Visitor Center:**

- General Information: (435) 719-2313
- Backcountry Reservation Office: (435) 259-4351
- Island in the Sky Visitor Center: (435) 259-4712

**Park Accessibility:**

- Okay for 2WD and RVs, 4WD in some areas
- Day and Overnight Use

**Experience Level:**

- Family Friendly to Backcountry Hiker

**Camping in Park:**

- Willow Flat Campground: 12 T/RV, no water, vault toilets, no hookups, first come-first served, open year round

**Lodging and Dining in Park:**

- None

**Nearest Town with Amenities:**

- Moab, UT is 30 mi / 48 km from park

**Getting There:**

- From Moab, UT: Take US-191 North and UT-313 West 30 mi / 48 km to park entrance

*Canyonlands from Green River Overlook*

## What Makes Canyonlands – Island in the Sky Special

- Each view holds a lifetime of hiking possibilities
- Largest National Park in Utah and yet the least visited
- Holds Cataract Canyon, Utah's biggest and most challenging rapids

Canyonlands National Park is big. In fact, it is the largest national park in Utah. It is broken into three districts. Island in the Sky is closest to Moab, UT and Arches NP. Then there is the hiker friendly Needles District followed by the Maze District, which is canyoneer and desert backcountry paradise.

The bulk of Canyonland's Island in the Sky District is a large mesa banded on either side by the Colorado and Green Rivers. Much of this District can be seen simply by driving on top of the island mesa, while 4-wheel drive enthusiasts will enjoy taking the serpent like narrow dirt roads that lead down into the many basins that surround the mesa.

Beyond the overlooks, there are more than a dozen hikes in this district as well. These include Upheaval Dome, a huge circular oddity that continues to baffle geologists as to its existence. In the Island in the Sky, the rock is deep red and the cliffs dramatic and sheer. The one word for this district is "epic" and perhaps it can be labeled as the definition of desert wilderness. It is not gentle here, the land is unforgiving and dry and yet vast and incredible in its beauty. The desert hiker looks out from the top of the Island and sees a lifetime of exploration, the canyoneer a lifetime of ascents and rappels. Canyonlands calls to those who hear it in the way the ocean calls a sailor, yearning to explore every current but knowing the impossibility of being able to doing so in one lifetime.

## Hiking in the Island in the Sky District of Canyonlands NP

### Neck Spring

Moderate – (5.8 mi / 9.3 km), round trip, allow 4 -5 hours, elev. Δ: 300 ft / 91 m, trailhead at Shafer Canyon Overlook

Neck Spring is popular for many reasons. It's a loop and while it does have some elevation gain and loss, the trail isn't as steep as some of the other routes that take the hiker off the mesa top. It's also close to the visitor center as well as Shafer Trail Road, which is fun to watch as 4WD cars snake their way down the side of a cliff. Neck Spring Trail has thick patches of pinyon juniper and overall much plant diversity.

The trail is very well marked, giving both views of interior canyon cliff faces as well as some panoramic views. Remains of old watering troughs and a cabin remnant can be found, indicating the historic ranching days that preceded the park. A small portion of the loop parallels the road.

### Lathrop Canyon

Strenuous – (21.6 mi / 34.8 km), round trip, multi day backpacking trip, elev. Δ: 2,000 ft / 610 m, trailhead is two miles into park from visitor center

With 2,000 feet in steep elevation gain/loss, this is one of the more strenuous hikes in the park. The trail heads off the mesa, steeply down to the Colorado River. The first 2.6 miles are single track across open low brush meadows and some slickrock. This portion makes for an easy hike to the rim of the mesa and incredible views.

The next jaunt is steeply down another three miles to connect with White Rim Road. Much of this portion is on open rock with markers. While the cairns are

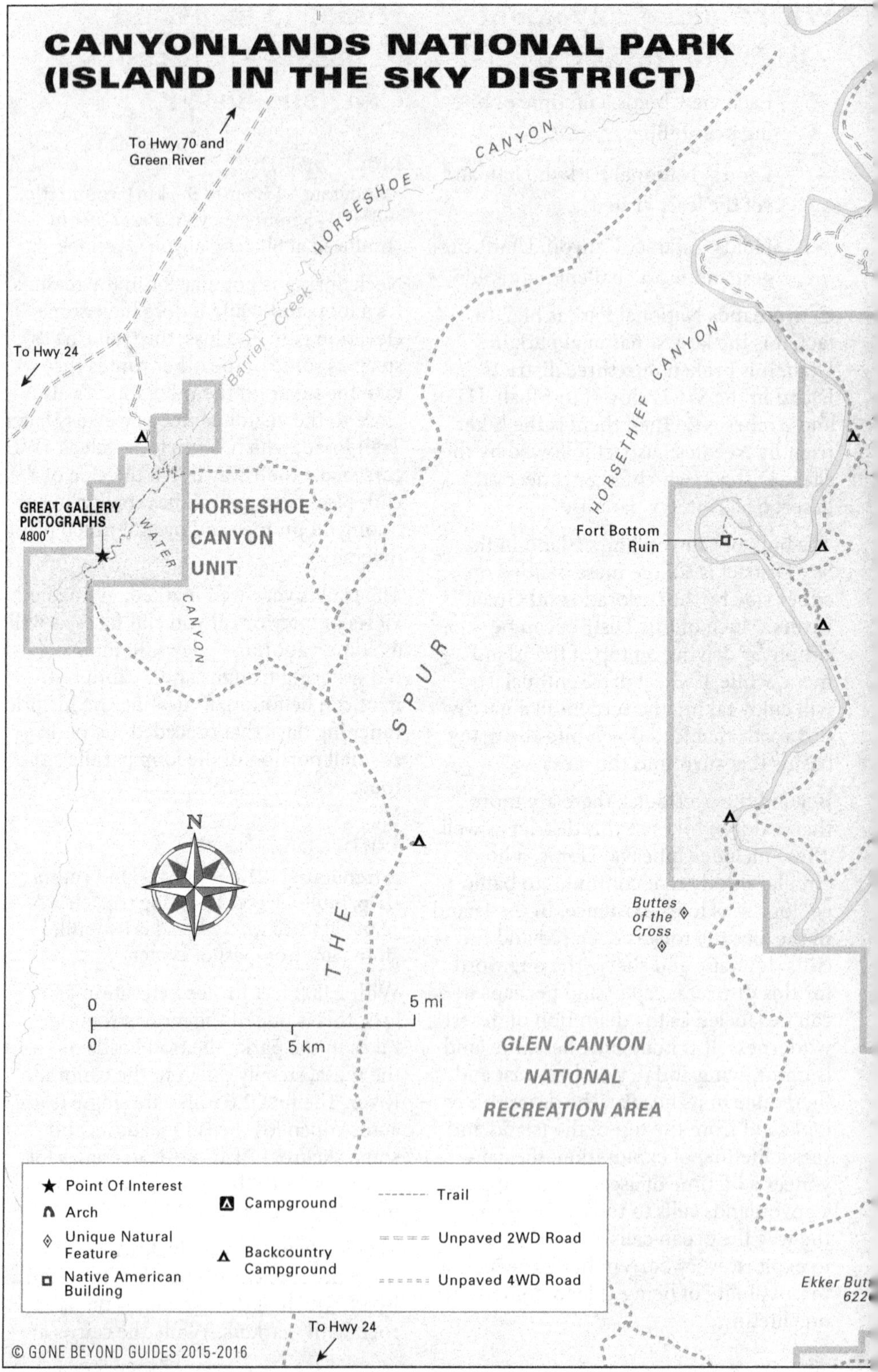
CANYONLANDS NATIONAL PARK
(ISLAND IN THE SKY DISTRICT)
To Hwy 70 and Green River
HORSESHOE CANYON
To Hwy 24
Barrier Creek
HORSETHIEF CANYON
GREAT GALLERY PICTOGRAPHS 4800′
HORSESHOE CANYON UNIT
WATER CANYON
Fort Bottom Ruin
THE SPUR
N
Buttes of the Cross
0
5 mi
0
5 km
GLEN CANYON NATIONAL RECREATION AREA
Point Of Interest
Arch
Unique Natural Feature
Native American Building
Campground
Backcountry Campground
Trail
Unpaved 2WD Road
Unpaved 4WD Road
To Hwy 24
© GONE BEYOND GUIDES 2015-2016

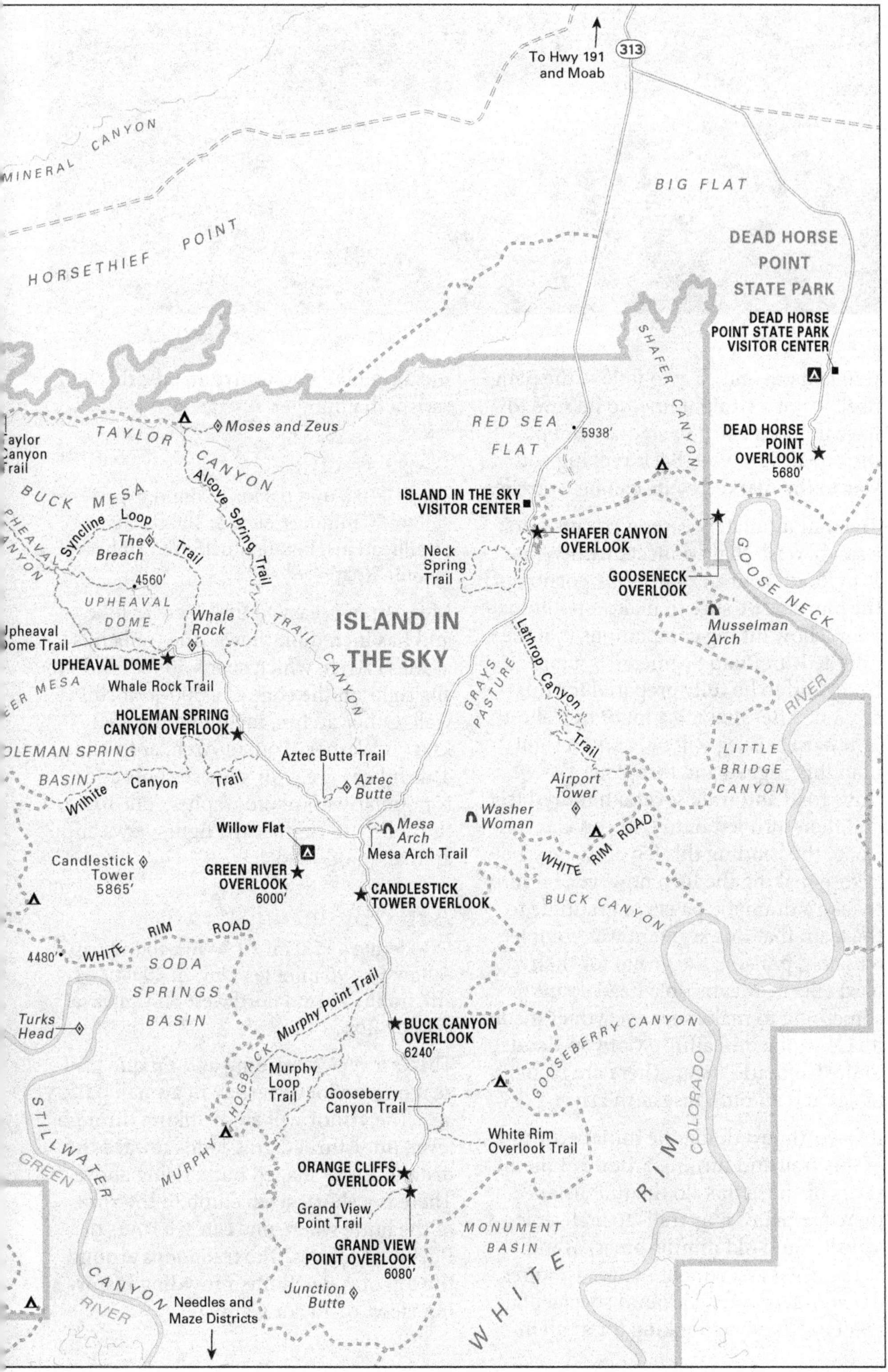
To Hwy 191
and Moab
313
MINERAL CANYON
BIG FLAT
HORSETHIEF POINT
DEAD HORSE
POINT
STATE PARK
DEAD HORSE
POINT STATE PARK
VISITOR CENTER
SHAFER CANYON
Moses and Zeus
RED SEA
FLAT
5938′
DEAD HORSE
POINT
OVERLOOK
5680′
Taylor
Canyon
Trail
TAYLOR
CANYON
Alcove Spring Trail
BUCK MESA
ISLAND IN THE SKY
VISITOR CENTER
SHAFER CANYON
OVERLOOK
Syncline Loop Trail
The Breach
UPHEAVAL
Neck
Spring
Trail
GOOSENECK
OVERLOOK
GOOSE NECK
4560′
UPHEAVAL
DOME
Whale
Rock
TRAIL CANYON
ISLAND IN
THE SKY
Lathrop Canyon Trail
Musselman
Arch
Upheaval
Dome Trail
UPHEAVAL DOME
Whale Rock Trail
GRAYS PASTURE
RIVER
MESA
HOLEMAN SPRING
CANYON OVERLOOK
HOLEMAN SPRING
BASIN
Wilhite
Canyon
Trail
Aztec Butte Trail
Aztec
Butte
LITTLE
BRIDGE
CANYON
Airport
Tower
Washer
Woman
Willow Flat
Mesa
Arch
Mesa Arch Trail
WHITE RIM ROAD
Candlestick
Tower
5865′
GREEN RIVER
OVERLOOK
6000′
CANDLESTICK
TOWER OVERLOOK
BUCK CANYON
WHITE RIM ROAD
4480′
SODA
SPRINGS
BASIN
Murphy Point Trail
Turks
Head
BUCK CANYON
OVERLOOK
6240′
GOOSEBERRY CANYON
HOGBACK
Murphy
Loop
Trail
Gooseberry
Canyon Trail
COLORADO
STILLWATER
White Rim
Overlook Trail
MURPHY
GREEN
ORANGE CLIFFS
OVERLOOK
Grand View
Point Trail
WHITE RIM
MONUMENT
BASIN
GRAND VIEW
POINT OVERLOOK
6080′
CANYON
RIVER
Junction
Butte
Needles and
Maze Districts

*Through Mesa Arch to Washer Woman*

well laid out and easy to follow, the path itself is not a straight line, so be sure to have the next cairn in sight as you pass the one next to you. Backtracking your way to the marked route can be a puzzler.

The trail ultimately eases as it cuts into a sandy wash that connects with White Rim Road, your next arduous portion of the journey. Be sure to make a point to your fellow hiking companions that the "White Rim Road Segment" is about to begin and to be fully prepared for this section. After making a lot of fuss about how hard this leg will be, make a right onto this rugged and torturous 4WD drive road and walk several hundred feet and then turn left onto Lathrop Canyon Road, thus ending this leg of the journey. Before making the turn however, be sure to take a dramatic pause in gratitude to the team that this segment was completed safely, praising the group for their hard efforts. Maybe do a head count or something to make sure everyone "made it". Continue on Lathrop Canyon Road to the Colorado River. There are picnic tables and an outhouse at the river.

It is worth just doing the initial portion of this trail and turning around at the rim. For those that do the full distance, there are many spur trails to archaeological sites and old mining areas, as well as the usual assortment of arches, spires, flat boulders and all around spectacular scenery. If you are looking for a full immersion hike into Canyonlands, this will satisfy that hunger.

## Mesa Arch

Easy – (0.5 mi / 0.8 km), round trip, allow 30 minutes, elev. Δ: 100 ft / 30 m, trailhead just before junction to Upheaval Dome Road

Mesa Arch is easy to find, easy to hike and has incredible views. The trail ends at Mesa Arch, which spans 50 feet and sits right on the edge of a 500-foot cliff wall. Other arches, including the well-known Washer Woman Arch, are visible. This hike is great for sunrise shots and is popular with photographers due to the ability to capture the light, views and arch all in one shot.

## Aztec Butte

Moderate – (2.0 mi / 3.2 km), round trip, allow 60 - 90 minutes, elev. Δ: 200 ft / 61 m, trailhead 1 mi northwest on Upheaval Dome Road

This is a very rewarding and unique trail as it offers a lot of variety in a small package. The visitor will enjoy hiking through level, undisturbed grasslands toward the distant dome-shaped butte rising above. There is a short, steep climb to the rim of the butte where one can see ruins of Pueblo granaries. The trail loops around the top of Aztec Butte, providing inspiring views of Taylor Canyon.

## Murphy Point

Moderate – (3.6 mi / 5.8 km), round trip, allow 2 hours, elev. Δ: 100 ft / 30 m, trailhead is 3 mi south on main park road from Upheaval Dome junction

See Murphy Loop for some additional elements of the trail description. The trail starts nicely across a flatland of short brush and then down a cairn marked area of slickrock to Murphy Point. Elevation gain is a modest 168 feet. Murphy Point offers an overlook to panoramic views of the many canyons that feed into the Green River. It's an immersive alternative to the drive up overlooks without having to do a steep descent off the mesa.

## Murphy Loop

Strenuous – (10.8 mi / 17.4 km), round trip, allow 5 – 6 hours, elev. Δ: 1,100 ft / 335 m, trailhead at Murphy Point trailhead

Murphy Loop is similar to many of the hikes in Island in the Sky District. The hike begins well enough along a blissfully flat section of brushy flatlands, followed by an insane descent via a bunch of short switchbacks leading to the lower regions of Canyonlands. Going clockwise on this loop puts one into an epic wash before connecting briefly with White Rim Road. From here, the trail climbs up a hogback ridge and follows it back to the loop junction. Some areas of steep slickrock, exposed ledges and need for navigational skills are involved in completing this trail.

*View from Aztec Butte Trail*

Highlights to be found on this trail include Murphy Point which gives commanding views of Murphy Basin and down into the Green River. (See Murphy Point for details on that spur trail). The other highlight is Murphy Hogback, a mesa narrow enough to feel as if you are walking across an ancient land bridge but wide enough to give the full pleasure of walking on the flatlands of a mesa top. This thin plateau allows for amazing views on either side.

## Grand View Point

Easy – (2.0 mi / 3.2 km), round trip, allow 1 hour, elev. Δ: 50 ft / 15 m, trailhead at Grand View Point

If you have been driving on the park's Grand View Point Road and on getting to the end, wish you could go just a little bit further, Grand View Point Trail is the answer. Starting at the parking lot for Grand View Point Overlook, the short little trail gets the hiker away from all those pesky cars and to very edge of Island in the Sky Mesa. This is an excellent hike for those limited on time.

## Gooseberry Canyon

Strenuous – (5.4 mi / 8.6 km), round trip, allow 4 - 5 hours, elev. Δ: 1,400 ft / 427 m, trailhead at Grand View picnic area

This is one crazy steep trail that leads off the mesa top down to Gooseberry Canyon, which is an impressive draw draining into the Colorado River. The trail drops down some 1,200 feet in just 0.7 miles via a series of well-built switchbacks. Make sure whatever time it took to get down is doubled for the trip back up. The trail then follows a dry wash to White Rim Road near Gooseberry Canyon.

Gooseberry provides some great views, starting with a 200-foot cliff face on all sides of the canyon and then stretching to the canyon floor. Peering over the edge into the canyon allows for the realization that you started this hike by peering across an overlook and then hiked for miles to end at another equally impressive overlook. This hike really shows the magnitude of Canyonlands NP.

## Wilhite Canyon

Strenuous – (12.2 mi / 19.6 km), round trip, allow 6 – 7 hours, elev. Δ: 1,600 ft / 488 m, trailhead on Upheaval Dome Road

Wilhite Canyon Trail starts amongst open brush flats and then descends at a very rapid rate (850 feet in 0.65 miles) dropping into Upper West Basin. From there, the trail winds around some impressive cliffs and then down a wash to West Rim Road. Highlights include great views of the Green River, Holeman Spring and Upper West Basins as well as a prominent monolith named Candlestick Tower to the southwest. This trail has some tough spots containing slickrock and talus rock combined with steep inclines. All in all, a typically strenuous trail, especially on the steep parts that reward the hiker with great views at each step. There is a cool slot canyon just over the road and it is possible to venture into it for a bit before needing canyoneering gear. Note that this canyon is easier to get down into then it is to get out of, moderate scrambling is required here.

## Taylor Canyon

Strenuous – (20.0 mi / 32.2 km), round trip, multi day backpacking trip, elev. Δ: 2,000 ft / 610 m, trailhead at Trail Canyon trailhead on Upheaval Dome Road

Taylor Canyon shares a few similarities to the Lathrop Canyon trek described below. Both step off of the mesa and require long steep descents, both are incredibly scenic and worth the effort and both lead to one of the major rivers of the Southwest. In Taylor Canyon's case, the water source in question is the Green River versus the Colorado River for the Lathrop Canyon trail. As described, the trail is a nice two-day loop, which includes Upheaval Dome and the gravity defying spires named Moses and Zeus.

Take Upheaval Dome Road to the Trail Canyon trailhead pullout and begin the steep descent into Trail Canyon. This trail does require a fair amount of skill, as there are several areas where minor scrambling and trail finding is needed. The trail makes its way to an obvious sandstone fin on the north side of the canyon, which can be used as a guide. The canyon bottom is reached after 2.1 miles.

From here, head north to a juncture where Trail Canyon merges with Taylor Canyon and the loop trail around Zeus and Moses. These two spires are quite impressive, shooting straight up, the tallest being 410 feet. Take the right trail to do the short loop around the spires and then left into Taylor Canyon. After a short distance is Taylor Campground, which is a dry camp with one pit toilet. This campsite has a lot to offer in views as it sits at the juncture of two canyons with the spires of Zeus and Moses framing the left of the camp. Good coffee, your favorite breakfast foods, and the campsite's view help make for a perfect morning moment.

Continuing on, the trail becomes a 4WD road. Travel on Taylor Canyon Road west for 5.2 miles passing humongous rocks the size of semi-trucks. At now 12 miles into the hike, you are at the Green River and Labyrinth Campground, a second choice for rolling the bag out for the night. Labyrinth does offer the lush, cooling Green River as a backdrop and is a great choice. Reservations are recommended if you plan to stay here and there is a fee of $30.

From the campground pick up White Rim Trail and continue for about a mile and then turn left at the junction into Upheaval Canyon. The trail now heads up a gorge of loose talus, making for a sluggish slow uphill stretch.

Some navigation is needed as the trail gets a little hard to follow in some spots. Keep heading up, 1,300 feet in all until the rim is once more under your feet. Check out Upheaval Dome on your way out and back to where you started.

## Whale Rock

Moderate – (1.0 mi / 1.6 km), round trip, allow 60 minutes, elev. Δ: 100 ft / 30 m, trailhead just before Upheaval Dome parking area

Whale Rock Trail gives an alternative view of Upheaval Dome. There is a short climb up a large rock that indeed does look like a whale. The trail ends with a nice "big picture" view of Upheaval Dome.

## Upheaval Dome

Easy – (2.0 mi / 3.2 km), round trip, allow 60 minutes, elev. Δ: 150 ft / 46 m, trailhead at Upheaval Dome parking area

Upheaval Dome as a geological feature is explained in some detail in the Canyonlands Geology section of this book. As a hike, it allows the visitor to get out and into the slick rock of the park without much fuss. It is only a mile (1.6 km) to the first overlook. It is well worth the extra effort to the second overlook, which will take you right to the dome's edge. Be sure to follow the cairns that have been laid out to mark the way, as in some portions the trail is simply walking on slick rock with the cairns as guides.

## Syncline Loop

Strenuous – (8.3 mi / 13.4 km), round trip, allow 5 - 6 hours, elev. Δ: 1,300 ft / 396 m, trailhead at Upheaval Dome parking area

For a longer hike, take this loop that circles the entirety of Upheaval Dome. There is a spur trail that leads to the center of the crater as well. Allow another 3 miles (4.8 km) for the spur trail. Another spur trail along the loop (7 mi / 11.2 km) leads to the Green River. The elevation change is about 1,300 feet. Note that this is a very rugged and strenuous trail and includes a mixture of boulder fields, steep switchbacks and plenty of slickrock. This is a fine example of a challenging hike that puts you inside one of the more remote sections of Canyonlands.

Warning: nearly all rescues in Canyonlands NP come from this trail. Route finding can be very difficult and there are many false spur trails. Also, given the various ups and downs on this loop, the actual elevation change is closer to 2900 feet. This trail is for experienced hikers only.

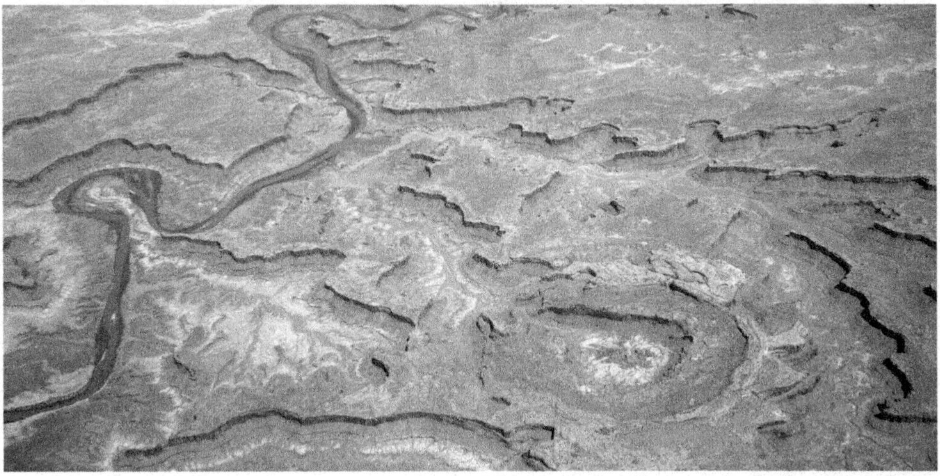

*Aerial shot of Upheaval Dome and the Green River*

# Canyonlands National Park - Needles District

## Quick Facts

**Official Park Website:** www.nps.gov/cany

**Visitor Center:**

- General Information: (435) 719-2313
- Backcountry Reservation Office: (435) 259-4351
- Needles Visitor Center: (435) 259-4711

**Park Accessibility:**

- Okay for 2WD and RVs, 4WD in some areas
- Day and Overnight Use

**Experience Level:**

- Family Friendly to Backcountry Hiker

**Camping in Park:**

- Squaw Flat Campground: 26 T/RV, plus 3 group campsites, drinking water, vault toilets, no hookups, first come-first served

**Lodging and Dining in Park:**

- None

**Nearest Town with Amenities:**

- Monticello, UT is 46 mi / 74 km from park

**Getting There:**

- From Moab, UT: Take US-191 South and UT-211 West 30 mi / 48 km to right turn onto Lark Hart road and the park's entrance

*View from BLM Managed Needles Overlook*

## What Makes Canyonlands – Needles District Special

- Some of the best and most accessible hiking in the Grand Circle
- Druid Arch, a natural arch that looks like a massive version of Stonehenge
- The two major rivers of the Southwest, the Colorado and the Green River, join forces here.

The Needles District is a hiker's paradise, with trails as numerous as they are varied in experience needed. Once in Needles, nearly all trailheads start from a paved road. Needles hiking is a mixture of fun and endurance, wonder and skill. It contains some of the best desert hiking in the Grand Circle.

## Hiking in the Needles District of Canyonlands NP

### Roadside Ruin

Easy – (0.3 mi / 0.5 km), round trip, allow 20 minutes, elev. Δ: negligible, trailhead is 0.4 mi from visitor center, left side of road

This quick loop starts right from the road and walks amongst desert brush and pinyon juniper within a wide valley, giving expansive views of sculptured sandstone off in the distance. The highlight of the trail is a small cylindrical granary tucked underneath a large alcove. The granary dates to 1270 to 1290 CE and is nicely preserved.

### Cave Springs Trail

Easy – (0.6 mi / 1.0 km), round trip, allow 30 minutes, elev. Δ: 50 ft / 15 m, trailhead at Cave Spring trailhead

This tidy little loop leads to a series of small overhangs. Taking the loop counterclockwise leads to a historic and well-preserved cowboy camp complete with a corral, benches, and other items left behind. It is quite a refreshing look at a more recent chapter of history. There is a second overhang that contains a number of treasures, ranging from fern grottoes, small springs, and petroglyphs. The trail includes two ladders to help up some steep slick rock that leads to some drier alcoves as the trail winds back to the trailhead. All in all, a fun little hike.

### Pothole Point Trail

Easy – (0.6 mi / 1.0 km), round trip, allow 30 minutes, elev. Δ: negligible, trailhead is 6.2 mi from visitor center on Big Spring Canyon Overlook Scenic Drive

Another easy little hike with very little elevation gain. The trail is almost entirely on slickrock with cairns marking the way. While the namesake of the trail is important to note, the main reason to hike this one are the spectacular views. Along the way, look for little potholes that when filled with water, maintain an ecosystem for shrimp, who have figured out how to thrive out in the desert. At Pothole Point, there is a small spur trail south that heads to an overlook of the Needles.

### Slickrock Trail

Moderate – (2.4 mi / 3.9 km), round trip, allow 90 minutes, elev. Δ: 150 ft / 46 m, trailhead is 6.2 mi from visitor center on Big Spring Canyon Overlook Scenic Drive

Slickrock has a bit of everything that Needles offers. There are four viewpoints that give commanding views of Island in the Sky District to the north and different views into the canyons below. The trail passes by a fragile arch and travels on both slickrock and actual trail. Each viewpoint is different and some offer long views into the canyons cut by the Colorado River. The Needles can also be seen in the distance.

# CANYONLANDS NATIONAL PARK (NEEDLES AND MAZE DISTRICTS)

SOUTHEAST UTAH

Canyonlands - Needles

French Spring

To Hwy 24

NORTH TRAIL CANYON

PETES MESA

GREE

MAZE OVERLOOK
5120'

Chocolate Drops

Elaterite Butte
6552'

Harvest Scene
Pictographs

RIVE

THE MAZE

ELATERITE BASIN

O R A N G E    C L I F F S

Chimney Rock
5563'

The Plug

LAND
OF STANDING
ROCKS

Lizard Rock
The Wall

Lower Red
Canyon Tra

Bagpipe
Butte
Overlook

Bagpipe
Butte
6679'

The Doll
House

THE FINS

ERNIES    COUNTRY

CATARACT    CANYON

BUT
F

COLORADO    RIVER

CROSS CANYON

THE GRABENS

Teapot
Rock
6221'

To Hwy 95

WATERHOLE FLAT

GLEN CANYON
NATIONAL
RECREATION AREA

IMPERIAL    VALLEY

BEEF    BAS

## Legend

| | | |
|---|---|---|
| ★ Point Of Interest | ∩ Arch | -------- Trail |
| ◪ Campground | ◈ Unique Natural Feature | ==== Unpaved 2WD Road |
| ▲ Backcountry Campground | ▢ Native American Building | ===== Unpaved 4WD Road |

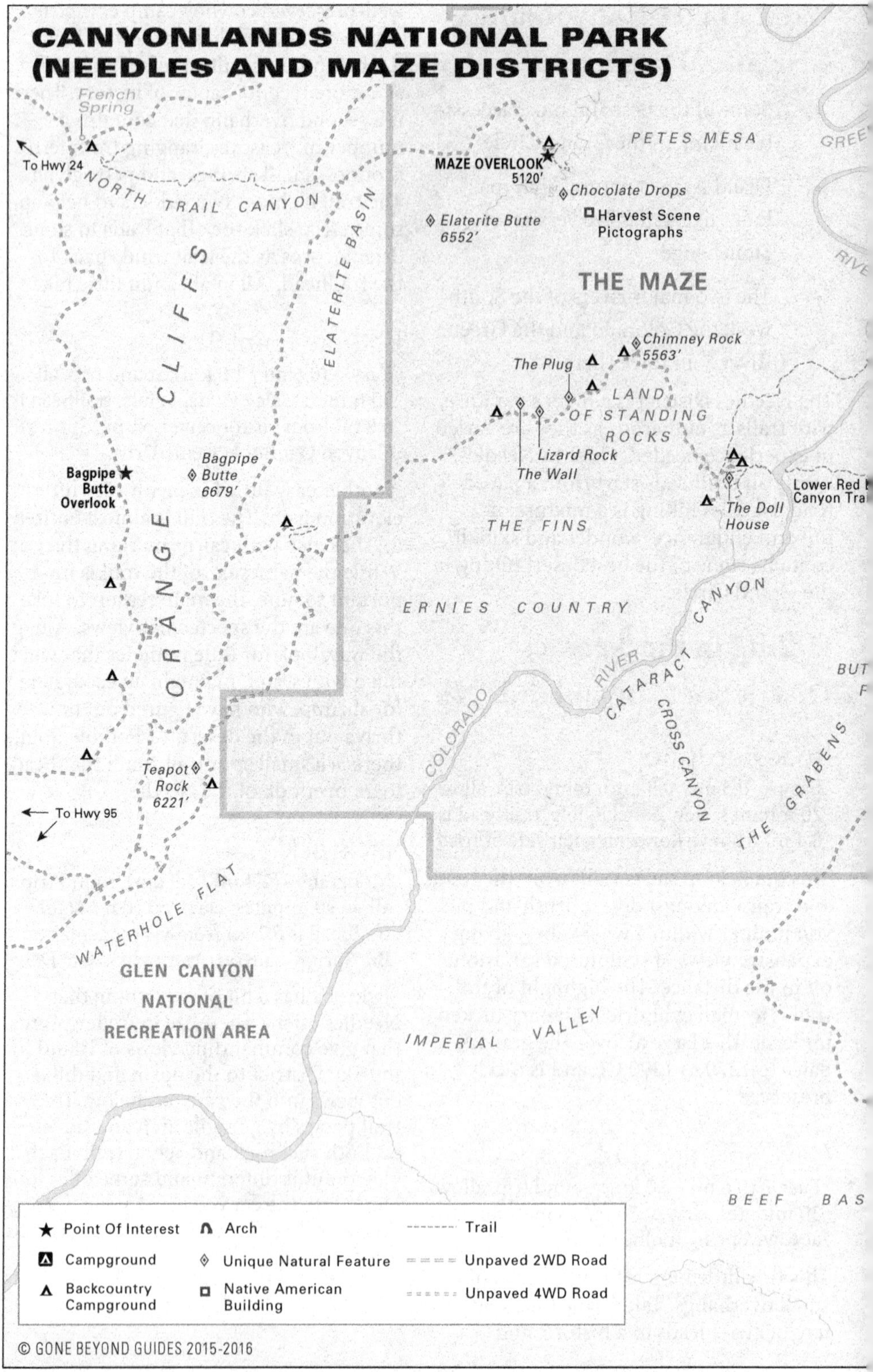

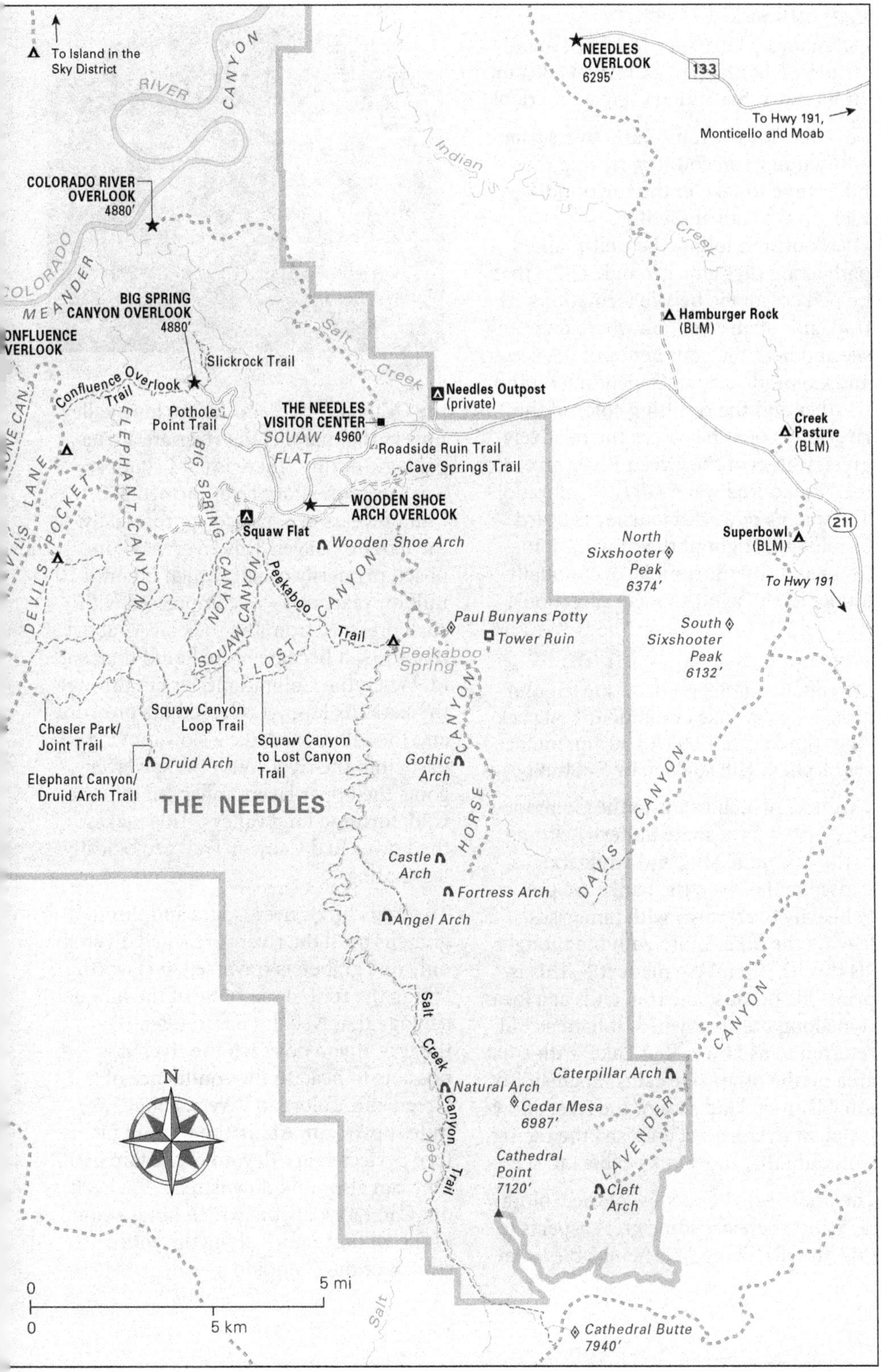
To Island in the Sky District
RIVER
CANYON
COLORADO RIVER OVERLOOK 4880′
COLORADO
MEANDER
BIG SPRING CANYON OVERLOOK 4880′
ONFLUENCE
VERLOOK
Slickrock Trail
Confluence Overlook Trail
Pothole Point Trail
ELEPHANT CANYON
BIG SPRING
DEVILS LANE
DEVILS POCKET
THE NEEDLES VISITOR CENTER 4960′
SQUAW FLAT
Salt Creek
Indian Creek
NEEDLES OVERLOOK 6295′
133
To Hwy 191, Monticello and Moab
Hamburger Rock (BLM)
Needles Outpost (private)
Creek Pasture (BLM)
Roadside Ruin Trail
Cave Springs Trail
WOODEN SHOE ARCH OVERLOOK
Squaw Flat
Wooden Shoe Arch
CANYON
Peekaboo Trail
SQUAW CANYON
LOST CANYON
Paul Bunyans Potty
Tower Ruin
Peekaboo Spring
North Sixshooter Peak 6374′
Superbowl (BLM)
211
To Hwy 191
South Sixshooter Peak 6132′
Squaw Canyon Loop Trail
Chesler Park/ Joint Trail
Squaw Canyon to Lost Canyon Trail
Druid Arch
Elephant Canyon/ Druid Arch Trail
Gothic Arch
HORSE CANYON
THE NEEDLES
DAVIS CANYON
Castle Arch
Fortress Arch
Angel Arch
Salt Creek Canyon Trail
CANYON
Caterpillar Arch
Natural Arch
Cedar Mesa 6987′
LAVENDER
Cathedral Point 7120′
Cleft Arch
N
0
5 mi
0
5 km
Salt
Cathedral Butte 7940′

## Confluence Overlook

Strenuous – (10.0 mi / 16.1 km), round trip, 5 - 6 hours, elev. Δ: 1,250 ft / 381 m, trailhead at Big Spring Canyon Overlook

This hike for the most part covers a fair amount of open country, leaving the hiker time to take in the surroundings. Pick up the trail at the Big Spring Canyon Overlook and follow the well-marked path along the same geologic faults that helped create the needle formations. The trail ends at an overlook where one can see and hear the confluence of the Green and Colorado rivers. Depending on the weather and the resulting color of the rivers, it is possible to see the relatively green waters of the Green River mix into the Navajo Red waters of the Colorado. The water's powerful journey is heard echoing throughout the canyon, sometimes as a distant rumble, occasionally louder as the wind changes directions.

## Lower Red Lake Canyon

Strenuous – (18.8 mi / 30.3 km), round trip, long day hike or multiday backpacking trip, elev. Δ: 1,000 ft / 305 m, trailhead at Elephant Hill and Squaw Flat trailheads

This hike, which heads to the Colorado River, does have some underwhelming parts. It is quite long and while it does end up at the river, the banks are pretty heavily overgrown with tamarisks, leaving the hiker more with the thought, "Is this it?" then "We made it!!" This is primarily because the trail ends at a location along the river where it flattens out, referred to as Lower Red Lake, with a flat area on the other side called Spanish Bottom. This wetland area of the river allows for plant overgrowth and isn't the raging Colorado that most folks expect to see.

The unexpected first view of the Colorado aside, there are some great aspects to this hike. The biggest is being able to see

*The famous Needles*

the Grabens first hand. These long valley fingers that parallel the river are a true geologic oddity. There is (or I suppose was) a sedimentary layer formed 300 million years ago named appropriately, the Paradox Layer. This layer was composed primarily of salt, which up until 10 million years ago was compressed with such pressure from the rock layers above that the salt became more liquid than solid. When the Colorado River cut through the Paradox layer, it released the pressure and the salt moved like a slow moving paste into the river. With the salt layer gone, the upper layers collapsed into the void, forming long valleys. This makes the Lower Red Canyon Trail geologically fascinating.

The trail climbs over ridges and through grabens until the river is reached. Even if only one graben is traversed, it is worth taking the trail to see some of the unique geology that Needles has to offer. By the way, if you do reach the river, it is possible to head to the confluence of the Green and Colorado Rivers, about 3.6 miles upstream. Along the way are picture perfect spots, devoid of the tamarisk. One can also walk downstream to check out Cataract Canyon, which holds some of the wildest rapids along the entire stretch of the Colorado.

## Elephant Canyon / Druid Arch

Strenuous – (11.0 mi / 17.7 km), round trip, allow 5 - 6 hours, elev. Δ: 1,000 ft / 305 m, trailhead at Elephant Hill trailhead

This is arguably one of the best hikes in Needles, with incredible views along the entire trail ending at Druid Arch. A quick glance at a park map will show that there are many routes from which to choose. This description starts at the Chesler Park access trail and follows up Elephant Canyon.

The entire route is well marked and while the trail is long and it is not otherwise terribly strenuous except for the end. Once on the canyon floor you'll find it contains some sand and loose gravel, which makes hiking slower. This continues to the end of the canyon, where the last pitch is a steep climb of a quarter mile (0.4 km) involving a little scrambling up slick rock and even climbing a ladder.

Druid Arch itself is well worth the hike. The views along Elephant Canyon are spectacular and the arch is one of the more unique-looking arches, with much angularity and several keyhole windows within a fin-like blade of rock. The one thing any picture doesn't do is portray the enormity of the structure, which is humbling.

*Druid Arch*

## Joint Trail

Moderate – (11.0 mi / 17.7 km), round trip, allow 5 - 6 hours, elev. Δ: 560 ft / 171 m, trailhead at Elephant Hill trailhead

This wonderful trail holds views of red rock monoliths amongst grassland meadows. In these sections, the sky is wide and the land holds a peaceful warmth, with inviting grasses, folding into the banded colored rocks and typically deep blue skies. This area is known as Chesler Park, surrounded all around by the famous Needles spires.

Then there is the Joint Trail itself. The trail leads to a narrow slot canyon that contains a tunnel and deep narrow crevices that require some mild scrambling to travel through. Part of what makes Joint Trail special is in the way it was formed. Unlike the water carved slot canyons typical of most of the Grand Circle, this canyon is an actual fracture in the rock just wide enough to walk through. It is a very different type of canyon and when combined with Chesler Park, the Joint Trail is a contender for one of the best hikes in the Needles District.

## Squaw Canyon Loop

Strenuous – (7.5 mi / 12.1 km), round trip, allow 4 hours at Squaw Flat trailhead, elev. Δ: 700 ft / 213 m, trailhead at Squaw Flat trailhead

There are some pretty steep patches and about 500 feet in elevation gain, but gives a really nice immersion into the Needles backcountry. The trail, as described here, starts in Squaw Canyon and travels to its head. From there, it's up and over into Big Spring Canyon for the return.

At the trailhead, walk within a large desert valley to a juncture. Staying left puts you into Squaw Canyon. The canyon itself starts out wide and inviting and then narrows. Stay on the trail to Squaw Canyon, avoiding the two junctures to the left to Lost Canyon. At a well-marked juncture, the trail goes up and over some slick rock, which may look challenging but is fairly easy to navigate when dry.

Take a moment at the ridge to enjoy the views and the canyon you just walked up and then come on down the other side into Big Spring Canyon. The trip down into the canyon has some steeper spots, but these are short. Note that while the slickrock offers firm holds when dry, it's a different story when wet or frozen, so use proper judgment here.

The trail ambles through Big Spring Canyon before climbing out and following closer to the Squaw Canyon side of the ridge back over and down again to the trailhead. Big Spring Canyon offers nice vegetation and great views of the Needles as you make the return.

## Squaw Canyon to Lost Canyon

Strenuous – (8.7 mi / 14.0 km), round trip, allow 5 -6 hours, elev. Δ: 380 ft / 116 m, trailhead at Squaw Flat trailhead

This trail is similar to the one described above for Squaw Canyon. The hike heads up Squaw Canyon and then diverts left to Lost Canyon, traveling up that canyon and then crossing over again up and back over into Squaw. So, Squaw Canyon up, ridge climb over, Long Canyon up (if doing the canyon clockwise), ridge climb over, Squaw Canyon down and out.

*Along the way in Elephant Canyon*

There are some notable differences. This trail is a bit longer and there is reliable water to be found. The trail is marked with cairns but can be hard to follow at times, requiring a sharp eye. This hike offers a bit more challenge and skill, different views and a great hike all in all.

## Peekaboo Trail

Strenuous – (10.0 mi / 16.1 km), round trip, allow 5 - 6 hours, elev. Δ: 550 ft / 112 m, trailhead at Squaw Flat trailhead

Peekaboo is an extension from Lost Canyon Trail. From the Squaw Canyon Trailhead, head up and take the first junction left towards Lost Canyon. Look for the junction again left through open country to Peekaboo Spring. The spring is situated near Salt Creek. Look for granaries hidden away in alcoves as well as some interesting pictographs and hand symbol petroglyphs. Some scrambling is required and there are two ladders that must be climbed to complete the journey. This is a great hike for the skilled desert hiker, offering a bit of challenge in navigation with amble rewarding views, hoodoos, large meadows, and blue sky touching red rock.

## Salt Creek Canyon

Strenuous – (22.5 mi / 36.2 km), round trip, long day hike or multiday backpacking trip, elev. Δ: 1,650 ft / 503 m, trailhead at end of 4WD road up Salt Creek or from Peekaboo Trail

This trail expands on the Peekaboo Trail listed above and continues along Salt Creek. As the creek holds water generally year long, this line of life holds plenty of archaeological sites, pictographs, petroglyphs, farming areas and numerous granaries. There is also an old log cabin built in the 1890's by a rancher named Rensselaer Lee Kirk showing some of the more recent history in Salt Creek Canyon.

## Quick Facts

**Official Park Website:** www.nps.gov/cany

**Visitor Center:**

- General Information: (435) 719-2313
- Backcountry Reservation Office: (435) 259-4351
- Hans Flat (Maze) Ranger Station: (435) 259-2652

**Park Accessibility:**

- 4WD recommended
- Primarily Overnight Use

**Experience Level:**

- Experienced Hiker to Backcountry Hiker

**Camping in Park:**

- No developed campground, backcountry camping okay with permit

**Lodging and Dining in Park:**

- None

**Nearest Town with Amenities:**

- Hanksville, UT is 61 mi / 98 km from park

**Getting There:**

- From Moab, UT: Take US-191 South, I-70 West and UT-24 to Lower San Rafael Road to Hans Flat Road. Total distance to Hans Flat Ranger Station is 134 mi / 216 km.

*Portion of the Great Gallery*

## What Makes Canyonlands – Maze District Special

- The Great Gallery Petroglyphs – a 200-foot-long wall of floating ghost like figures that are so timeless that reproductions hang in the New York Museum of Modern Art
- One of the most remote places in the United States, takes a full day's drive on rough dirt roads just to get to the entrance of the park
- Only 3% of Canyonlands visitors go here, it is too remote for a day hike, thus unattainability is part of the charm.

## Hiking in the Maze District of Canyonlands NP

The Maze is true desert wilderness and the trails are for the most part, more routes than actual trails. The area is remote and folks that had out this way usually plan on taking a minimum 4-5-day backpacking trip. Part of the reason is it takes nearly a full day just to get to the access points.

There is one developed trail in the Maze District and a very special one at that, Horseshoe Canyon. It is not inside the main section of the district and is an easier trip, relatively speaking. Horseshoe Canyon is definitely one of the pinnacle trails in all of the Grand Circle. To learn why, read the description below.

### Horseshoe Canyon

Strenuous – (7.0 mi / 11.3 km), round trip, allow 4 -5 hours, elev. Δ: 800 ft / 244 m, trailhead described below

The one exception to this is Horseshoe Canyon. It is a protected island of land separate from the main park that was added in 1971 to protect one of the most significant examples of rock art in North America. It is arguably the best example of Barrier Canyon Style rock art. It is also one of the most recognizable. The life sized anthropomorphic figures with their unique trapezoidal shapes sit as reproductions in both the Denver Natural History Museum and the Museum of Modern Art in New York.

The centerpiece of Horseshoe Canyon is the Great Gallery. Within it is a panel of rock measuring 200 feet long (61m) and 15 feet (4.6m) high. The panel contains 20 elongated floating limbless humanoid figures, all life-sized, with one measuring over seven feet (2.1m) tall. The figures seem to float as ghosts on the rock, having no feet and distinctive trapezoidal shoulders. A visit to the Great Gallery is certainly a high-water mark for any trip.

Horseshoe Canyon is a separate unit from the main section of Canyonlands NP. It is best accessed from the west near Goblin Valley State Park at Highway 24. This road is often accessible for two-wheel drive vehicles and is okay for smaller RVs. It is graded along the 30 miles (48 km). You can also take a 47-mile (75 km) dirt road from Green River, but it has similar caveats and is longer.

Once out to the Horseshoe Canyon unit, it is an additional 7-mile (11 km) round trip hike to the Great Gallery. Allow about four hours for the hike, leaving plenty of time, water and food for the strenuous climb back out of the canyon. During the spring and fall, guided walks are held by the park's rangers. Aligning with these guided tours is an excellent way to see the petroglyphs and pictographs. The rangers do an amazing job of tying in the interesting details of what you are seeing and bringing historical context to your trip.

Go to www.discovermoab.com for a complete list of guided tours to Horseshoe Canyon and for rafting, jeep, and horseback riding tours.

Note that the roads may be closed seasonally during monsoon season. Check with the ranger station before heading out.

## Quick Facts

**Official Park Website:** http://stateparks.utah.gov/parks/dead-horse/

**Visitor Center:** (435) 259-2614

**Park Accessibility:**

- Okay for 2WD and RVs
- Day and Overnight Use

**Experience Level:**

- Family Friendly to Casual Hiker

**Camping in Park:**

- The Kayenta Campground: 21 T/RV + 3 yurts, hook-ups, drinking water (limited), restrooms, 4 sites are first come-first served, rest are reservable through Reserve America: (800) 322-3770 or online at www.reserveamerica.com

**Lodging and Dining in Park:**

- Pony Express Coffee Shop, closed in winter

**Nearest Town with Amenities:**

- Moab, UT is 28 mi / 45 km from park

**Getting There:**

- From Moab, UT: Take US-191 North to I-70 West to UT-24 West. Total distance is 101 mi / 162 km to park

*Colorado River from Dead Horse Point*

*The iconic view from Dead Horse Point with the La Sal Mountains in the background*

## What Makes Dead Horse Point State Park Special

- Amazing trails for both hikers and mountain bikers
- If you love Canyonlands, you will love this park, same great location, but different views
- One of the most dramatic overlooks of the Colorado River

Dead Horse Point State Park is located adjacent to the Island in the Sky District of Canyonlands as well as the town of Moab. The state of Utah has done a great job in providing a great camping, hiking and mountain biking experience within the park's boundaries. Given the popularity of mountain biking in Moab, Dead Horse Point has become a mecca for mountain bikers, especially those that are just starting out in the sport. There is no exposure and none of the trails requires a lot of experience to enjoy them.

There are a number of trails that are designed specifically for the mountain bike, though hikers can use them too. And while this book is geared more for the hiker, there really is nothing quite like tearing through a single track, finding that satisfying center point between your bike and your body, even when the bike is outstretched to the right while your body is angled to the left.

For those hikers that aren't crazy about sharing the road at 2 - 3 miles an hour with something that can go a lot faster, there are hiking only trails too. But hopefully, with over 79 parks and hundreds of trails described, certainly dear hiker, you won't mind if the mountain biking loops are described first for this park.

## Mountain Biking in Dead Horse Point State Park

All mountain bike loops in Dead Horse Point State Park can be hiked by foot as well. In some cases, the hiking and mountain biking trails parallel each other, making it easy to cross over to the hiking only trails if you are on foot.

There are three loops in the park, ranging in ease and distance traveled, from 1.4 miles to 9.0 miles round trip. Many folks do all three in one session.

### Intrepid Loop

Easy – (1.4 mi / 2.3 km), round trip, allow 20 – 30 minutes for bikers, 45 minutes for hikers

This is the most laid back of the three loops and the shortest. Mostly level, with minor bits of uneven terrain. High points include the Colorado Overlook, which is easily accessible. Good for a pleasant family bike outing.

## Great Pyramid Loop

Moderate – (4.2 mi / 6.8 km), round trip, allow 1 hour for bikers, 2 hours for hikers

Similar red rock terrain as Intrepid Loop, but with more elevation up and down as well as a slight increase in the amount of uneven terrain and one spot that is more slick rock than trail. For folks that only mountain bike a little, this is a fun bit of single track. The trail connects with the Colorado Overlook as well as Pyramid Canyon Overlook.

## Big Chief Loop

Moderate – (9.0 mi / 14.5 km), round trip, allow 2 hours for bikers, 4 hours for hikers

The longest of the three loops. The trail starts out on the Great Pyramid Loop and then continues on to Big Chief. Both loops together make up the nine-mile loop. Big Chief Loop is similar in difficulty to Great Pyramid and in fact for much of the journey is a little easier. The highlights of this trail are Big Chief Overlook, which offers great views of the distant La Sal Mountains and added remoteness. If you want to do all three loops, allow about 2 hours 30 minutes.

# Hiking Dead Horse Point State Park

## Nature Trail

Easy – (0.3 mi / 0.5 km), round trip, allow 10 minutes

Pick up a brochure at the visitor center for this pleasant interpretive walk. The brochure will point out different aspects of the geology and flora at numbered locations.

Now, as you start out on this trail you will pass a snack shack and they have some tempting items, which can be a problem for this hike. There are two ways to manage the snack shack. Either a) realize you have no willpower whatsoever and completely give into temptation before you even hit the trail under the justification that it's still a trail and you need sustenance or b) hold off until after the hike as a reward for conquering this paved quarter-mile long monster. Either way, have a little fun and get something for yourself, you deserve it!

## Colorado Overlook Trail

Easy – (1.0 mi / 1.6 km), round trip, allow 30 minutes

This trail parallels the Intrepid Loop for half its length. Hike is along the rim with great views of the Colorado River.

## East Rim Trail

Easy – (4.0 mi / 6.4 km), round trip, allow 2 hours

The distance listed for this trail is round trip just for East Rim plus the spur trail out to Basin Overlook. Many visitors do both the East and West Rim, which is 5.7 miles with all the overlook spur trails. This trail gives nonstop panoramic views of the canyon and surrounding area. Basin Overlook provides a glimpse of Chimney Rock and Pyramid Butte.

## West Rim Trail

Easy – (6.2 mi / 10.0 km), round trip, allow 3 hours

Similar to East Rim in commanding views, West Rim mileage noted here is if the trail was done as a there and back including the spur trails to Rim, Shafer Overlook and Meander Overlooks. Again, it is a better hike overall to combine the East and West Rim trails and make it a loop.

## Big Horn Overlook Trail

Easy – (3.4 mi / 5.5 km), round trip, allow 90 minutes

This trail heads cross-country through pinyon juniper woodlands to an overlook and some large pothole formations. Similar views as West Rim Trail.

# Arches National Park

## Quick Facts

**Official Park Website:** www.nps.gov/arch

**Visitor Center:** (435) 719-2299

**Park Accessibility:**

- Okay for 2WD and RVs
- Day and Overnight Use

**Experience Level:**

- Family Friendly to Backcountry Hiker

**Camping in Park:**

- Devils Garden Campground: 50 T/RV, no water, restrooms, some pull thru sites, no hookups, all sites can be reserved and are typically full in summer. Reserve at http://www.recreation.gov/

**Lodging and Dining in Park:**

- None

**Nearest Town with Amenities:**

- Moab, UT is 5 mi / 8 km from park

**Getting There:**

- From Moab, UT: Take US-191 North 5 mi / 8 km to park entrance

*Delicate Arch, arguably the most recognized arch in the world*

## What Makes Arches Special

- Contains over 2,000 natural stone arches, the highest concentration of arches in the world
- Landscape Arch, the longest arch in North America and second largest in the world
- Seeing Delicate Arch, the most photographed and recognized arch on the planet

Arches National Park contains some of the most recognized arches in the world. At the top of the list is Delicate Arch. Most everyone who visits the park takes this hike in spite of the steep incline at the front end of the trail. The hike to Delicate Arch has amazing views along the way and just at the moment the weary hiker feels they really do not want to go any further, the trail opens up and there's the arch, big as life, with the often-snow-capped La Sal Mountains in the background. You can even stand under nearby Frame Arch to capture a unique picture of the famous Delicate Arch.

Then there is Landscape Arch, the longest arch in North America, with a span of 306 feet base to base. It is an easy 1.6-mile (2.4 km) hike and baffles the imagination with its threadlike frailty. It has in fact lost a bit of itself with three decent stone slabs falling from the arch in recent years. In 1991, the trail to walking under the arch closed as a result.

There is something wonderful and even magical about stepping through an arch. For everyone who comes, the arch draws them in, invites them to stand underneath these bows of rock and step through them to see what they look like from the other side. Watch your fellow visitor. They walk up to the arch, look up underneath it, and then carry through to see it from the other side. Arches fascinate, and at Arches NP, there is a lot of fascination. Nowhere in the world is there a place quite like this park. The arches are an invitation, every one of them.

## Hiking Arches National Park

### Park Avenue

Easy – (2.0 mi / 3.2 km), round trip, allow 1 – 2 hours, elev. Δ: 330 ft / 101 m, trailheads at Park Avenue or North Park Avenue parking areas

Park Avenue has a small elevation change as it descends steeply into a wide canyon with amazing thin-walled fins of rock that sheer upwards hundreds of feet into the air. The scenery is best described as epic southwest, as grand as anything the Colorado Plateau has to offer. Once in the canyon, the walk is easy enough, allowing one to take in the view of the Courthouse Towers, including The Organ, a massive sandstone fin tower. Other notables are Sheep Rock, which looks like a lamb on a rock, and the Three Gossips, which resemble three figures standing around. If you are of the paranoid type, the Three Gossips are definitely talking about you! If you look to your left of Sheep Rock, you can see a newly forming arch that some have nicknamed "Baby Arch." Sheep Rock itself is thought to have once been part of a double arch. See if you can make out the remnant towers that have sparked this theory.

The area is well marked and is one of the first pull-offs as you enter the park. To get back to your car, either return the way you came or arrange for a shuttle car to pick you up at the end of the trail. The Park Service discourages hikers from walking on the park road.

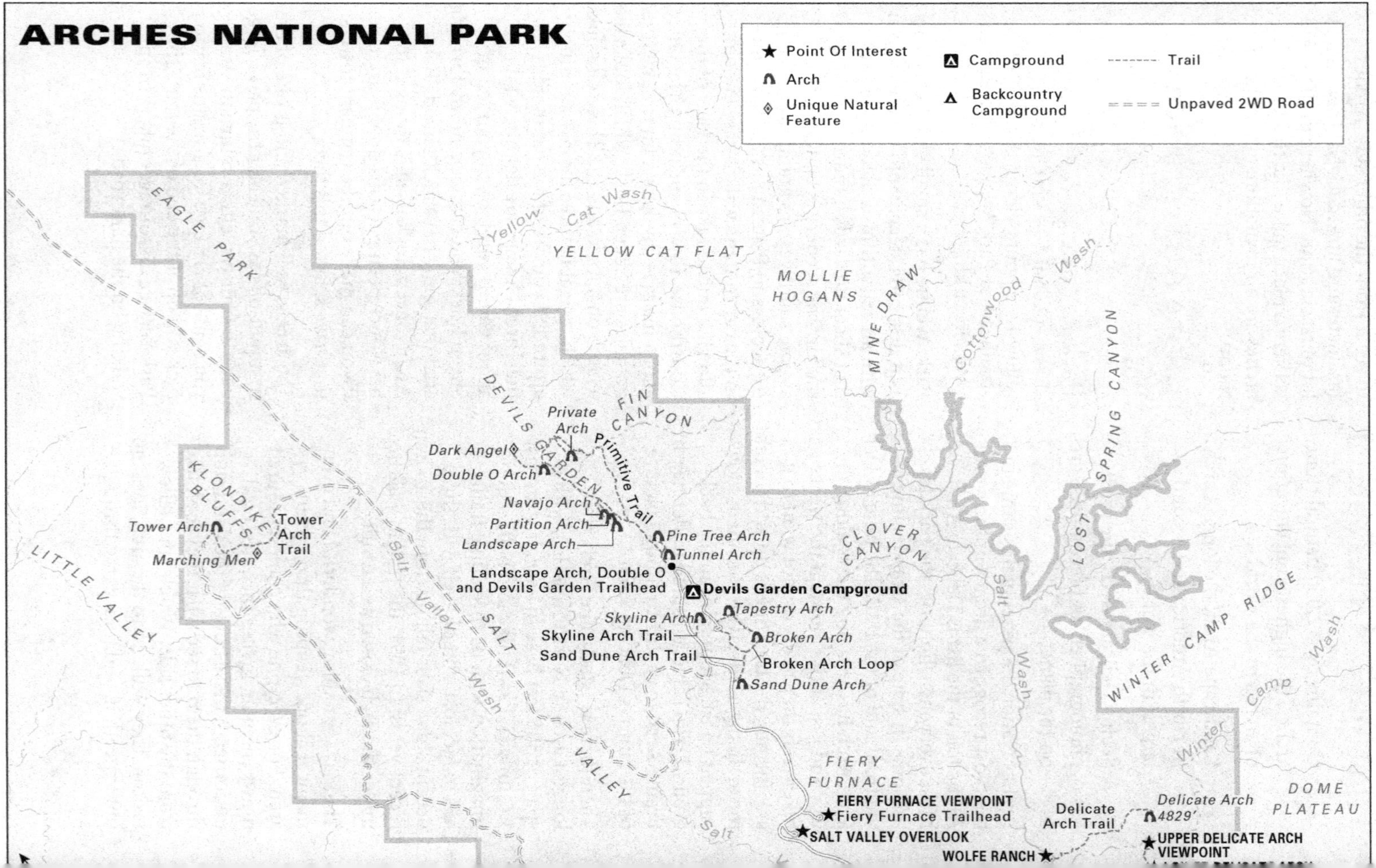
ARCHES NATIONAL PARK
Point Of Interest
Arch
Unique Natural Feature
Campground
Backcountry Campground
Trail
Unpaved 2WD Road
EAGLE PARK
Yellow Cat Wash
YELLOW CAT FLAT
MOLLIE HOGANS
MINE DRAW
Cottonwood Wash
SPRING CANYON
LOST
DEVILS GARDEN
FIN CANYON
Private Arch
Primitive Trail
Dark Angel
Double O Arch
Navajo Arch
Partition Arch
Landscape Arch
Pine Tree Arch
Tunnel Arch
Landscape Arch, Double O and Devils Garden Trailhead
Devils Garden Campground
Tapestry Arch
Skyline Arch
Skyline Arch Trail
Sand Dune Arch Trail
Broken Arch
Broken Arch Loop
Sand Dune Arch
CLOVER CANYON
Salt Wash
WINTER CAMP RIDGE
Winter Camp Wash
KLONDIKE BLUFFS
Tower Arch
Tower Arch Trail
Marching Men
LITTLE VALLEY
Salt Valley Wash
SALT VALLEY
FIERY FURNACE
FIERY FURNACE VIEWPOINT
Fiery Furnace Trailhead
SALT VALLEY OVERLOOK
Salt
WOLFE RANCH
Delicate Arch Trail
Delicate Arch 4829′
UPPER DELICATE ARCH VIEWPOINT
DOME PLATEAU

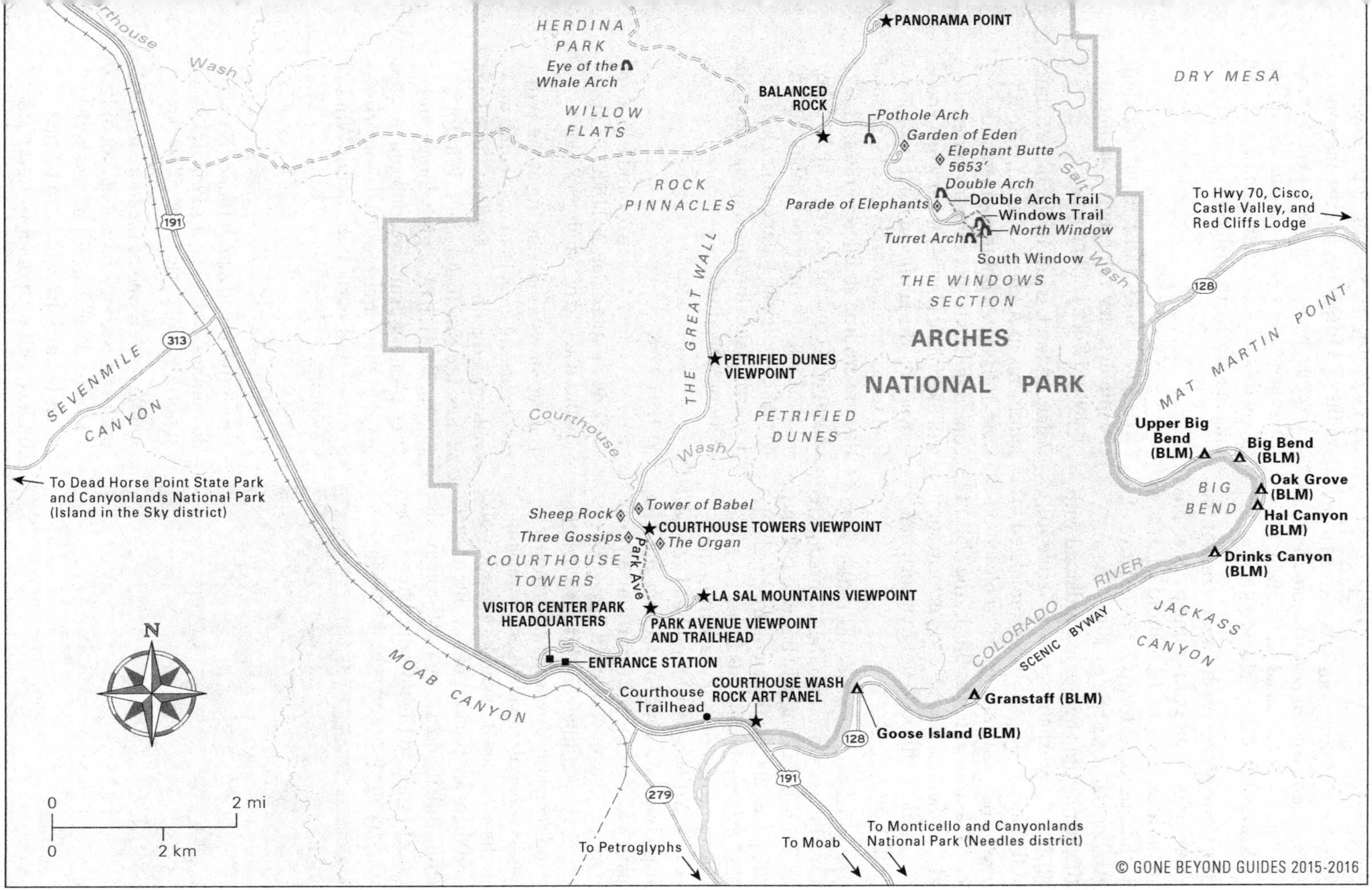
PANORAMA POINT
HERDINA PARK
Eye of the Whale Arch
WILLOW FLATS
BALANCED ROCK
Pothole Arch
Garden of Eden
Elephant Butte 5653′
Double Arch
Double Arch Trail
Windows Trail
North Window
Turret Arch
South Window
Parade of Elephants
DRY MESA
Salt Wash
To Hwy 70, Cisco, Castle Valley, and Red Cliffs Lodge
128
ROCK PINNACLES
THE GREAT WALL
THE WINDOWS SECTION
ARCHES NATIONAL PARK
PETRIFIED DUNES VIEWPOINT
PETRIFIED DUNES
MAT MARTIN POINT
Upper Big Bend (BLM)
Big Bend (BLM)
BIG BEND
Oak Grove (BLM)
Hal Canyon (BLM)
Drinks Canyon (BLM)
Courthouse Wash
191
313
SEVENMILE CANYON
To Dead Horse Point State Park and Canyonlands National Park (Island in the Sky district)
Sheep Rock
Tower of Babel
COURTHOUSE TOWERS VIEWPOINT
Three Gossips
The Organ
Park Ave
COURTHOUSE TOWERS
LA SAL MOUNTAINS VIEWPOINT
VISITOR CENTER PARK HEADQUARTERS
PARK AVENUE VIEWPOINT AND TRAILHEAD
ENTRANCE STATION
COLORADO RIVER
SCENIC BYWAY
JACKASS CANYON
MOAB CANYON
Courthouse Trailhead
COURTHOUSE WASH ROCK ART PANEL
Granstaff (BLM)
Goose Island (BLM)
N
0
2 mi
0
2 km
279
To Petroglyphs
To Moab
To Monticello and Canyonlands National Park (Needles district)
© GONE BEYOND GUIDES 2015-2016

## Courthouse Wash Rock Art

Moderate to Strenuous – (5.5 mi / 8.9 km), round trip, allow 6 – 8 hours, elev. Δ: 210 ft / 64 m, trailhead on Highway 191, 0.5 mi north of the Colorado River

The Courthouse Wash Panel is one of the more colorful and intriguing petroglyphs in the area. It shows humanoid figures with trapezoidal forms representative of Barrier Canyon Style rock art. The anthropomorphic figures are ordained with abstract, almost alien, heads. While still full of color, the panel was vandalized in 1980 when someone splashed bleach on it. As disappointing as this is, the National Park Service was able to perform some restoration, although not to its original grandeur.

The panel sits just inside the outlet of Courthouse Wash into the Colorado River. There is parking off Highway 191 and the panel sits less than a quarter mile (1.2 km) upstream from this lower trailhead. The route described here is from the upper Courthouse Wash Trailhead accessed from the main park road. Come into the park and look for the Courthouse Wash parking area on your right, just across the obvious bridge. The hike is a delight, winding gently down the Courthouse Wash either alongside it or by walking in the creek itself. It can be a sandy walk, and there are pockets of non-life-threatening quicksand as you cut through tall canyon walls to the lower trailhead. The route is one way and is best pre-planned with a shuttle car waiting at the lower trailhead. Otherwise, admire the panel and return by walking back upstream. There are several side canyons to explore along this hike, the first encountered that cuts in a northerly fashion is a favorite.

*Courthouse Wash Rock Art*

## Balanced Rock

Easy – (0.3 mi / 0.5 km), round trip, allow 30 minutes, elev. Δ: negligible, trailhead at Balanced Rock parking area

Balanced Rock is one of the more iconic landforms in Arches NP and the Southwest. It has been photographed and copied in movie sets so many times; it will likely be a familiar form when you first see it. The landform itself is a 128-foot tower of different layers of sandstone that are eroding at different rates. The capstone is eroding slower, which makes for the look of a large rock balancing on a smaller pedestal. Balanced Rock can be accessed just before turning right into the Windows Section.

## Windows

Easy – (1.0 mi / 1.6 km), round trip, allow 30 – 60 minutes, elev. Δ: 115 ft / 35 m, trailhead at end of Windows Road

The Windows Trail, starting at the Windows parking area, is an easy climb up a well-graded path that leads to three huge arches, the North and South Windows and Turret Arch. A slightly longer and often pleasant primitive loop can be used to get to these arches as well. The primitive loop trail starts at the South Window viewpoint.

## Double Arch

Easy – (0.5 mi / 0.8 km), round trip, allow 30 minutes, elev. Δ: 62 ft / 19 m, trailhead at north end of circle for Windows arches

Double Arch is one of the more magical landforms within Arches NP. Not only is it a true double arch, but also both arches are massive and seem to interconnect with each other from certain

*Double Arch*

angles. It is tough to make out the nature of this landform from the road, and it is easily overlooked by folks who just got back in their vehicle from the Windows trailhead. That said, this is not a formation you want to miss; it is one of the highlights of the park. The trail from the parking lot is sandy and flat. It is possible to scramble up into the bases of both arches.

## Delicate Arch

Strenuous – (3.0 mi / 4.8 km), round trip, allow 2 – 3 hours, elev. Δ: 500 ft / 152 m, trailhead at Wolfe Ranch parking area

The hike up to Delicate Arch is not as strenuous as some will tell you. Granted, there is no shade, so bring plenty of water and wear a hat and sunscreen. There is a decent 500-foot ascent on slick rock after a half mile (0.8 km) of easy hiking. Once you summit the ascent, the trail levels out for the most part and is fairly straightforward. There is a rock ledge about 200 yards long that is navigable for two-way traffic. The nice thing about this hike is that the arch is hidden from you until you are right on it. You turn a corner and bam, there it is, Delicate Arch.

The arch is a juxtaposition of themes for the viewer, with the often-snowcapped La Sal Mountains in the distance framing the fiery and dry sandstone in the foreground. Front and center to it all is the showpiece, the most famous arch in the world. The lighting can be nothing less than spiritual at sunset, though be prepared to share your life moment with your fellow hikers during peak season.

## Devils Garden (full loop)

Strenuous – (7.2 mi / 11.6 km), round trip, allow 30 minutes, elev. Δ: 355 ft / 108 m, trailhead at Devils Garden trailhead

This is the longest maintained trail in the park and covers many of the north canyon fins and arches of Salt Valley. Expect a fair amount of scrambling and generally rugged terrain as you span farther into the canyon. The hike is worth doing, weaning out many of the visitors looking for shorter hikes and providing views of eight arches total, including the solemn Navajo Arch and the remote Private Arch.

## Sand Dune Arch

Easy – (0.3 mi / 0.5 km), round trip, allow 30 minutes, elev. Δ: negligible, trailhead at Sand Dune Arch parking area

Sand Dune Arch is a secluded arch that is an easy hike along an orange red sand path. The arch is between two large fins, giving a sense of isolation within a very short hike. During windy days, be prepared to get a little sandblasting exfoliation, especially around the shins.

## Broken Arch Loop

Easy – (2.0 mi / 3.2 km), round trip, allow 60 minutes, elev. Δ: negligible, trailhead at Sand Dune Arch parking area

Broken Arch is an easy loop that makes for a nice walk from Devils Garden Campground, especially in the cooler times of morning or evening. The trail ambles across a large meadow to an arch with a visible crack in the middle of it, hence the name. Clear views of the La Sal

Mountains can be seen in the distance. There is also a short spur trail to the triple arch feature called Tapestry Arch as well as a connection to Sand Dune Arch.

## Skyline Arch

Easy – (0.4 mi / 0.6 km), round trip, allow 30 minutes, elev. Δ: negligible, trailhead at Skyline Arch parking area

This trail is straightforward and very short, crossing a small meadow area to Skyline Arch, which is one of the characteristically visible arches from the road. A large boulder fell out of the arch in 1940, doubling the size of the opening. This is a nice trail to take in the twilight hours for a chance to see wildlife. There are many spur trails at the end to entice the hiker for more adventure within the rock garden surroundings.

## Landscape Arch

Easy – (1.6 mi / 2.6 km), round trip, allow 60 minutes, elev. Δ: 60 ft / 18 m, trailhead at Devils Garden trailhead

What makes Landscape Arch so popular is that it defies logic. It is fragile, seemingly ribbon thin in spots, yet it is the longest arch in the park and the second largest in the world. Landscape Arch is so fragile it prompted the Secretary of the Air Force to put a stop to supersonic jet flight over or even near national parks in 1972 after an outcry from local citizens. The arch measures 306 feet from base to base and can be accessed via a fairly flat gravel trail.

This trail can be a destination in itself or the beginning of the longer hikes to Double O Arch and the Devils Garden Loop. There are nice spur trails down to the Tunnel Arch and quaint Pine Tree Arch.

## Double O Arch

Strenuous – (4.0 mi / 6.4 km), round trip, allow 2 – 3 hours, elev. Δ: 277 ft / 84 m, trailhead at Devils Garden trailhead

Double O Arch is listed in case you don't want to do the more primitive loop portion of the Devils Garden Loop or some of the other spur trails to other arches. Double O is an arch on top of an arch, hence the name. It is one of the cooler landforms in the park, looking like a fin of sandstone Swiss cheese. Dark Angel, a monolithic tower of darker sandstone, is off a spur trail another 0.5 mi (0.8 km) further on.

## Fiery Furnace

Strenuous – (2.0 mi / 3.2 km), round trip, allow 2 – 3 hours, elev. Δ: 250 ft / 76 m, trailhead at Fiery Furnace Viewpoint

Fiery Furnace is a special section of Arches. The area itself is a labyrinth of rock, containing no trails, and lots of scrambling, wedging, and the need for equal helpings of agility and endurance. It is best seen through the park's ranger-led programs, as this minimizes the damage that has been caused of late through too much hiker love. You can

*Landscape Arch*



access the area on your own, but only if you obtain a permit at the visitor center and watch a minimum impact video. The fee for a permit is $6 for each adult and $3 for children 5 through 12 and can be purchased at the visitor center. For both the permit and the ranger-led programs, children under five are not permitted.

The ranger-led tour is a tremendous amount of fun for an active family but isn't for everyone. Once you start on the hike, you are committed to completing it. The hike includes squeezing through narrow gaps, scrambling up at times, jumping over small gaps, and navigating through a maze of rock containing the usual assortment of narrow ledges, loose sandstone, and broken rocks.

This ranger-led program contains a fair number of historical and geographical descriptions from likely one of the most passionate advocates of the park you will meet. Bring good hiking shoes, plenty of water and a backpack to store everything because you will be using your hands from time to time to make your way through the terrain.

Tickets for the ranger-led program are by reservation during the peak season. They can be purchased up to six months in advance through www.recreation.gov. Like the campground in Arches, this program is quite popular and requires a bit of planning, tenacity, and patience to get the spot you want. Tickets during November and early spring can be obtained at the visitor center. Costs are $16 for adults and $8 for children 5 through 12.

## Tower Arch

Strenuous – (3.4 mi / 5.5 km), round trip, allow 2 – 3 hours, elev. Δ: 450 ft / 137 m, trailhead at Devils Garden trailhead

Fins, hoodoos, and arches, oh my! This trail is off the beaten track in the northwestern Klondike Bluffs. This is a fun little area, with a bit of elevation gain to keep you in shape, but providing one sandstone oddity after the other along the way. Even the end point, Tower Arch, is unusual, giving clear sight to an arch, but with what looks like a big submarine, complete with an observation control tower on top. The "submarine" clearly overshadows the poor arch. The whole place has an M. C. Escher meets Salvador Dali element to it with fins tilted to the winds and hoodoos standing like kids getting in trouble or others that resemble little Buddhas having tea. If you are good at finding patterns in clouds, this is the place for you.

From the park map, the trail shows unpaved roads on either end. Take the Salt Valley Road and turn at the second left into the Klondike Bluffs. It is possible to enter the trail from the other end, but this is a seldom-traveled high clearance 4WD road.

# Goosenecks State Park

## Quick Facts

**Official Park Website:** http://stateparks.utah.gov/parks/goosenecks/

**Visitor Center:** none, contact park at (435) 678-2238

**Park Accessibility:**

- Okay for 2WD and RVs
- Day Use Only

**Experience Level:**

- Family Friendly – Experienced Hiker

**Nearest Town with Amenities:**

- Mexican Hat, UT is 8 mi / 13 km from park

**Getting There:**

- From Page, AZ: Take AZ-98 East to US-160 East to US-163 North to UT-261 North to UT-316 West. Total distance is 151 mi / 243 km to park

## What Makes Goosenecks State Park Special

- Peering over the edge to see the neatly layered rock cut like artwork by the deep meander of the San Juan River
- Driving away from the general viewing area down a dusty dirt road to hike the Honaker Trail to the river's shore and becoming for a brief moment, part of this artwork
- Learning about and seeing a gooseneck

Goosenecks State Park is an easy side trip for those traveling from the Moab area parks south towards Arizona. The park has its own state highway, UT-316, which travels 3.5 miles from its juncture with UT 261 to the Goosenecks overlook and parking area. What to do once you are there is limited.

At a modest 10 acres of park, most folk's park, head to the railing and look down at the meandering San Juan River. In this section of the river, there are a number of U shaped river course ways that have been cut dramatically and deeply into the underlying strata. The view is well worth the five minutes to get there. There is also one trail that takes the more adventurous traveler down to the San Juan River shoreline.

By the way, if you are asking yourself why the river doesn't just carve a straight line, the answer has to do with the river itself. The flow of water erodes the outer banks at a faster rate, while simultaneously depositing sediment on the slower moving inner course of the river. The result of this erosional process causes a snaking pattern to form as the river cuts through the valley. Any flowing body of water can carve out a meandering course, as the principles are the same no matter the volume of the water. In the course of sandstone, this process starts very early and then essentially sets in place, eroding straight down thereafter.

## Hiking Goosenecks State Park

### Honaker Trail

Strenuous – (5.0 mi / 8.0 km), round trip, allow 3 - 4 hours

This is a steep route built in 1893 by prospectors during the short-lived gold rush in this territory. Honaker Trail proved too steep even for pack animals or so the legend goes, so if you do take this trail and make it the bottom, you'll have the bragging rights that you out hiked a mule. The trail is 1.5 miles northeast from the Goosenecks SP parking lot. Look for a water tank and a metal sign that says Honaker. The road travels below the first rim to the non-descript cairn-marked trailhead. From here, it's 1,000 feet over 2.5 miles to the bottom. At about 1.5 miles down, you'll notice an abundance of fossilized brachiopods (fossilized shells). It is nearly impossible to avoid walking on them in this spot. Once at the bottom, take a look up to where you came from. As a sign at the Grand Canyon reminds us hikers at times like these, "Down is optional. Up is mandatory". Keep this mind as you take the strenuous hike back up.

*View from Goosenecks State Park Overlook*

# Edge of the Cedars State Park

*Sun Sculpture at Edge of the Cedars*

**Official Park Website:** http://stateparks.utah.gov/parks/edge-of-the-cedars//

**Visitor Center:**

(435) 678-2238

**Park Accessibility:**

- Okay for 2WD and RVs
- Day Use Only

**Experience Level:**

- Family Friendly

**Camping in Park:**

- None

**Lodging and Dining in Park:**

- None

**Nearest Town with Amenities:**

- The park is located in the town of Blanding, UT

**Getting There:**

- From Moab, UT: Take US-191 South to Blanding, UT. Total distance is 76 mi / 122 km to park.

## What Makes Edge of the Cedars State Park Museum Special

Edge of the Cedars sits within the town of Blanding, Utah, lying south of Moab and Monticello, UT and north of the Four Corners and Mesa Verde NP. While the Ancestral Pueblo ruins are worth exploring, the highlight here is the museum, which holds a diverse selection of pottery and other artifacts. This is a great place to see the actual tools of these people and is worth seeing.

Blanding, UT is a solid little small town of about 3,500 residents. Besides being a gateway town, serving tourists on their way to the next natural park, it has economic ties within the mineral processing and agriculture industries. This is a good place to stock up on goods and grab a bite to eat.

## Quick Facts

**Official Park Website:** http://www.nps.gov/nabr

**Visitor Center:** (435) 692-1234 ext. 16

**Park Accessibility:**

- Okay for 2WD and RVs
- Day and Overnight Use

**Experience Level:**

- Family Friendly to Casual Hiker

**Camping in Park:**

- Natural Bridges Campground: 13 T/RV, no water, vault restrooms, no dump station, no hookups, first come-first served
- Several backcountry campgrounds

**Lodging and Dining in Park:**

- None

**Nearest Town with Amenities:**

- Blanding, UT is 44 mi / 71 km from park

**Getting There:**

- From Blanding, UT: Take UT-95 North to UT-275 North 44 mi / 71 km to park entrance

*As above, so below. The Owachomo Bridge*

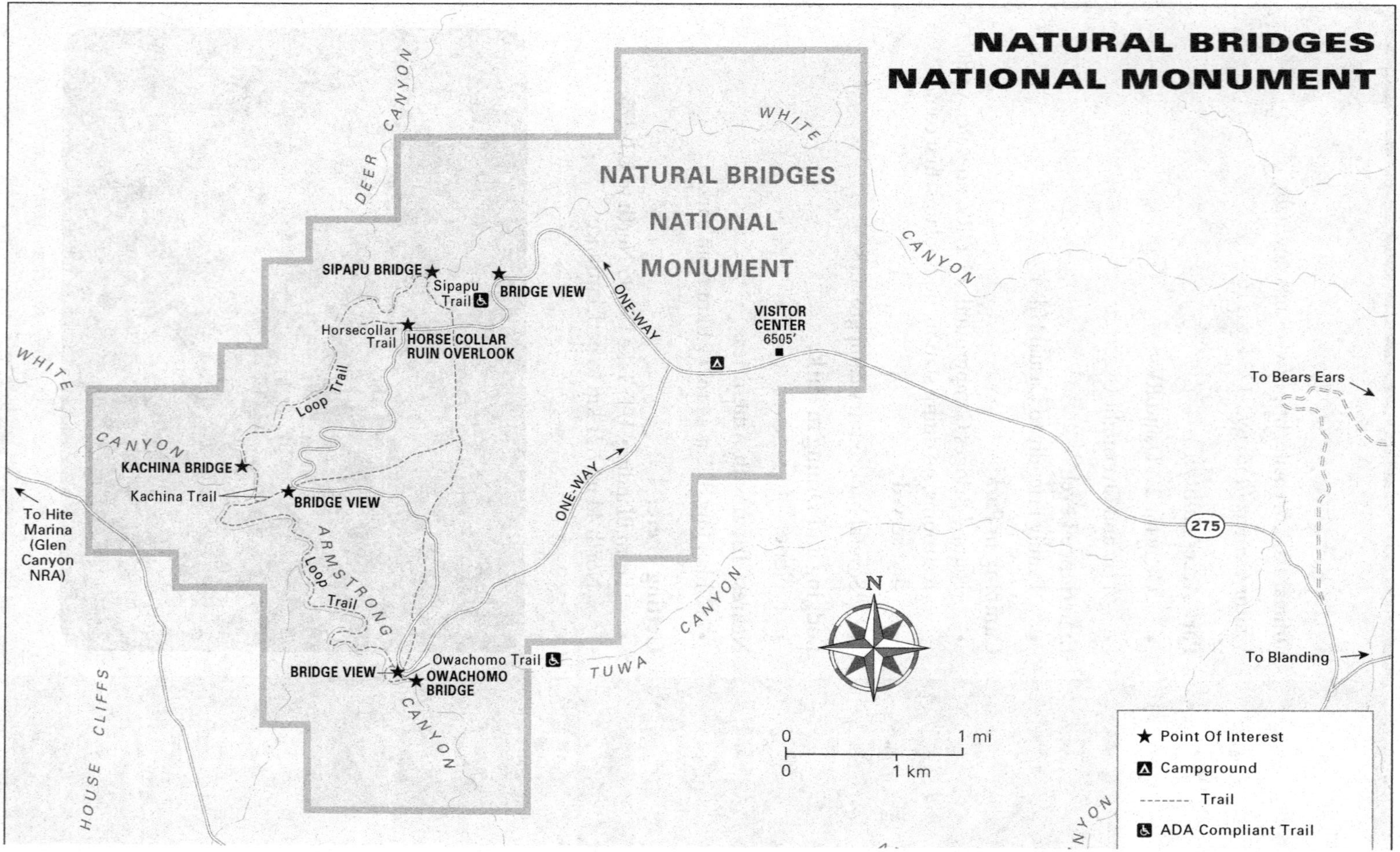
NATURAL BRIDGES
NATIONAL MONUMENT
NATURAL BRIDGES NATIONAL MONUMENT
VISITOR CENTER 6505'
ONE-WAY
ONE-WAY
SIPAPU BRIDGE
Sipapu Trail
BRIDGE VIEW
Horsecollar Trail
HORSE COLLAR RUIN OVERLOOK
Loop Trail
KACHINA BRIDGE
Kachina Trail
BRIDGE VIEW
ARMSTRONG
Loop Trail
BRIDGE VIEW
Owachomo Trail
OWACHOMO BRIDGE
CANYON
WHITE
CANYON
DEER CANYON
WHITE
CANYON
TUWA CANYON
HOUSE CLIFFS
To Hite Marina (Glen Canyon NRA)
To Bears Ears
To Blanding
275
N
0 1 mi
0 1 km
Point Of Interest
Campground
Trail
ADA Compliant Trail

## What Makes Natural Bridges Special

- The reverence of seeing three massive stone bridges that cross over deep canyons in a lush pinyon juniper forest setting
- Knowing they were formed by a gooseneck that is so close together that it eroded through and pinched off the lower portion of the "neck", leaving the top layer of rock intact as a true natural bridge
- One of the easier side trips if you just want to peer over from the top and see what a natural bridge looks like

Natural Bridges National Monument is a unique place in that there are a total of three natural bridges here. From above, the overlooks peer down to the canyon below, which seems to be a confusing maze of twists and turns with huge spans of rock arching across streambeds of pale white sandstone. In reality, the area has had a number of gooseneck meanders, where the stream has created a U-shaped canyon into the strata. At three places, the water eroded through the bottom layer of the meander, leaving the top layer as a natural bridge.

Most folks take the short trips to the various overlooks and peer down to the bridges below. The scenic drive takes about an hour to see all three, not including the trip to the visitor center to get all the necessary brochures. Hiking down below is more immersive and more strenuous, as the canyon floor is about 500 feet below. All of the trails as well as the bridges themselves have awesome mythological names from the Hopi tradition, which adds to the overall ambiance of this park.

## Hiking Natural Bridges National Monument

### Horsecollar Ruin Overlook Trail

Easy – (0.6 mi / 1.0 m), round trip, allow 30 minutes

A fairly level trail leading to the edge of White Canyon where an Ancestral Puebloan cliff dwelling can be seen in a large alcove. This ruin is best known for its two granaries, which look like large circular barrels with doorways that look like horse collars (hence the name).

*Horsecollar Ruins*

### Sipapu Bridge Trail

Easy – (1.2 mi / 1.9 km), round trip, allow 1 hour

Sipapu Bridge is the second largest natural bridge in the world, second only to Rainbow Bridge at Rainbow Bridge NM. The name Sipapu is a Hopi term for the gateway of souls into the spirit world. The trip down is steep but once on the canyon floor, the going is easier, though a bit uneven. The elevation gain/loss here is 500 feet and there is a staircase and three wooden ladders to help hikers get down safely. At the top of the stairway, look for a set of logs reaching from the cliff wall to a large fir. Early visitors used this fir, climbing up and down it to get to the canyon floor. At the base of the tree, you can still see remnants of the earlier staircase.

## Kachina Bridge Trail

Easy – (1.4 mi / 2.3 km), round trip, allow 1 hour

Kachina Bridge is considered the youngest formed of the three bridges and is also the least dramatic from the overlook above due to the angle. Take switchbacks down 400 feet to the bridge.

## Owachomo Bridge Trail

Easy – (0.4 mi / 0.6 km), round trip, allow 30 minutes

The easiest of the bridges to get to, Owachomo, meaning "rock mound" in the Hopi language is also the most delicate of the three bridge formation. The bridge's form suggests that it is eroding more quickly than the others. It is also considered the most pleasing to the eye, due to its thin span of rock that stretches across the sky.

## Loop Trail

Strenuous – (8.6 mi / 13.8 km), round trip, allow 4 -5 hours

The Loop Trail gives the complete package of all three bridges with return options along the mesa top. At the mesa, the loop has a juncture that allows for a shorter hike. Start the hike at any of the parking areas. Starting at Sipapu gives the most flexibility if you need to return early as you pass by Sipapu and Kachina before climbing back out. If you do continue to Owachomo Bridge, follow the trail up the left side of the canyon after Kachina Bridge in order to more easily navigate past the Knickpoint pour-off, a dry fall that pours water runoff into a pool below when it rains.

*Sipapu Bridge*

*Kachina Bridge*

# Hovenweep National Monument

## Quick Facts

**Official Park Website:** http://www.nps.gov/hove

**Visitor Center:** (970) 562-4282 ext. 10

**Park Accessibility:**
- Okay for 2WD and RVs
- Day and Overnight Use

**Experience Level:**
- Family Friendly to Casual Hiker

**Camping in Park:**
- Hovenweep Campground: 31T sites, some sites will accommodate RV's, drinking water, flush toilets, no hookups, one ADA compliant site, first come-first served

**Lodging and Dining in Park:**
- None

**Nearest Town with Amenities:**
- Bluff, UT is closer by 5 miles but Cortez, CO has more amenities. Cortez is 45 mi / 72 km from the park

**Getting There:**
- From Cortez, CO: Take US-491 N/N Broadway and turn left onto Road Bb, which becomes County Road 10 in Utah. Total distance is 45 mi / 72 km to park entrance

*The round ruins of Hovenweep*

## What Makes Hovenweep NM Special

The feeling of discovery as you walk from one ruin to another

Understanding the harmony of man-made and natural structures under the warm glow of a late afternoon sun

The sacredness of being in the middle of nowhere

Hovenweep National Monument is a small park protecting several small villages of the Ancestral Puebloans on the borders of Utah and Colorado. What is unique here is the setting. Unlike the deep alcoves of Mesa Verde or the immensity of Chaco, Hovenweep was built in an arid flatland that at first glance would appear to have no surprises. Upon arrival however, it feels as if the visitor has stumbled upon something, the ruins feel unexpected and special. There is a sentiment of solitude that the land brings to one's visit which invokes thoughts that Hovenweep was more sanctuary than village. The harmony of the structures and their natural disposition against the frame of nature itself brings a sense of peace as one walks among these ruins. Hovenweep is a bit off the beaten path, but if any drive can lead to a place that inspires the spirit, then that is a road worth traveling on.

## Hiking Hovenweep National Monument

There are six villages protected at Hovenweep. Of these, the most popular is Square Tower, which also contains the only maintained trails. The other five villages are best viewed by driving to the sites and walking amongst the ruins via short trails that are less maintained. The other five sites are Cajon, Cutthroat Castle, Holly, Horseshoe, and Hackberry and are spread out over 20 miles. A good first step in exploring Hovenweep is picking up a visitor's guide to get an understanding of the general layout of the park.

### Rim Trail Loop

Easy – (1.5 mi / 2.4 km), round trip, allow 1 hour

The Rim Trail Loop is picked up just outside the visitor center and covers some of the most iconic ruin imagery in the park. Here one can see the Square Tower, Hovenweep Castle, the circular Twin Towers, and the Stronghold House, which is the first ruin found from the visitor center.

### Tower Point Loop

Easy – (0.5 mi / 0.8 km), round trip, allow 20 – 30 minutes

This a quick loop that travels along a peninsular section of the mesa ending at Tower Point. The canyon drops on both sides with the ruins as a backdrop, creating a nice view of the surrounding area.

### Horseshoe and Hackberry Trail

Easy – (1.0 mi / 1.6 km), round trip, allow 1 hour

This slightly more primitive trail is a nice loop covering both the Horseshoe and Hackberry sites. Highlights include the Horseshoe Tower and Horseshoe House as well as the Hackberry group, which is one of the largest ancestral population centers in the park.

### Cutthroat Castle Trail

Easy – (1.4 mi / 2.3 km), round trip, allow 1 hour

This site was added to the park in 1956 and showcases typical structures of the Ancestral Puebloans. It is possible to drive right up to the site, however from the trailhead junction; the road is not maintained and is suitable only for high clearance vehicles.

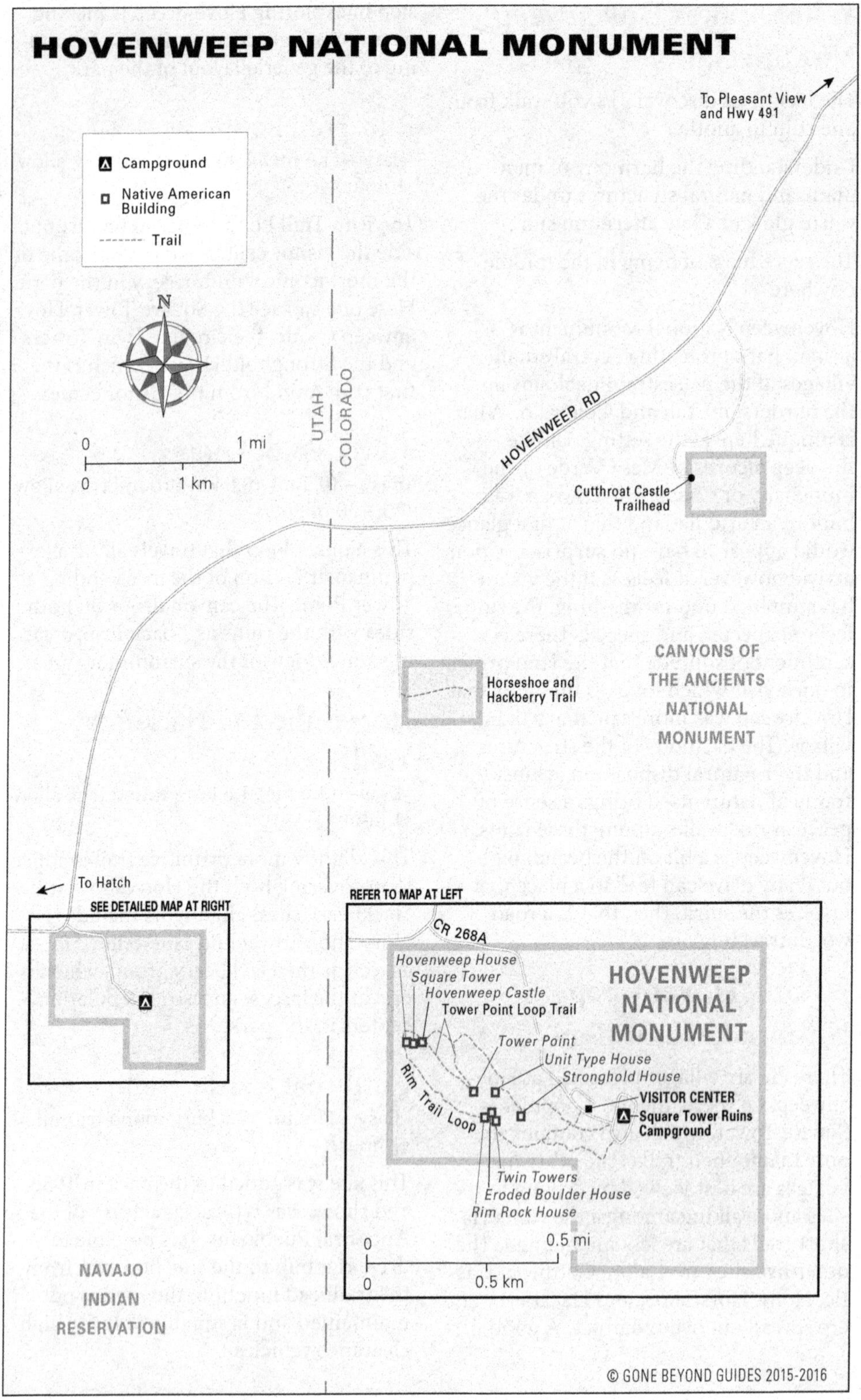
HOVENWEEP NATIONAL MONUMENT
Campground
Native American Building
Trail
N
0
1 mi
0
1 km
UTAH
COLORADO
To Pleasant View and Hwy 491
HOVENWEEP RD
Cutthroat Castle Trailhead
Horseshoe and Hackberry Trail
CANYONS OF THE ANCIENTS NATIONAL MONUMENT
To Hatch
SEE DETAILED MAP AT RIGHT
REFER TO MAP AT LEFT
CR 268A
Hovenweep House
Square Tower
Hovenweep Castle
Tower Point Loop Trail
HOVENWEEP NATIONAL MONUMENT
Tower Point
Unit Type House
Stronghold House
VISITOR CENTER
Square Tower Ruins Campground
Rim Trail Loop
Twin Towers
Eroded Boulder House
Rim Rock House
0
0.5 mi
0
0.5 km
NAVAJO INDIAN RESERVATION
© GONE BEYOND GUIDES 2015-2016

# Four Corners Monument

*Come on, you know you want to stand here!*

**Official Park Website:** http://www.navajonationparks.org/htm/fourcorners.htm

**Visitor Center:**

None in park, contact: Four Corners Monument Park Office, P.O. Box 861, Teec Nos Pos, AZ 86514, Phone: (928) 206-2540

**Park Accessibility:**

- Okay for 2WD and RVs
- Day Use Only

**Experience Level:**

- Family Friendly

**Camping in Park:**

- None

**Lodging and Dining in Park:**

- Seasonally open snack stand

**Nearest Town with Amenities:**

- Cortez, CO is 41 mi / 66 km from park

**Getting There:**

- From Moab, UT: Take US-191 South to UT-262 East to US-160 West to NM-597. Total distance is 145 mi / 233 km to park
- From Cortez, CO: Take US-160 West/US-491 South to NM-597. Total distance is 41 mi / 66 km to park
- From Gallup, NM: Take US-491 North to US-64 West to US-160 East to NM-597. Total distance is 124 mi / 200 km to park
- From Flagstaff, AZ: Take US-89 North to US-160 East to NM-597. Total distance is 227 mi / 365 km to park

## What Makes Four Corners Special

- The only place you can play a game of four state Twister!

- Being in the center of the Grand Circle! (Well, not really, in fact, not at all, but go with it)
- Trying to find that unique Four Corner keepsake from stall after stall of folks selling the same thing

If there is an anchor to the Grand Circle, it is the Four Corners. It isn't the center of the circle, which is a shame from a perfect symmetry standpoint, but it is the symbolic center. In this one spot are captured four of the five states that make up the Grand Circle, namely Utah, Colorado, New Mexico and Arizona. Part of the overall allure of the Grand Circle is "Where does that highway lead to?" The answer to this question here is it leads to a magical place where one can stand in four states at the same time.

The park is run by the Navajo Nation and consists of a large marker indicating the location of the four corners, suitable for family photos and what not. Surrounding this marker on all four sides is a row of vendor stalls. Each stall is run by a local merchant selling the usual collection of jewelry, carved stones, arrows, feathered earrings, dream catchers, and spirit animals. While it would seem that the initial intent was to have New Mexico crafts on one side and Colorado goods on the other, at this point all of the merchants are for the most part selling Navajo crafts. Sometimes there is some Zuni and Hopi representation as well.

The flea market vibe aside, the merchants are all great folk and perhaps the best part of the monument. They come each day; they all know each other and are worth getting to know a little. Most are willing to share a little of their life with you if you invite them into a conversation. There is Navajo bread and other goodies for sale and basic bathroom facilities, however true to being the center of nowhere, there is no electricity, phone service, or running water here.

*Time isn't used, it's experienced ~ Hopi proverb*

# South West Colorado

Mesa Verde National Park .......... 148
Canyons of the Ancients National Monument .......... 158
Yucca House National Monument .......... 159


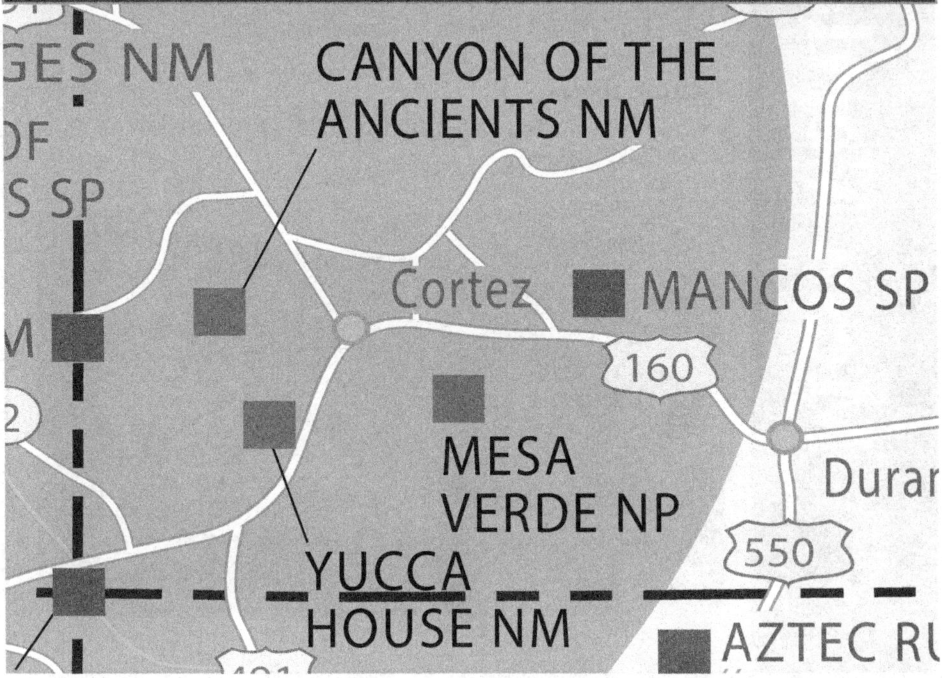

# Mesa Verde National Park

## Quick Facts

**Official Park Website:** http://www.nps.gov/meve

**Visitor Center:** (970) 529-4465

**Park Accessibility:**

- Okay for 2WD and RVs
- Day and Overnight Use

**Experience Level:**

- Family Friendly – Casual Hiker

**Camping in Park:**

- Morefield Campground: 267 T/RV sites restrooms, drinking water, showers, hookups, and a dump station. Some sites can be reserved at (800) 449-2288. Campground rarely fills up.

**Lodging in Park:**

- Far View Lodge, reservations by phone: (800) 449-2288 or online at http://www.visitmesaverde.com/accommodations/far-view-lodge.aspx

**Dining in Park:**

- Metate Room and Far View Terrace Restaurant

**Nearest Town with Amenities:**

- Cortez, CO is 10 mi / 16 km from park

**Getting There:**

- From Cortez, CO: Take US-160 E 10 mi / 16 km to park entrance

*Cliff Palace*

## What Makes Mesa Verde Special

- The largest archaeological preserve in the United States containing some of the most well preserved cliff dwellings in the world
- Seeing them via unique and immersive ranger guided tours, sometimes in character of historical figures
- Not just a cultural national park, Mesa Verde is also a World Heritage Site

Mesa Verde National Park is truly a standout. It is the oldest National Park within the Grand Circle, holding over five thousand archaeological sites and some six hundred cliff dwellings. This makes Mesa Verde the largest archaeological preserve in the US and is even recognized globally as a UNESCO World Heritage Site.

All these facts aside, perhaps what really makes this park amazing are the park ranger's ability to connect the visitor to the park and the sites themselves. There are several ranger led tours that really help the visitor fully enjoy the park. Some of the tours are actually done in character representing a time in the park's history. There are even some tours, again led by rangers, which are part hiking and part bicycle touring. The tours are described in much greater detail in the companion book A Family Guide to the Grand Circle National Parks. There are few archaeological sites in or outside of the Grand Circle that are as immersive as Mesa Verde National Park. The NPS does an outstanding job here in preserving the history of the area while allowing visitors to enjoy it first-hand.

## Guided Tours

As stated earlier, taking a guided tour is highly recommended. The rangers are all wonderfully passionate and well versed in what is known of the Mesa Verde inhabitants. There is no bad tour, nor is one better than another. They are all special. There are some tours that require climbing up a ladder or out onto an open rock face. The wording that the park provides causes the reader to wonder whether they will be putting themselves in danger. In reality, the wording is conservatively written to manage to the largest possible crowd. The climbing activities are easily achievable for most active visitors and are as fearful as climbing up a slide at a children's park. That said, rely on your own judgment in whether the more active tours are right for you.

There are some operating hour logistics to consider. The park runs in two seasons, each having its own operating hours. The summer/fall schedule typically runs from April/May to October/November, and the winter/spring schedule runs the rest of the year. In general, there are more tours and they are offered more frequently during the summer/fall schedule. The cost of each tour is $4 per person. You will need the ticket to take the tour and can purchase them at the visitor center. There are no refunds.

If you are going during peak season, it will help to have your preferred plan and a backup plan on which tours you want to take, as they do book up. The most popular tours are Cliff Palace and Balcony House. Given the demand, you may be asked to choose only one of these tours per day. Long House gets less traffic and can typically be combined with either the Cliff or Balcony House tours. The ticketing process can in itself take time, as there are a lot of folks there with you. Also, as stated earlier, make sure you factor in about an hour to get to the ruins and find parking.

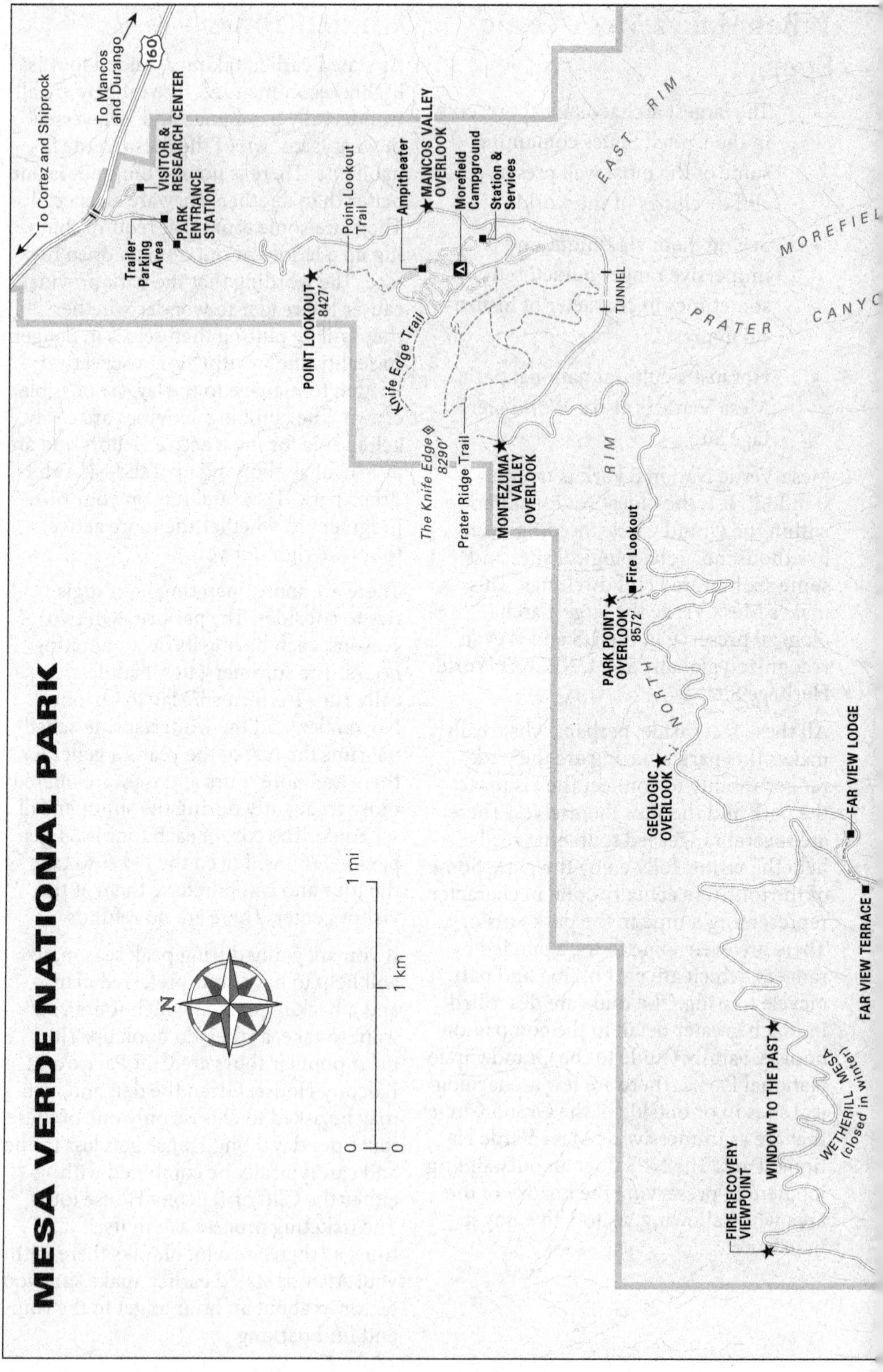
MESA VERDE NATIONAL PARK
To Cortez and Shiprock
To Mancos and Durango
160
VISITOR & RESEARCH CENTER
PARK ENTRANCE STATION
Trailer Parking Area
Point Lookout Trail
POINT LOOKOUT 8427'
Knife Edge Trail
The Knife Edge 8290'
Prater Ridge Trail
Ampitheater
MANCOS VALLEY OVERLOOK
Morefield Campground
Station & Services
EAST RIM
MOREFIELD
PRATER CANYON
TUNNEL
MONTEZUMA VALLEY OVERLOOK
RIM
Fire Lookout
PARK POINT OVERLOOK 8572'
NORTH
GEOLOGIC OVERLOOK
FAR VIEW LODGE
FAR VIEW TERRACE
WINDOW TO THE PAST
WETHERILL MESA (closed in winter)
FIRE RECOVERY VIEWPOINT
N
0 1 mi
0 1 km

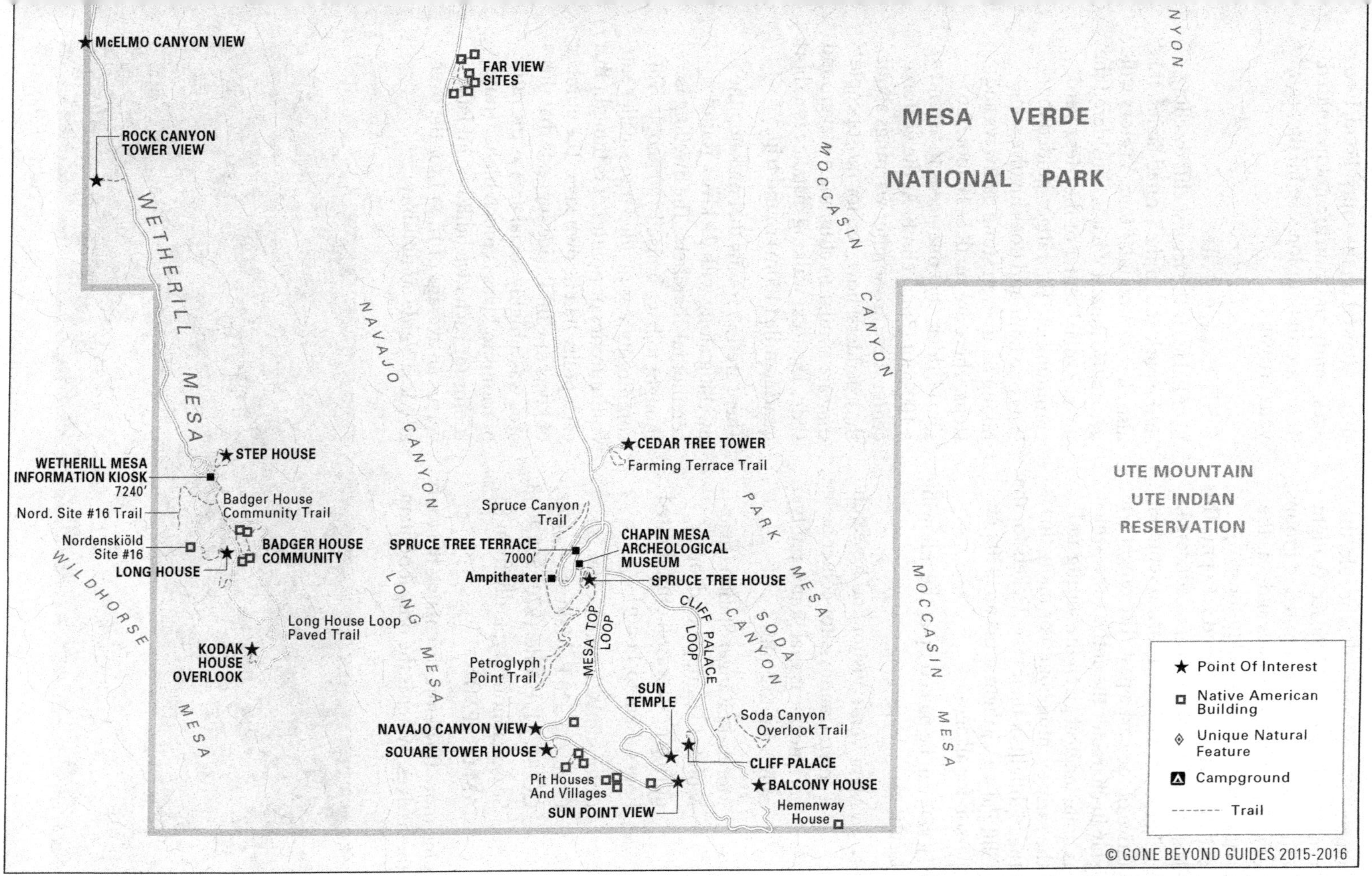
MESA VERDE
NATIONAL PARK
UTE MOUNTAIN
UTE INDIAN
RESERVATION
McELMO CANYON VIEW
FAR VIEW SITES
ROCK CANYON TOWER VIEW
WETHERILL MESA
NAVAJO CANYON
MOCCASIN CANYON
MOCCASIN MESA
CEDAR TREE TOWER
Farming Terrace Trail
STEP HOUSE
WETHERILL MESA INFORMATION KIOSK
7240′
Badger House Community Trail
Nord. Site #16 Trail
Nordenskiöld Site #16
BADGER HOUSE COMMUNITY
LONG HOUSE
WILDHORSE MESA
Long House Loop Paved Trail
KODAK HOUSE OVERLOOK
LONG MESA
Spruce Canyon Trail
SPRUCE TREE TERRACE
7000′
Ampitheater
CHAPIN MESA ARCHEOLOGICAL MUSEUM
SPRUCE TREE HOUSE
PARK MESA
SODA CANYON
CLIFF PALACE LOOP
MESA TOP LOOP
Petroglyph Point Trail
SUN TEMPLE
Soda Canyon Overlook Trail
NAVAJO CANYON VIEW
SQUARE TOWER HOUSE
CLIFF PALACE
BALCONY HOUSE
Pit Houses And Villages
SUN POINT VIEW
Hemenway House
Point Of Interest
Native American Building
Unique Natural Feature
Campground
Trail
© GONE BEYOND GUIDES 2015-2016

Mesa Verde

During the summer/fall schedule, the rangers also offer Cliff Palace Twilight tours. These tours are limited to groups of twenty, last 90 minutes and—as the name suggests—are led in the early evening between 6:30 and 7:15 pm. This is a chance for the ranger to educate in a character that is a historical representative of the park's past. The ranger will stay in character the entire time, which is quite magical given the setting and the early evening hour. For many this is the highlight of their stay. Tickets for the Cliff Palace Twilight tours are $20 per person for all ages.

Tickets can be picked up at the following locations:

- Mesa Verde Visitor and Research Center: (main visitor center near entrance, seasonal hours, but typically 8 am to 5 pm)
- Morefield Ranger Station (near Morefield campground, open during peak season only, limited hours, 7 am to 11 am)
- Colorado Welcome Center (in Cortez at 928 E. Main St., Cortez, CO 81321, Phone: (970) 565 4048. Seasonal hours typically from 8 AM to 5 PM)

One more tip before discussing the tours themselves: Water is the only food item that is allowed on the tours. Food, beverages, candy and gum are not permitted. Tours are an hour long, so fill up prior to your arrival.

## Cliff Palace Tour

Cliff Palace is the largest cliff dwelling in the park and in the United States. It is also the most popular tour. Visitors will get a close look at what is considered the former social center of the Mesa Verde communities. The ranger-guided tour lasts one hour and does involve some hiking on uneven stone pathways and steps. There are small 8–10 foot (2.6 -3m) ladders that one needs to ascend a 100-foot (30m) climb. At the visitor center there are somber warnings about these ladders; however, for most people they are similar to climbing a playground slide. The total walking distance is a short quarter-mile (400m) round trip.

There are 150 rooms that make up the dwelling along with 23 kivas, round ceremonial chambers. The dwelling is thought to have housed 100 people. This community was divided into smaller sub communities or polities. It is thought that each polity had its own kiva. The number of kivas in Cliff Palace suggests that this area was a highly social area as the ratio of rooms to kivas is much higher (nine rooms for each kiva built in Cliff Palace versus an average of 12 to 1 for the overall Mesa Verde community).

*Cliff Palace Panorama*

The structures are made of sandstone, mortar and wooden beams. Sandstone blocks were shaped using harder stones with mortar to seal and maintain structural integrity. In some places, small "chinking" stones were placed in larger gaps. Once finished, the walls were colored with earthen pigments. A sharp eye in Cliff Palace and in the other dwellings will note that the doorways are fairly small. The average man was 5'6" while the height of the average woman was around 5'.

One of the more prominent dwellings is a large square tower known as the Square Tower House. The Square Tower House was in ruins by the 1800s and has been restored by the National Park Service. It stands 26 feet tall and has four levels.

## Balcony House Tour

This one-hour ranger-guided tour is a little more adventurous than the Cliff Palace tour and explores a cliff dwelling sitting on a high ledge facing east. The eastern view meant colder winters, but the tradeoff for those living here was increased security. The ledge was only accessible via a series of small footholds carved into the cliff by the early dwellers. This is believed to be the only way into and out of the dwelling and was thus easy to defend.

Modern visitors are faced with a similar challenge, although the National Park Service has done a good job of making the journey adventurous but safe. The visitor will need to climb up a 32-foot ladder at the beginning of the tour. To get back out, one will need to bend low through a 12-foot-long tunnel to climb two 10-foot ladders. As with all of these tours, you will need to feel comfortable that you and your party can climb the ladders.

The Balcony House is smaller than the Cliff Palace, with 45 rooms and two kivas. Don't let the smaller size fool you.

*Kiva in Balcony House*

Given the Balcony House was harder to get to, it was placed into the park's hands in better shape than some of the other dwellings. Many of the wooden beams can still be seen supporting roofs and sticking out of room walls. The Balcony House gives an intimate look at the Mesa Verde cliff dwellings. Besides the wooden beams and roofs, another favorite feature is a T- shaped doorway that can be seen during the tour.

## Long House Tour

The Long House Tour is the longest, most in-depth and engaging tour offered. The tour is 90 minutes compared to the usual one-hour tours of Cliff Palace and Balcony House, includes a tram ride to and from the trailhead and is on the less traveled Wetherill Mesa. Unfortunately, it is also the hardest to get to for folks in an RV as vehicles over 25 feet are prohibited on the Wetherill Mesa Road. It is only open from Memorial Day to Labor Day each year. This tour is the most strenuous and requires a ¾-mile (1.2 km) hike round trip to access the dwellings.

The tour begins at the Wetherill Mesa information kiosk. Here you will board a tram that travels through a pinyon juniper forest undergoing recovery from a recent burn. Once at the Long House Trailhead, you follow a paved path downhill about 1/3 mile (0.54 km) to reach the ruins. At one point, there is a concrete staircase of 50 steps with railing.

The hike itself adds to the ambiance of discovery. The ruins are not in sight at first, only the tops of mesas and wide canyons. The hike descends through wonderful rock and pinyon juniper forests. In the summer, it is hot and dry and, while this leads to the strenuous aspects of the hike, it may give appreciation for what the early inhabitants faced. Once fully immersed in the surroundings, Long House comes into view.

After a short lecture near the ruins, the tour includes climbing two 15-foot (4.5m) ladders up into the site itself. No longer standing alongside the ruins, you are now inside them, bringing a personal aspect to experiencing the dwellings. The ruins themselves are fairly extensive, with more than 100 rooms, including multistory buildings. Long House is the second largest cliff dwelling in the park. The ranger will point out some petroglyphs along the way as well. The tour ends by taking the same trail back, this time uphill. On a hot day, the 50 concrete steps won't look as welcoming going up as they did going down. The tram will take you back to the Wetherill parking area.

## Self-Guided Tours

### Spruce Tree House (Chapin Mesa)

***Note: Spruce Tree House has been closed for the foreseeable future due to concerns relating to rock falls.***

During the winter months from November to early March, the Spruce Tree House is not only a ranger-led guided tour but is free. The tours last one hour and are given three times a day. The rest of the year, it is available as a self-guided tour.

Spruce Tree House is the third largest cliff dwelling (Cliff Palace and Long House are larger). It is also the best preserved of the cliff dwellings. The walking distance of the tour is ½ mile (0.8 km) round trip and begins at the Chapin Mesa Archeological Museum. Visitors can meander at leisure along paths that encourage a more relaxed experience. There are around 130 rooms and 8 kivas, which were believed to have housed 60 to 80 people. There are many multistory buildings to view and a kiva that one can enter as part of the tour.

### Far View Sites Complex (Chapin Mesa)

The Far View Sites are often overlooked on the drive to the more known sites at Chapin Mesa proper. The Far View Sites are unique in that these villages sit at the top of the mesa rather than in an alcove of a cliff. There were at one time 50 villages in the half square mile surrounding this area. The self-guided tour gives a nice walk among five of the villages plus a dry reservoir. The trail is unpaved but level and is ¾ mile (1.2km) long. These surface sites include Far View House, Pipe Shrine House, Coyote Village, Far View Reservoir, Megalithic House, and Far View Tower. This is a great hike if you want to round out the day's experience on your way back to the campground.

### Badger House Trail (Wetherill Mesa)

The Badger House Community is a series of four sites on a paved and gravel trail. The sites include Modified Basketmaker Pithouse, Developmental Pueblo village, Badger House and Two Raven House. Like Far View Sites Complex, these sites sit on top of the mesa. The trail is 2.5 mile (4km) if started at the Wetherill Mesa Kiosk or 1.5 miles (2.41 km) if you take the tram to the Badger House tram stop. The tour is both educational and peaceful.

## Step House (Wetherill Mesa)

The Step House is one of the more unique self-guided tours in that one can see clear distinctions pointing to two separate occupations of the site. The first inhabitants were the Modified Basketmakers, which dated to A.D. 626. Evidence of their habitation can be found between the old stone steps on the southern edge of the site and the large boulders to the north. The area was inhabited again in BCE 1226 as evidenced by the masonry structures seen within the rest of the site. Two standouts of the ruins are a pit house and the petroglyphs.

The trail is steep and ¾ mile (1.2 km) long along a winding path. Many visitors that come to Wetherill Mesa combine the Step House self-guided tour with the ranger-led Long House tour. Allow a good half day if you decide this is the right combination for you.

# Hiking Mesa Verde

## Point Lookout Trail

Strenuous – (2.2 mi / 3.5 km), round trip, elev. Δ: 510 ft / 155 m, trailhead at Morefield Campground

This is one of the three trails that start from the Morefield Campground. The trail does pass by some Ute structures and other ruins as it makes its way to a highpoint called Point Lookout. The point stands as a natural lookout tower for the entire Mesa Verde area. It was used by the United States Calvary to signal fellow mounted forces as well as earlier by the Utes.

There is an elevation gain of about 500 feet, most of it occurring in the first half mile as the trail winds on up via a series of switchbacks. The trail continues through Oak brush vegetation with a few more switchbacks and then more gently climbs the final half mile to the top. The trail here narrows to a knife ridge, but there is plenty of vegetation on either side. Here there are remnants of Ute structure, inscriptions, initials and other interested artifacts as you reach the top and the great views of the Mancos and Montezuma Valley.

## Knife Edge Trail

Easy – (2.0 mi / 3.2 km), round trip, elev. Δ: 59 ft / 18 m, trailhead at Morefield Campground

One of the other three hikes near the Morefield Campground, this short there and back trail gives some decent views of Montezuma Valley. The trail starts by passing between the Prater Ridge and an obvious little rock hillock called Lone Cone. There is a bit of elevation at first, but much of the trail is flat as it follows the old Knife Edge Road. The trail pretty much just ends at a sign that says, "STOP!! Trail End" indicating it's time to turn back. This short trail is nicely secluded on most days and provides a great place to take in a sunset.

## Prater Ridge Trail

Strenuous – (7.8 mi / 12.6 km), round trip, elev. Δ: 710 ft / 216 m, trailhead at Morefield Campground

This loop is the longest of the three trails that start from the nearby Morefield Campground. The trail climbs until it reaches Prater Ridge and then follows

*Weatherhill Mesa*

along the rim of the cuesta. Like all of the trails near the campground, it is light on ruins but big on nature. Prater Ridge gives expansive views of the Montezuma Valley. This is honestly one of the best of the longer hikes in the park. It makes a complete loop, giving a variety of views of the southern Colorado countryside. If you want to make it a smaller loop, there is an obviously marked cutoff trail that trims the loop by roughly half.



## Farming Terrace Trail

Moderate – (0.5 mi / 0.8 km), round trip, allow 15 minutes, elev. Δ: 120 ft / 37 m, trailhead on Chapin Mesa

While the distance of this small loop trail isn't terribly long, it is fairly well exposed and can get hot. This trail gives a nice peak into how the Ancestral Puebloans farmed the land. At first glance, it just looks like a bunch of terraces, but one learns that they made good use of water runoff, diverting it as it made its way downhill to provide much needed moisture to their crops. The whole thing is quite ingenious to see unfold before the hiker. The trail is also close to the Cedar Tree Ruins, which is worth exploring. Make a right once you retrace the loop back to the road to see a kiva and a tower remnant.

## Spruce Canyon Trail

Moderate – (2.4 mi / 3.9 km), round trip, elev. Δ: 529 ft / 161 m, trailhead on Chapin Mesa

Spruce Canyon Trail begins at the Spruce Tree House trail and gives the viewer a chance to experience the ecosystem of the canyon floor. The trail heads to the bottom of Spruce Tree Canyon and then back up along the mesa top in one nice loop. Like the Petroglyph Point Trail, the loop finishes at the Chapin Mesa Archeological Museum, which is well worth exploring in its own right.

## Petroglyph Point Trail

Moderate – (2.4 mi / 3.9 km), round trip, elev. Δ: 196 ft / 60 m, trailhead on Chapin Mesa

This trail begins from the Spruce Tree House trail and is one of the more pleasant hikes in Mesa Verde. The loop starts down below the mesa top, following what feels like an ancient trail used years ago. One winds through narrow rock passages among pinyon juniper forests with views of Spruce and Navajo Canyons. The trail "ends" at the petroglyphs, which are impressive and worth the hike. From the rock art, the trailheads up to the top of the mesa for a level and easy walk back to the parking area. The hike drops you at the Chapin Mesa Archeological Museum, which is well worth a visit in its own right. Across the street is the Spruce Tree Terrace Café to finish off the hike with a well-deserved snack.

A trail guide is available and registration (at the museum) is required.

## Soda Canyon Overlook Trail

Easy – (1.2 mi / 1.9 km), round trip, allow 30 minutes, elev. Δ: 72 ft / 22 m, trailhead on Chapin Mesa

This is an easy and flat hike that leads to three great overlooks from which several ruins can be viewed, including the Balcony House. There is a viewing scope installed at the canyon's edge at the middle overlook. The southernmost overlook gives the best views of Balcony House.

## Nordenskiöld Site No. 16 Trail

Easy – (1.0 mi / 1.6 km), round trip, allow 30 minutes, elev. Δ: 228 ft / 69 m, trailhead on Wetherhill Mesa

This trail found in the Wetherill Mesa section leads to an overlook of Nordenskiöld Site 16. The trail itself is flat and passes through a portion of the 2000 Pony Fire burn area. As a result, the land is a mixture of grasslands showing the wonder of recovery against a multitude of sentinel dead trees standing as silent evidence of the fire. The trail crosses a paved tram road occasionally. It is prohibited for hikers to walk the tram road, but okay to take the tram back if you want. The tram does make a stop at the Nordenskiöld site overlook, which is the end of the trail. The overlook gives a view into Site 16, a nice double alcove cliff dwelling. The site is named for Gustav Nordenskiöld, who made the first extensive excavations of the site back in 1891.

### Badger House Community Trail

Moderate – (2.3 mi / 3.7 km), round trip, allow 1 hour, elev. Δ: 52 ft / 16 m, trailhead on Wetherhill Mesa

This is a rather flat but exposed trail which was hit by the 2000 Pony Fire. The trail is straightforward with a mixture of pea gravel and paved trail, offering some self-guided sections displaying various aspects of the Badger top site ruins. The top site ruins do have different qualities then the alcove ruins, so the Badger House trail helps make for a rounded experience.

## Limited Backcountry Hikes

Each year, the Mesa Verde park rangers offer up exclusive and unique backcountry hikes and tours. The offerings are different each year and are definitely worth looking into. These hikes and guided ranger tours often go to areas that are not open or even publicized. The hikes typically require advance purchase of tickets and the number of tickets available each day is limited. Each hike is very special and even unprecedented in what the open up for visitors to see and experience.

For a list of the current year's hikes, check with the park for more information by going to the following link: http://www.nps.gov/meve/planyourvisit/backcountry_hikes.htm. Some of the hikes that seem to be perennial offerings are listed below. That said, each year they change them enough to warrant going to the website for current details.

### Wetherill Mesa Bike and Hike Adventure

Strenuous – (9.0 mi / 14.5 km), round trip, allow 4.5 hours, not including driving time

Tickets are $18.00 for adults. Tours are limited to 15 people. Bike not included (you need to bring your own). There are rental bikes available, call (970) 529-4631 for information on local bike rental places.

Kokopelli Bike and Board offers bikes for rental in Cortez (130 W Main St, Cortez, CO 81321. (970) 565-4408). Also, tour times were limited to Wednesdays and Sundays as of this writing.

This is likely one of the coolest ranger led hikes in the entire Grand Circle. You get to hike with a ranger for four miles and bike alongside for another five miles. This isn't a tram stuffed full of people and some guy reciting into a megaphone, this is a full immersion bimodal journey into depths of Mesa Verde accompanied by an expert.

The entire trip is filled with great views of cliff dwellings with in depth trips to Nordenskiöld #12, Double House and even includes a short hike to Long House. Allow about six hours total for the hike and driving time to the starting point from the visitor center. The trip is okay for young adults able to travel 9 miles comfortably. Also, bring plenty of water, snacks, sunscreen, and a hat. Folks must be in good overall shape for this adventure.

# Canyons of the Ancients National Monument

**Official Park Website:** http://www.blm.gov/co/st/en/nm/canm.html

**Visitor Center:**

No visitor center at park. Park is administrated by BLM in conjunction with Canyons of the Ancients and Anasazi Heritage Center, 27501 Highway 184, Dolores, Colorado USA 81323, Phone: (970) 882-5600. Visitors are encouraged to stop here first for orientation before visiting the park.

**Park Accessibility:**

- High clearance 4WD
- Primarily Overnight Use

**Experience Level:**

- Experienced Hiker – Backcountry Hiker

**Camping in Park:**

- No developed campground, backcountry camping allowed with some limitations, see park website for details.

**Lodging and Dining in Park:**

- None

**Nearest Town with Amenities:**

- Cortez, CO is 18 mi / 29 km from the park

**Getting There:**

- From Cortez, CO: Take US-491 South turn right onto County Road G. Continue on Road G for about 14.4 miles. Total distance is 18 mi / 29 km to park entrance

The Canyons of the Ancients National Monument is unlike any other park set aside for the preservation of Ancestral Puebloan lands. It is in a very true sense an outdoor museum meant primarily to preserve the past. To date, more than 6,000-recorded sites have been discovered over the park's 176,056 acres (roughly half the size of Canyonlands National Park). The trails are more routes and even roads into the park are scarce. Many of the ruins in this park are not publicized.

To explore this monument, it is highly encouraged that the visitor first visits the Anasazi Heritage Center for orientation and current conditions. The center is located at 27501 Highway 184, Dolores, Colorado USA 81323, Phone: (970) 882-5600. Even before going to the center, it's a good idea to watch the video created by the park's stewards from the website link below.

Canyons of the Ancients is a very special place and any visit here carries with it a sense of responsibility for any visitor. One steward of the area stated it best; the only thing you can take is that which fills your heart. Enjoy the ruins with respect and ideally from a distance. Resist the urge to take a piece of pottery or a grinding stone home with you. Even resist the urge to move them for others to see. This is a sacred and spiritual area for many.

To get a much better idea of the park, take about 10 minutes to watch the below video by the stewards of this area. These are the words of the descendants of the people who lived here and are found on the park's home page. Besides giving a good idea of the landscape of some of the ruins in the area, their message is a strong one. Visit with respect. Take nothing. Say thank you when you leave. The video can be found here. www.youtube.com/watch?v=AvAuUeJoTIQ

# Yucca House National Monument

**Official Park Website:** http://www.nps.gov/yuho

**Visitor Center:**

No visitor center at park. Park is administrated by Mesa Verde NP: (970) 529-4465

**Park Accessibility:**

- Okay for 2WD and RVs
- Day Use Only

**Experience Level:**

- Family Friendly – Casual Hiker

**Camping in Park:**

- None

**Lodging and Dining in Park:**

- None

**Nearest Town with Amenities:**

- Cortez, CO is 12 mi / 19 km from the park

*Yucca House NM Entrance*

**Getting There:**

- From Cortez, CO: Take US-491 South turn right onto County Road B. After 0.8 miles, turn right onto County Road 20.5. Total distance is 12 mi / 19 km to park entrance

The park holds one of the larger Ancestral Puebloan sites, with hundreds of rooms. What makes Yucca House special however is what isn't there. There are no facilities, no visitor guides, no campsites, and no trails to be found. There is an easement access for a road to be built, but since its inception in 1919, there is no road. All that defines Yucca House is a lone-gated entrance. You walk up to it, you open the gate, and from here, you are on the same page as any other archaeologist and visitor. The place is yours to discover.

There are some paths created from use, follow these to find various mounds, some with bits of walls and other elements of ancient structures revealing themselves. The fascination is how quickly nature has taken back these lands. To walk around what is a 600 plus room complex and seeing more scrub and faint traces is a wonder in its own right.

Yucca House is a great place to stop as a side trip to Mesa Verde. It is a quick 20-minute drive from Cortez, Colorado via Highway 160E. The park is not well marked, but can be found easily with GPS navigation apps on most smartphones.

# Northern Arizona

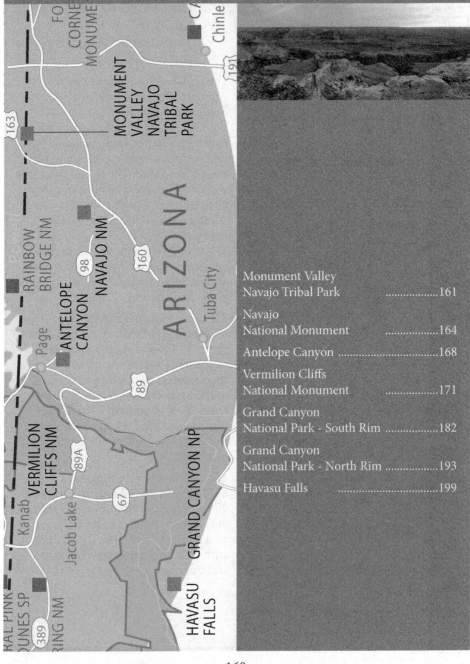

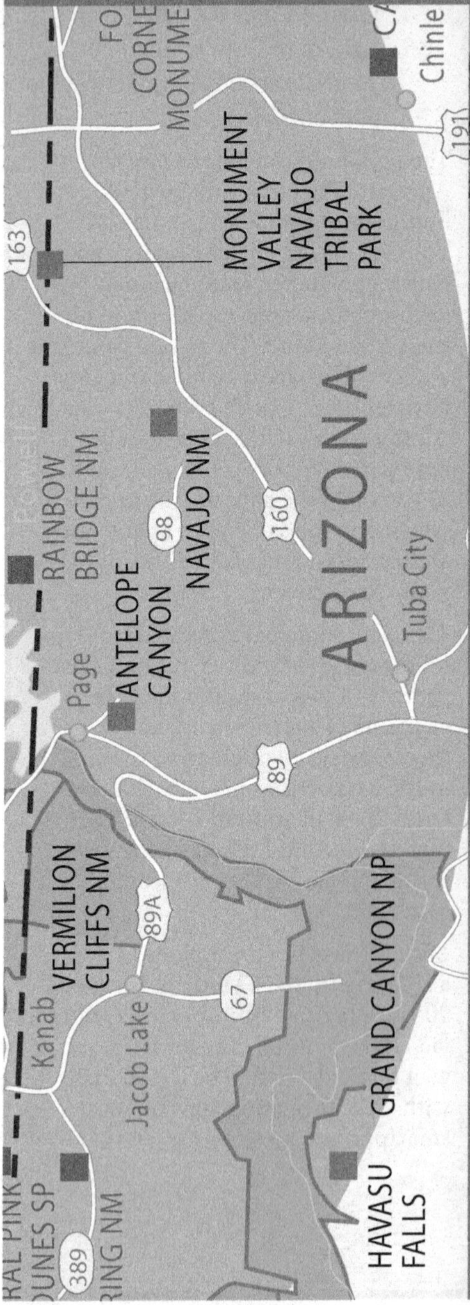

Monument Valley
Navajo Tribal Park ..................161

Navajo
National Monument ..................164

Antelope Canyon ..................168

Vermilion Cliffs
National Monument ..................171

Grand Canyon
National Park - South Rim ..................182

Grand Canyon
National Park - North Rim ..................193

Havasu Falls ..................199

## Quick Facts

**Official Park Website:**

- http://www.navajonationparks.org/htm/monumentvalley.htm

**Visitor Center:**

- Contact Monument Valley Navajo Tribal Park at: PO Box 360289, Monument Valley, Utah 84536, Phone: (435) 727-5874, (435) 727-5879, (435) 727-5870

**Park Accessibility:**

- Okay for 2WD and RVs
- Day and Overnight Use

**Experience Level:**

- Family Friendly – Casual Hiker

**Camping in Park:**

- The View Campground: 90 T/RV, no water, no hookups, restrooms, shower, reservations: (435) 727-5802

**Lodging in Park:**

- The View Lodge, reservations: (435) 727-5555

**Dining in Park:**

- The View Restaurant

**Nearest Town with Amenities:**

- Oljato-Monument Valley, UT – adjacent to park

**Getting There:**

- From Flagstaff, AZ: take US-89 North, US-160 East and US-163 North to Monument Valley Rd in Oljato-Monument Valley
- From Moab, UT: take US-191 South to Oljato-Monument Valley
- From Cortez, CO: take UT-162 West and US-163 South to Oljato-Monument Valley

## What Makes Monument Valley Special

If you have ever watched the classic movie Stagecoach, one of the top westerns of all time, you will notice one thing. No matter where that stagecoach is heading, they are always passing through Monument Valley. The movie was John Wayne's breakthrough role and arguably put Monument Valley on the map for America. From 1939, when the movie was made, to present, Monument Valley has become THE definitive icon of the Southwest.

The problem with any icon is it tends to become larger than reality itself and we are let down when we finally meet it. The good news with Monument Valley is it will not disappoint in this way. It is as sweeping and epic in real life as it is on film. It is a place where time seems to slow down and watching the late afternoon sun slowly slip off the monuments is a memory that will stick with you for life.

Monument Valley is easy to drive through, but to capture the impact of this area it is recommended to stay overnight. The campground set up by the Navajo Tribal Park offers some of the best viewing real estate in the park. The campsites sit on a sandy hill overlooking many of the most recognized monuments, including the Mittens. The View Hotel nearby is also recommended. The famed Goulding's Lodge is another favorite place to stay and was home for the cast and crew of the movie Stagecoach and other westerns.

In terms of hiking, the land is privately owned and actively used by the Navajo. The Wildcat Trail is the only hike that a visitor can take without a Navajo escort in the park. The trail is a 3.2-mile loop that goes completely around the West Mitten. The trail starts at The View Hotel and once down in the valley is fairly flat. Allow 2 – 3 hours to complete this hike and bring water.

There is also a 17-mile scenic drive on a maintained unpaved road, which is highly recommended. The drive is suitable for most cars and is open for day use only. If you are looking for more immersion, you can take a guided tour. These tours are really the only way to see some of the places within the park. All of the official tour operators are listed here: www.navajonationparks.org/htm/monumentvalleytours.htm

*West Mitten Butte, Monument Valley*

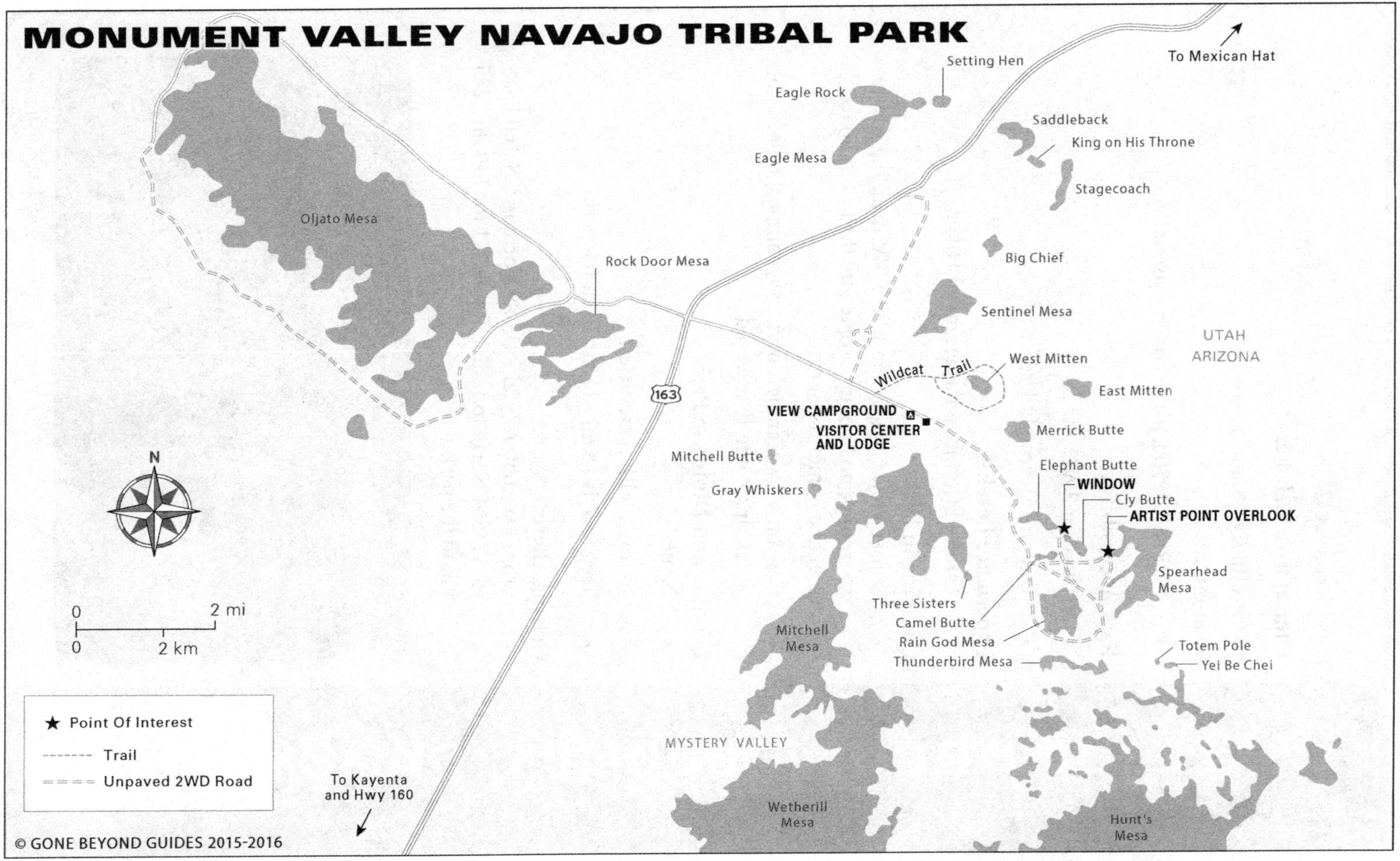
MONUMENT VALLEY NAVAJO TRIBAL PARK
To Mexican Hat
Setting Hen
Eagle Rock
Eagle Mesa
Saddleback
King on His Throne
Stagecoach
Oljato Mesa
Rock Door Mesa
Big Chief
Sentinel Mesa
UTAH
ARIZONA
Wildcat Trail
West Mitten
East Mitten
163
VIEW CAMPGROUND
VISITOR CENTER AND LODGE
Merrick Butte
Mitchell Butte
Elephant Butte
WINDOW
Cly Butte
ARTIST POINT OVERLOOK
Gray Whiskers
Spearhead Mesa
Three Sisters
Camel Butte
Rain God Mesa
Thunderbird Mesa
Mitchell Mesa
Totem Pole
Yei Be Chei
N
0
2 mi
0
2 km
Point Of Interest
Trail
Unpaved 2WD Road
MYSTERY VALLEY
To Kayenta and Hwy 160
Wetherill Mesa
Hunt's Mesa
© GONE BEYOND GUIDES 2015-2016

# Navajo National Monument

## Quick Facts

**Official Park Website:**

- http://www.nps.gov/nava

**Visitor Center:**

- (928) 672-2700, park is open seasonally

**Park Accessibility:**

- Okay for 2WD and RVs
- Day and Overnight Use

**Experience Level:**

- Family Friendly – Experienced Hiker

**Camping in Park:**

- Sunset View Campground: 33 T/RV, drinking water, restrooms, no hookups, some pull thru sites, no fee site, first come-first served
- Canyon View Campground: 14T, compost toilets, no water, first come-first served

**Lodging and Dining in Park:**

- None

**Nearest Town with Amenities:**

- Tsegi, AZ is 18 mi / 11 km from the park

**Getting There:**

- From Flagstaff, AZ: take US-89 North to US-160 East to AZ-564 North to Indian Route 221 for 140 mi / 225 km to the park

*Large alcove protecting Betatakin ruins*

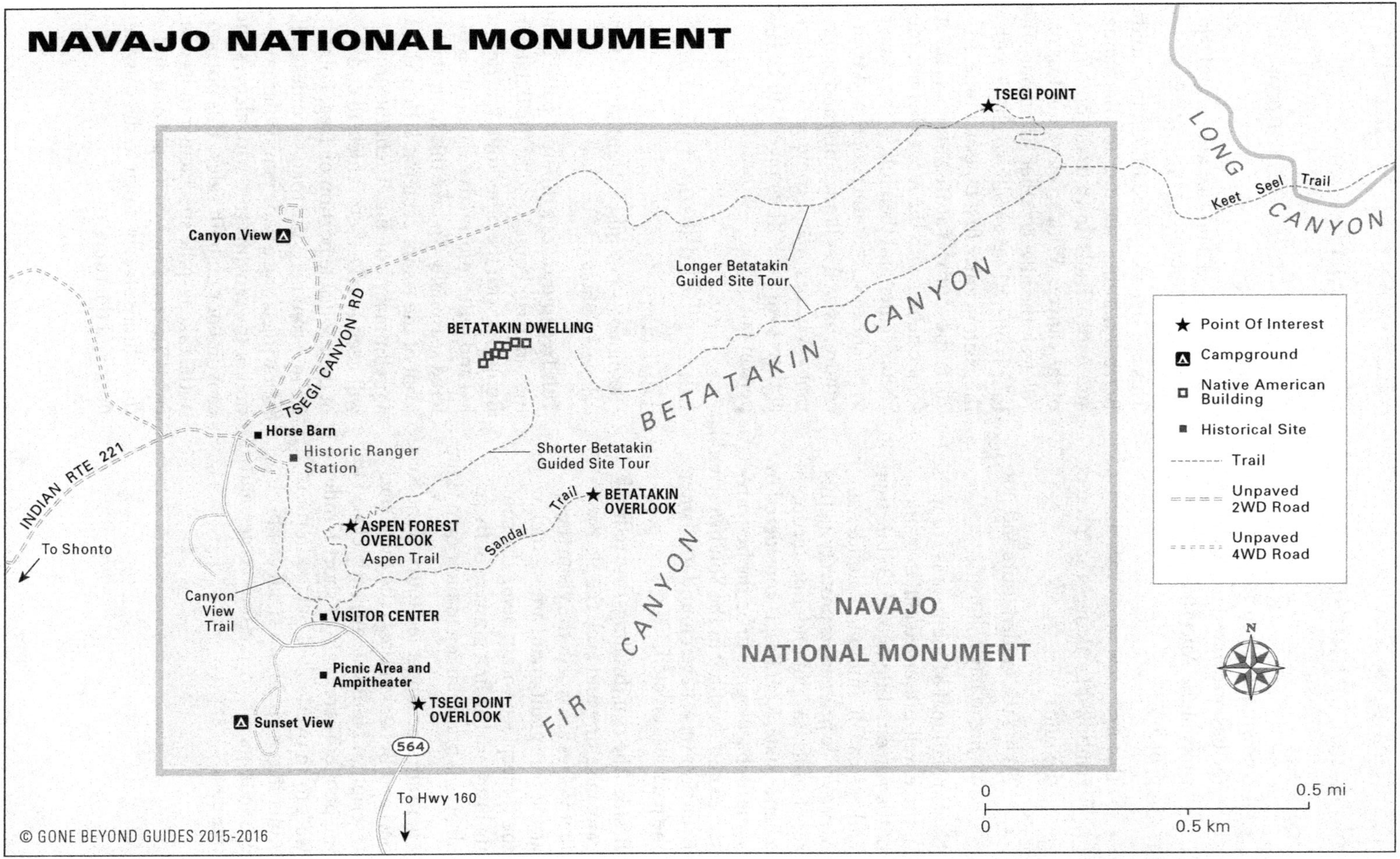
NAVAJO NATIONAL MONUMENT
TSEGI POINT
LONG CANYON
Keet Seel Trail
Canyon View
Longer Betatakin Guided Site Tour
BETATAKIN CANYON
TSEGI CANYON RD
BETATAKIN DWELLING
Horse Barn
Historic Ranger Station
INDIAN RTE 221
Shorter Betatakin Guided Site Tour
Sandal Trail
BETATAKIN OVERLOOK
ASPEN FOREST OVERLOOK
Aspen Trail
To Shonto
Canyon View Trail
VISITOR CENTER
FIR CANYON
NAVAJO NATIONAL MONUMENT
Picnic Area and Ampitheater
TSEGI POINT OVERLOOK
Sunset View
564
To Hwy 160
Point Of Interest
Campground
Native American Building
Historical Site
Trail
Unpaved 2WD Road
Unpaved 4WD Road
N
0
0.5 mi
0
0.5 km

## What Makes Navajo National Monument Special

- Knowing that you are arguably at the best preserved cliff dwelling ruins of the Ancestral Pueblo people
- That first view of the massive rock rainbow-like alcoves that protect the ruins
- Taking the guided tours and not having to pay a dime

Navajo National Monument is comprised of three well-preserved cliff dwellings of the Ancestral Puebloans. While there had been a fair amount of plunder at Mesa Verde prior to its protection, this set of ruins was put under protection in a better state. Keet Seel is considered by some archaeologists to be the best-preserved cliff dwelling in the Southwest and Betatakin wasn't even found until after the park was created.

Besides the cliff dwellings, the redrock canyon setting and even the alcoves themselves are worth the visit. These alcoves are giant grand arcs of rock, with the centerpiece within being the ruins themselves. The first glimpse of these alcoves is breathtaking in their own right.

There are free ranger led tours of the Keet Seel and Betatakin sites. The third site, Inscription House, is currently closed to the public. There is also a short 1-mile walk to an overlook of Betatakin ruins. Amenities include two small campgrounds, picnic area, visitor center, and museum.

## Hiking Navajo National Monument

### Shorter Betatakin Guided Site Tour

Strenuous – (3.0 mi / 4.8 km), round trip, allow 3 – 4 hours

This is a free ranger led hiking tour to the Betatakin Ruins. The tour follows Sandal and Aspen Trails down to the bottom of the canyon. With an elevation loss of 700 feet, the hike is rather strenuous. The tour is offered seasonally, so check with the visitor center first on exact time. In 2015, the tour was at 10 AM. Folks meet for a briefing with the ranger behind the visitor center and then follow the ranger as he/she describes the people and their culture, as well as flora, fauna and geography. Visitors are welcome to walk back at their own pace. The ranger will be last person out.

### Longer Betatakin Guided Site Tour

Strenuous – (5.0 mi / 8.0 km), round trip, allow 3 – 5hours

This free tour takes a different path, using the old Tsegi Point Road to the Betatakin Ruins. As with the other tour, it is ranger led and quite informative. The tour is offered seasonally. To take this tour, start in front of the visitor center at 8:15 AM for a preliminary briefing. Then, the group will need to take their vehicle to end of the navigable portion of Tsegi Point Road. From here, the road becomes trail, following along a wide peninsular portion of the canyon's rim, with alcoves and canyon floor on both sides. This portion of the hike is quite spectacular in its own right. The road ends at Tsegi Point and then climbs steeply down to the canyon floor and the ruins.

## Keet Seel

Strenuous – (17.0 mi / 27.4 km), round trip, full day or overnight backpacking trip

It is possible to visit the ruins of Keet Seel. This is considered by some to be the best-preserved cliff dwelling in the Southwest. The ruins are laden with artifacts, both in volume and variety. These include pieces of jewelry, arrowheads, and corncobs. Many of the rooms have the original ceiling beams and exterior plaster still intact. There is a ranger on site who will lead you around once you arrive. For visitors that feel 17 miles is too long for a day hike, there is a primitive campground nearby.

The park limits the number of visitors to Keet Seel to 20 per day. Advanced reservation and a backcountry permit are required. Before receiving a permit, one must listen to orientation, which is held daily at 8:15 AM and 3:00 PM. Keep the permit with you at all times as you hike. Fortunately, it is not difficult to obtain a permit due to the monument's location and the trail's distance.

The route starts in a similar manner as the "Longer Betatakin Guided Site Tour". A permitted visitor takes Tsegi Road to Tsegi Trail down to the canyon floor. From there, look for signs indicating the side canyon for Keet Seel. This primitive trail heads up canyon, crossing the stream multiple times and passes a 100-foot, awe-inspiring waterfall.

Keet Seel is not open in the winter and early spring. In addition, during the summer monsoon season, the park may cancel reservations due to potential flash flooding in the park.

## Sandal Trail

Easy – (1.0 mi / 1.6 km), round trip, allow 30 minutes

A paved and accessible trail that leads to an overlook of Betatakin cliff dwelling and surrounding canyon.

## Aspen Trail

Moderate – (0.8 mi / 1.3 km), round trip, allow 30 minutes

A spur trail off Sandal Trail that heads lower into the canyon and an old growth grove of Aspen trees.

## Canyon View Trail

Easy – (0.4 mi / 0.6 km), round trip, allow 30 minutes

This is an easy walk along the rim, leading from the visitor center and campground to the historic ranger station

*Betatakin ruins*

# Antelope Canyon

## Quick Facts

**Official Park Website:**

- http://navajonationparks.org/htm/antelopecanyon.htm

**Visitor Center:**

- Contact Lake Powell Navajo Tribal Park Office, P.O. Box 4803, Page, AZ 86040, Phone: (928) 698-2808

**Park Accessibility:**

- Okay for 2WD and RVs
- Day Use Only

**Experience Level:**

- Family Friendly – Casual Hiker

**Camping in Park:**

- None

**Lodging and Dining in Park:**

- None

**Nearest Town with Amenities:**

- Page, AZ – most tours begin in Page.

**Getting There:**

- From Flagstaff, AZ: take US 89 North to Page, AZ
- From Cortez, CO: take US 160 West to AZ 98 West to Page, AZ
- From Kanab, UT: take US 89 South/East to Page, AZ

*It really is this beautiful*

## What Makes Antelope Slot Canyon Special

- One of the most stunning and easily accessible slot canyons in the Grand Circle
- Knowing you are taking photographs that are typically seen in art studios
- Special enough to be one of the only attractions in this book that is not a national or state park!

Antelope Slot Canyon is, on the surface, one of the most incredible and beautiful sights one can see on a trip to the Grand Circle. If you are fortunate enough to book a high noon tour, when the beams of sunlight shine down onto the sands of the canyon floor, the experience is transcendent. Antelope Slot Canyon is a delight to the eye, with narrow water carved walls of multihued sandstone, towering high above into an infinitely blue sky. The contrast of light combined with shadow play brings out an experience that is certainly worth the trip and is often a highlight of any vacation to the southwest.

This is despite the downsides of the slot canyon. Once an unknown secret canyon revealed occasionally by photographers in desert themed coffee table books, the canyon is now wide open to the public via tours given by the Navajo. Herein lies the flipside of this heavenly experience. The narrow canyon is packed with tourists. Look up and the views are stunningly divine. Look at eye level and it's like being at Times Square on New Year's Eve. Adding to this is the equally dichotomous Navajo sentiment towards the site; a people torn between guarding a place held sacred and exploiting this "outdoor church" for money.

This is not in any way meant to discourage one from going; the trip is definitely

*High noon sunbeams*

worth it. In addition, what is described above is reflective of peak season traffic. If you go in the off-season, the experience can be more intimate.

There are almost as many tour groups going to the slot canyon as there are layers of sandstone in the canyon. Some are recommended below. There are also two major sections to visit, the upper and lower slot canyons. Most tours go to the upper canyon due to access and popularity. The lower canyon can be more intimate though it too is getting more crowded with each passing year.

The best time to go for photography and effect is during the high noon tour. There is direct sunlight into the canyon at this time and the guides will toss sand high up which brings out filtered streams of light, which make for incredible photos. (Wait until the dust settles a bit for the best photos). The canyon is so narrow the sun penetrates like beams from heaven, bright and with crisply defined lines. Keep in mind that this is peak time, so expect to take your shot quickly before being herded along. If you don't like crowds, your best bet is to take one of the early morning or evening tours.

Logistically, each tour group gets into the back of an open-air truck that has been retrofitted to carry people. The driver heads into a sandy wash at a decent speed until the entrance of the canyon is reached. One tour driver pretended to be stuck in the sand, presumably to invoke the thrill of adventure. Keep your hats in your lap or tightly on your head, there is no stopping. Once out of the vehicle, the tour guide does his or her genuine best to make the trip as intimate as possible for his group. The biggest advice is stay with your tour lead. Getting left behind has happened, but more typically, your late return to the vehicle will be met with glib looks from the fellow tour group members. Some tours feature a hoop dance back at the tour guide headquarters.

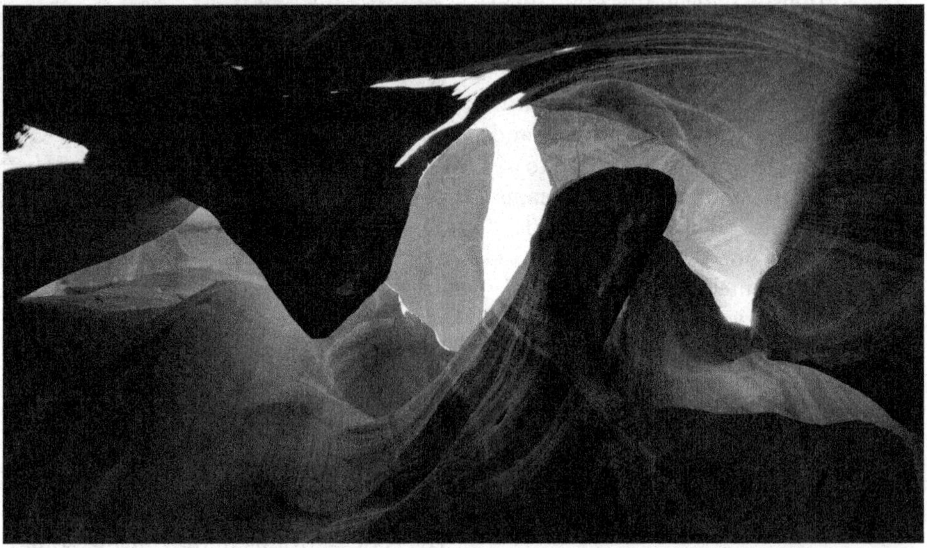

*Looking up within the slot canyon*

## Antelope Slot Canyon Tours

### Adventurous Antelope Canyon Photo Tours

Highway 98, Page, AZ 86040, Phone: (928) 380-1874, www.navajoantelopecanyon.com

### Antelope Slot Canyon Tours by Chief Tsosie

55 S Lake Powell Blvd, Page AZ 86040, Phone: (928) 645-5594, www.antelopeslotcanyon.com

### Ken's Guided Tour of Lower Antelope Canyon

Indian Route 222, Page, AZ 86040, Phone: (928) 606-2168, lowerantelope.com

### Dixie Ellis' Lower Antelope Canyon Tours

Indian Route 222, Page, AZ 86040, Phone: (928) 640-1761, antelopelowercanyon.com

## Quick Facts

**Official Park Website:**

- http://www.blm.gov/az/st/en/prog/blm_special_areas/natmon/vermilion.html

**Visitor Center:**

None in park, for a ranger contact:

- BLM St. George Field Office: 345 E. Riverside Drive, St. George, UT 84790-6714, Phone: (435) 688-3200
- Hours: 7:45 a.m.-5:00 p.m. Monday through Friday, 10:00 a.m.-3:00 p.m. Saturday, Closed Sunday

**Park Accessibility:**

- No paved roads, high clearance/4WD vehicles required for most of the park
- Primarily Overnight Use

**Experience Level:**

- Experienced Hiker – Backcountry Hiker

**Camping in Park:**

- Stateline: 4 T, no water, no trash, restrooms, first come/first served, open year round
- White House: 5 T, no water, no trash, restrooms, first come/first served, open year round

**Lodging and Dining in Park:**

- None

**Nearest Town with Amenities:**

- Page, AZ, 40 mi / 64 km to Marble Canyon entrance

**Getting There:**

- Southern Section: From Flagstaff: head north on US 89 to 89A at the Bitter Springs off ramp. From US I-15: take AZ 389 East to US 89A South
- Northern Section: From Kanab, Utah: take US 89 to the east or US 89A to the south. From US I-15: take UT 9 East to US 89 South

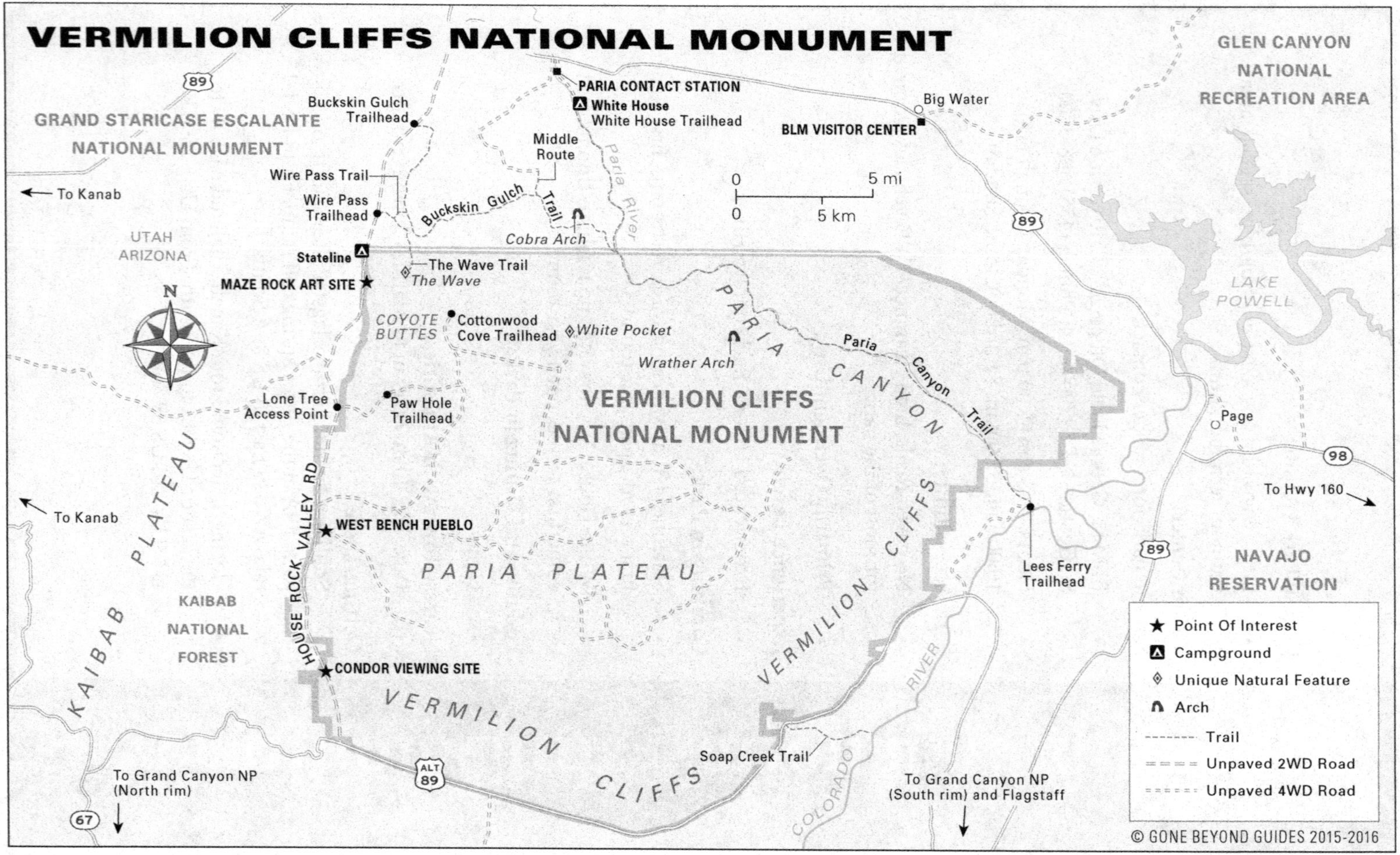
VERMILION CLIFFS NATIONAL MONUMENT
GRAND STARICASE ESCALANTE
NATIONAL MONUMENT
89
To Kanab
UTAH
ARIZONA
N
To Kanab
KAIBAB PLATEAU
KAIBAB
NATIONAL
FOREST
To Grand Canyon NP
(North rim)
67
Buckskin Gulch
Trailhead
Wire Pass Trail
Wire Pass
Trailhead
Stateline
MAZE ROCK ART SITE
Lone Tree
Access Point
HOUSE ROCK VALLEY RD
WEST BENCH PUEBLO
CONDOR VIEWING SITE
ALT 89
PARIA CONTACT STATION
White House
White House Trailhead
Middle
Route
Buckskin Gulch Trail
Cobra Arch
Paria River
The Wave Trail
The Wave
COYOTE
BUTTES
Cottonwood
Cove Trailhead
White Pocket
Paw Hole
Trailhead
PARIA PLATEAU
VERMILION CLIFFS
Big Water
BLM VISITOR CENTER
0
5 mi
0
5 km
PARIA CANYON
Wrather Arch
Paria Canyon Trail
VERMILION CLIFFS
NATIONAL MONUMENT
VERMILION CLIFFS
Lees Ferry
Trailhead
Soap Creek Trail
COLORADO RIVER
To Grand Canyon NP
(South rim) and Flagstaff
GLEN CANYON
NATIONAL
RECREATION AREA
LAKE
POWELL
Page
98
To Hwy 160
NAVAJO
RESERVATION
Point Of Interest
Campground
Unique Natural Feature
Arch
Trail
Unpaved 2WD Road
Unpaved 4WD Road
© GONE BEYOND GUIDES 2015-2016

## What Makes Vermilion Cliffs National Monument Special

Vermilion Cliffs National Monument is certainly a candidate for one of the top park destinations within the Grand Circle. Nearly as large as all of the three sections of the Canyonlands and yet relatively new and unheard of, this is one of the most unspoiled parks to be found. It is also one of the most remote. The park is located north of Grand Canyon and east of the Navajo lands, touching the border of Utah, referred to as the Arizona Strip. There is no visitor center, few roads, little previous development, and only a scattered handful of trails.

Vermilion Cliffs is true desert wilderness. It is untouched, insufferable, rugged, and pure. There are places within it where it feels as if no person has ever stepped foot. For the most part, Vermilion Cliffs is pure virgin sandstone, quietly being shaped over millions of years.

It was only made into a national monument in 2000, though the land had been protected under other measures prior. Much of the 280,000 acres protects the Paria Plateau, a significant mesa that spans over 20 miles and is roughly square in shape. The plateau itself is a vast desert island oasis, invoking freedom and being on top of the world. However, it is the areas along the edges of the plateau that offers some of the most amazing sections in the park, such as The Wave, a striated

### Before heading out:

Here are some tips to ensure a safe and successful trip:

- First, get a permit. Overnight access to Buckskin Gulch is limited to 20 folks per day. The online process is listed in the web URL above.
- Speak to the BLM rangers. The rangers are the best versed in current conditions, what to expect and general guidance on how to prepare and execute this hike. Kanab Field Office – 318 North 100 East, Kanab, UT 84741 – Phone: (435) 644-4600 Fax: (435) 644-4620 or by email: utknmail@blm.gov
- Use a shuttle or two cars. These are long distances, so if you are short on time, this is best way to do this hike. Try Paria Outfitters (www.paria.com) for shuttle services. At the very least, check out their site for the cool pics of the areas they serve.
- Check the weather forecast. Backpacker Magazine puts this as one of the 10 most dangerous hikes, primarily due to flash flood risks. As they put it, "Should thunderstorm-bloated flood waters come charging down the tunnel, you're no better than a bug in a firehose."
- Bring water shoes, plenty of drinking water, and multiple layers of clothing. There are points where the watercourse is the trail so bring some decent water shoes. While there are seeps, pools and water, it can be downright murky, so best to bring in what you need. Finally, fires are not permitted in the area, so make sure you have layer coverage for the temperature range of the trip.

section of carved sandstone that has to be seen to be believed. Then there is Buckskin Gulch, a tributary of the Paria River and at a length of 20 miles is a contender for the longest slot canyon in the world.

It must be stated that not all of this wonder and remote beauty comes without some caution and regulations. Much of the land is accessed by permit only. While day use permits are more available, overnight permits are limited and can be obtained by going to the URL below and following the online instructions: www.blm.gov/az/st/en/arolrsmain.html. The caution is that this land can be extremely challenging. Flash floods, venomous reptiles and insects, sun exposure, and remoteness make this park much different than say, taking the shuttle from the Zion Lodge and taking a hike. This area is ideally suited for experienced hikers and desert backpackers.

A quick note on the permitting system. One consistent theme within all of these parks is finding a balance between preservation of the land and the ability to share it for the enjoyment and recreation of others. Vermilion Cliffs NM pushes this balance more on the preservation side. There is a capacity to the number of visitors allowed to use the park each day and while it may be frustrating if you are the unfortunate soul that didn't get a permit, you have to respect the process. The desert is fragile and takes a very long time to recover. Some parks, especially the national parks, are pushing the balance more towards recreation and the wear on them does show. Having explored all of these parks since the 1980's, the impact over just 35 years is quite evident and not in a good way. Vermilion Cliffs NM continues to retain that pristine hallowed ground of desert experience because of the permit process. Not everyone will get to go, especially for those permitted areas only available by lottery, but those that do will experience the difference.

*Vermilion Cliffs*

## Hiking Vermilion Cliffs National Monument

### Paria Canyon Trails

#### Buckskin Gulch Trail

Moderate – (5.7 mi / 9.2 km), one way to Wire Pass Trailhead, allow 3 hours

Strenuous – (23 mi / 37 km), one way, to White House Trailhead, full day hike or 2-day backpacking trip

Strenuous – (47 mi / 76 km), one way, to Lee's Ferry Trailhead, 3-5-day backpacking trip

Buckskin Gulch is the longest and deepest slot canyon in the Grand Circle. The narrows extend nearly 15 miles, with some sections being but 10 feet in width. The terrain and views are as inspiring as they are varied, making this a popular hike. The slot canyon leaves for very few exits during a flash flood and rain as far as Bryce Canyon 50 miles away can drain into Buckskin. The gulch is also known for muck pools, where in the middle of summer you may find yourself with no other choice but to wade through residual pools that become foul smelling mud pots. They are normally no more than 3 feet deep, but some folks have noted being chest deep in one pool. Additionally, expect to do a fair amount of scrambling and even rappelling. In many spots, there is a rope left behind as a gesture of courtesy to rappel down the 15 foot drops, but you'll want to bring rope just in case.

There are many entry points into Buckskin Gulch. There is the Buckskin Gulch Trailhead or Wire Pass Trailhead to the east, heading downstream to a juncture where you can either head north to White House Trailhead or southeast through Paria Canyon down to Lee's Ferry. The most popular hike is from Wire Pass Trailhead to White House Trailhead. This section describes the route starting from Buckskin Gulch Trailhead. Use this route if you want to say you hiked the full extent of Buckskin Gulch.

Take Highway 89 east from Kanab, UT 38 miles or west from Page, AZ for 34 miles and turn onto House Valley Road. This will be a right if coming from Kanab. The Buckskin Trailhead is 4.5 miles down a dirt road and is suitable for 2WD vehicles. That said, the clay-based soils are super sticky in some areas and like driving on ice in others when wet. It is not recommended, even in a 4WD vehicle, to drive this road when wet.

There is no established campground here, but camping is allowed at the trailhead. The trail is obvious and dry for most of the year to the junction to Wire Pass Trailhead, starting off fairly wide relative to the narrows later on. From the junction to Wire Pass, the canyon begins its journey as the longest narrows in the Southwest. The next big milestone is Buckskin Gulch Junction (1.8 miles, 1 hour). Here, (and beyond), the narrows are quite spectacular. Every turn is a different "wow!" moment. Along this section are The Cesspools, a stretch of murky, muddy, god-awful water that you have to wade through to continue.

The trek through this section of the narrows is 6.5 miles long, with the next milestone being Middle Route. Allow 4 hours for this part. Middle Route is yet another passage into Buckskin over a 4WD drive road and is described later in the book.

From Middle Route to Rock Fall (aka Rock Jam) is another 3 miles (allow 2 hours). This area has some rock problem areas that require scrambling. In spots, it can get quite dark, though not enough for a flashlight. Rock Fall presents the toughest of the areas where scrambling is needed. The scramble is easy enough, with some footholds into the rock for the down climb or hikers can opt for the Rabbit Hole, which is the easiest of methods to get through this scramble of rock (look for a way down through the rocks rather than up). From Rock Fall the campground and Paria River Confluence is in sight and is the spot for an overnight rest for most folks. The distance here is 1.3 miles to the campground and another quarter mile to the confluence. Allow 1 hour. It is not recommended to camp at the confluence due to potential risk of "going to Lee's Ferry prematurely" due to flooding. The campground sits higher up providing some protection from rising waters.

The hike to the confluence is dry for the most part, aside from the mud pots and stronger seeps and springs providing some run off. While it may be tempting to get the water from these sources, it is not recommended. You will need 1.5 to 2 gallons of water for this leg in the summer, more depending on distance traveled and time spent.

If you are continuing upstream to White House Trailhead, you have another 4 hours and 7.5 miles ahead of you. This route is possible to do as a day trip, but it is a full day.

Heading downstream will take you Lee's Ferry. The total distance to Lee's Ferry from Buckskin Gulch Trailhead is 47 miles. Plan on a 3 - 5-day backpacking trip and definitely use a shuttle. Along

with Paria Outpost listed above, Circle Tours, (888) 854-7862 and End of the Trail Shuttles, (928) 355-2252 offer shuttle services.

## Wire Pass Trail

Moderate – (5.7 mi / 9.2 km), one way to Buckskin Gulch Trailhead, allow 3 hours

Strenuous – (21 mi / 34 km), one way, to White House Trailhead, full day hike or 2-day backpacking trip

Strenuous – (44 mi / 71 km), one way, to Lee's Ferry Trailhead, 3-5-day backpacking trip

Wire Pass Trail offers an alternate entrance into Buckskin Gulch through Wire Pass Gulch. Wire Pass Trailhead is often chosen over entering directly from the Buckskin Gulch Trailhead because it is shorter and the gulch is itself a very nice set of narrows. It only cuts off 2 miles from any destination but does offer help satisfy the "slot canyon" fix a little faster than starting from Buckskin Gulch Trailhead. This trailhead is also used as the starting destination for a popular sandstone formation known as The Wave, described later on.

To get here, just follow the directions above to Buckskin Gulch Trailhead and continue on House Rock Valley Road another 3.8 miles (8.3 miles from Highway 89). Again, permits are needed as is reading all the tips provided in the Buckskin Gulch Trail description. Stateline Campground is one-mile south of the Wire Pass Trailhead and camping is allowed at the trailhead if campground is full. There are restrooms here, but no water.

## Middle Route

Strenuous – (1.4 mi / 2.3 km), one way to Buckskin Gulch, allow 1 - 2 hours

The Middle Route is a good alternative if you are looking to bypass many of the cold stagnant pools of water as you wind through the narrows of Buckskin Gulch. It also saves a day of hiking. It is a short easy route to navigate into the gulch via a long, sandy, unsigned, and at times impassable 4WD road with multiple forks to consider.

About midway through Buckskin Gulch, the walls of the canyon lower down to about 100 feet. Here there is a very steep crack that is possible to scramble up if one needs an early exit out of the gulch or as a means to down climb into the slot canyon. This is Middle Route. This crack is definitely for the experienced canyoneer and bringing a 50-foot rope is highly recommended for lowering packs. The crack contains steep drop offs and climbing down slickrock. Exposure aside, this is a Class 3 - 4 scramble and doesn't require any technical climbing per se.

Getting to Middle Route is not straightforward as hinted at above. It's best to

*Coyote Buttes South*



consult with the Paria Contact Station for directions, road conditions and even a video of Middle Route.

## White House Trail

Strenuous – (23 mi / 37 km), one way to Buckskin Gulch Trailhead, full day hike or 2-day backpacking trip

Strenuous – (21 mi / 34 km), one way, to Wire Pass Trailhead, full day hike or 2-day backpacking trip

Strenuous – (38 mi / 61 km), one way, to Lee's Ferry Trailhead, 3-5-day backpacking trip

Continuing in our long list of trails that lead to Buckskin Gulch, let's add White House Trail.

Following the directions in the Buckskin Gulch Trail description, take the dirt road towards the Paria Contact Station and turn onto the obvious dirt road just before it. Follow this 2WD road for 2 miles to the trailhead.

White House trail is a popular exit route for Buckskin because of the possibility to utilize a shuttle or second car. It is also adjacent to the White House Campground. There is no water here but there are restrooms. The trail follows the Paria River downstream as it heads towards Lee's Ferry and the Colorado River. It is 7.5 miles to Buckskin Gulch. This section does require some wading at times, with the occasional spot of quicksand. Wrap gear and wear water shoes for this section. See the Buckskin Gulch Trail for more information.

## Lee's Ferry Trailhead

See Glen Canyon National Recreation Area

# Coyote Buttes North

## The Wave

Strenuous – (5.6 mi / 9.0 km), round trip, from Wire Pass Trailhead, allow 3 – 4 hours

If ever there was a destination that could compete with Buckskin Gulch, the longest slot canyon in the Southwest and perhaps even the world, it a little place called The Wave. In the Grand Circle there is a lot of red rock, so much in fact, that after a few weeks within it, one starts dreaming of fantastic mashups of slickrock canyons and formations that don't actually exist. The Wave is a place that is so fantastic; it is as if it came from one of these dreams. Seeing an image of The Wave is to reset the art of the possible within the realm of red rock. To see it in person can be surreal, as if it shouldn't exist, yet it does. As an added bonus, the whole terrain getting to it and around it is cool to explore.

*The Wave*

This area is part of the Coyote Buttes North. This is a day use only area and requires a permit. Permits are limited to 20 people a day with 10 folks chosen through a walk in lottery process the day before and 10 folks obtaining the permit via an online process via (www.blm.gov/az/paria/obtainpermits.cfm?usearea=CB).

For the online process, the lottery opens up 4 months prior to the use date. Generally, online permits for the Coyote Buttes North are hard to obtain. The cost to apply is $5 per group and you can select up to three dates. See the lottery schedule below for exact dates, but in general, the process works like this. For a permit in say the month of May, one would apply

## Coyote Buttes North Lottery Schedule

| Apply between | for a permit during | Lottery Run at 1:05 p.m. MST for remaining permits available |
|---|---|---|
| January 1 - 31 | May | February 1 |
| February 1 - 28 | June | March 1 |
| March 1 - 31 | July | April 1 |
| April 1- 30 | August | May 1 |
| May 1 - 31 | September | June 1 |
| June 1 - 30 | October | July 1 |
| July 1 - 31 | November | August 1 |
| August 1 - 31 | December | September 1 |
| September 1 - 30 | January | October 1 |
| October 1 - 31 | February | November 1 |
| November 1 - 30 | March | December 1 |
| December 1 - 31 | April | January 1 |

at any time four months earlier, from January 1-31, in this case. On February 1, at 1:05 PM MST, the permits holders are chosen. If you are successful, you will be notified via email and will then need to pay $7 per individual.

There is no established trail to The Wave. There are two routes, however. The most readily accessible method is to start from Wire Pass Trailhead. The drive is easy enough and more straightforward of a hike then the other method known as The Notch. The route from Wire Pass Trailhead will be described here.

Start by following the instructions to Wire Pass Trailhead listed above. Enter into Wire Pass Gulch across the road and travel down the wash for about half a mile. Take the juncture to the right, marked Coyote Buttes, where you will find an obvious trail. The trail climbs up a hill and across a desert field ending at a wash. Total distance of the trail is approximately 0.65 miles.

From here on out the trail becomes route and the area is by permit only. On the other side of the wash is a slickrock incline that is typically marked with cairns. Climb this saddle and head towards the BLM marker ahead of you. This saddle is a great point to mark if you have a GPS, as it will greatly aid in finding the trail on the return.

Continue to follow the BLM markers south, heading towards and staying to the left of a landmark known as Twin Buttes. Once you pass by this landmark, you are about 0.6 miles from the Utah – Arizona border and 1.0 mile from the Wave. The next landmark to aim for is a narrow crack like gully in the cliffs as you continue south. As you get closer to the gully look for a small sand dune left of the gully. Climb the sand dune, then the slickrock to arrive at The Wave. There are many other features to check out in the area, including The Second Wave, The Alcove, and some petroglyphs and dinosaur tracks. See the below website for a list of all of them.

One exceptional site dedicated to The Wave feature is a site called "thewave". It covers everything outlined here and has a virtual tour of the hike itself, sunset/sunrise calculator, weather, and other details. Go here: www.thewave.info/CoyoteButtesNorthCode/Map.html

### Maze Rock Art Site

Just beyond Wire Pass Trailhead and State Line Campground is a trailhead to a rich petroglyph site. There are numerous examples of Ancestral Puebloan art, including the namesake, a petroglyph that looks like a maze. Head south from State Line Campground on House Valley Road for about a mile to find the trailhead.

## Coyote Buttes South

The Coyote Buttes South region of Vermilion Cliffs NM is, like its northern counterpart, accessed by permit only. The good news is the permits are much easier to obtain for this region. Just go online and follow the instructions.

https://www.blm.gov/az/paria/obtainpermits.cfm?usearea=CB

All of the hiking here is for the experienced. Beyond needing a permit, you'll need a 4WD vehicle and topo maps. Per the BLM, these are both mandatory. As the BLM site indicates these aren't really trailheads, they are access points. After driving through deep sands and rough terrain, after figuring out on numerous occasions which junction you should take at the many spur roads on the way, you find yourself parking at the beginning of your own adventure.

For all of the below access points listed below, there are no trails, no markers, direction signs, or navigational information once you leave the road that got you there. In places like these, there is this advice. You will find at least one piece of trash, typically a Budweiser can and you

*A land of soulfulness and escape*

will wonder how it got there. You will have the opportunity to step where no human has stepped, and see things that no one has seen in quite the same way. You will hopefully take solace in knowing that the closest Starbucks to your tent is a good 3 hours away and that when the sun sets, you will likely see one of the darkest skies you have ever seen. This is the middle of nowhere. It is desert nirvana, BFE, God's country. Whatever you call it, the place will leave its mark on the soul as days remembered for the rest of your life.

## Cottonwood Cove Trailhead

This access point leads to the Cottonwood Teepees, a series of cone shaped sandstone formations. In general, the red rock is twisted and deformed, resembling something more reminiscent to a Salvador Dali landscape.

The rocks at times look like huge spine fossils of some large monster, eroded away by time until only the backbone remains curved out on a pedestal of rock. There is also one teepee formation called the Queen, looking like a typical cone shaped formation but with the smallest of capstones on top.

Getting to Cottonwood Cove Trailhead starts by taking House Rock Road, the same road taken for Buckskin Gulch and Wire Pass Trailheads. Head south past Wire Pass for 20.2 miles and turn left on BLM 1017, (Pine Tree Road). If coming from the south, the distance on House Rock Road will be 9.4 miles to this intersection.

Mark the trip meter and take Pine Tree Road for 3.1 miles and then turn left on Red Pockets Road and begin heading in a northwest bearing. At 6.0 miles, you should see a cattle gate (leave as you found it, whether open or closed). At 8.3 miles, bear to the right and at 8.7 miles turn left onto Upper Pawhole Road. This area, called Poverty Flat has several out buildings worth checking out. At 9.0 miles keep to the right until you reach a closed gate with a sign that says Coyote Buttes Fee Area. End of the road worth driving on is at 11.4 miles. Park on your left, the Cottonwood Teepees are to the west.

## Paw Hole Trailhead

Paw Hole is close to Cottonwood Cove, offering slightly different topography. It is possible to do both in one trip. Paw Hole has some interesting, often delicate striations in the sandstone. Paw Hole is a small water hole that looks like, (wait for it), a paw. One recommended route is to stay at Cottonwood Cove the first night and then Paw Hole the next. This method allows for a loop back to House Valley Road.

Coming from Cottonwood Cove, double back to BLM 1079 and take it to the signs indicating Paw Hole. To head out, continue on BLM 1079 to connect back to House Valley Road. It is not recommended to take this road to Paw Hole directly from House Valley as it is uphill and is too steep for many vehicles.

### Lone Tree Access Point

This is an access point to Paw Hole and the Coyote Buttes South for folks that have a 2WD vehicle only. Take House Valley Road south to BLM 1079 and turn left. Drive on 1079 for 0.2 miles and park the car near the obvious lone tree. Continue hiking east to Paw Hole along BLM 1079 from here. It is approximately 2.4 miles to Paw Hole from the tree.

## Marble Canyon

### Soap Creek Trail

Strenuous – (8.0 mi / 12.9 km), round trip, allow 2 - 3 hours

Soap Canyon is a feeder canyon to the Colorado River. The trail passes much of its time within the Grand Canyon National Park, which protects either side of the river north to Glen Canyon NRA. The trail is found by driving south on Highway 89A approximately 9 miles from Marble Canyon, AZ. Look for mile marker 548 and thereafter a latched gate. Turn left onto this dirt road, pass some abandoned buildings, and drive about 0.6 miles to the trailhead.

Soap Canyon allows for a quick access to the Colorado River and is popular with anglers as a result. It does have two dryfalls that must be navigated. If you find yourself wondering how you are going to get down the first 10-foot one, then you might want to turn back as the second one is 25 feet high. The gradient is easy going at first and the canyon becomes narrower and steeper on its way to the river. Both dryfalls have alternate routes to allow access around them. The tributary opens up shortly after the second dryfall at the inspiring Soap Creek Rapids. If you plan to stay overnight, you will need to obtain a permit from Grand Canyon NP.

### Stone House

A woman by the name of Blanche Russell was driving through the area and her car broke down. She took it as fate and built a house where her car stopped in 1930. The ruins, called Stone House, as well as oddly eroded and balanced rocks can be found here. Stone House is 8.4 miles south of Marble Canyon, AZ and about 0.3 miles north of the Cliff Dwellers Lodge.

*Sunrise at Cottonwood Cove*

# Grand Canyon National Park - South Rim

## Quick Facts

**Official Park Website:**
http://www.nps.gov/grca

**Visitor Center:**

- General Visitor Information: (928) 638-7888
- Backcountry Information Center: (928) 638-7875

**Park Accessibility:**

- Okay for 2WD and RVs
- Day and Overnight Use

**Experience Level:**

- Family Friendly – Backcountry Hiker

**Camping in Park:**
Reservations strongly recommended at (877) 444-6777 or online at the http://www.recreation.gov/

- Mather Campground: 309 T/RV, open year round, drinking water, flush toilets, pull-thru sites, laundry and showers, no hookups, 30-foot total vehicle length, group sites available.
- Trailer Village RV: 80 RV, open year round, hookups, drinking water, flush toilets, accommodates vehicles up to 50 feet in length, pull-thru sites, shower and laundry
- Desert View: 50 T/RV, first come–first served, closed in winter, drinking water, restrooms, 30-foot total vehicle length, typically fills be early afternoon in summer.

**Lodging in Park:**

- 7 lodges in the South Rim, including Phantom Ranch. Go here for full details: http://www.nps.gov/grca/planyourvisit/lodging.htm. Reservations strongly recommended

**Dining in Park:**

- Multiple restaurants and markets for groceries. Go here for full details: http://www.nps.gov/grca/planyourvisit/restaurants.htm

**Nearest Town with Amenities:**

- Tusayan, AZ is less than 2 mi / 3 km from park

**Getting There:**

- From Flagstaff, AZ: take I-40 to US-180 North to South Rim park entrance

## What Makes the South Rim of the Grand Canyon Special

- Hiking in one of the most amazing natural wonders on the planet
- Knowing that if you make it the canyon floor, you are amongst rock that is 2.2 billion years old, some of the oldest exposed rock on earth
- The grandeur of the mesas, the magnitude of the various rock layers, the sheer immensity, it's the Grand Canyon!

## Hiking in the South Rim of the Grand Canyon

### Rim Trail

Easy – (13.0 mi / 21.0 km), one way, time varies on route taken, elev. Δ: 200 ft / 61m, trailhead at viewpoint at Grand Canyon Village and along Hermit Road

The Rim Trail is great for just strolling in the Grand Canyon with the view slowly changing before you. The trail starts at the South Kaibab Trailhead and extends to Hermit's Rest. It can be picked up from any overlook, and by utilizing the shuttle system one can pick up the trail and drop off it with a great deal of convenience. The trail is mostly paved and well traveled. For quieter moments, try walking it in tune to the sunrise or meander along its route in the late afternoon into dusk.

### Bright Angel Trail

Strenuous – (12.0 mi / 19.3 km to Plateau Point), round trip, allow 5-8 hours, elev. Δ: 3,039 ft / 926 m, trailhead west of Bright Angel Lodge

Strenuous – (17.6 mi / 28.3 km to Colorado River), round trip, allow 5-8 hours, elev. Δ: 4,888 ft / 1,490 m, trailhead west of Bright Angel Lodge

Bright Angel is a very well defined trail that ultimately leads to the Colorado River itself. While it is possible to do this in one day, as mentioned above, this is an all-day hike and not for the casual hiker. The thing to realize about Bright Angel is it is very inviting and gives wonderful views as you immerse yourself into the depths of the canyon. However, the trail is steep, which gives you the impression that you are "cooking with gas" as you travel downward. It is only on the return that you realize just how steep this trail is. Allow twice as much time for the return trip and bring twice as much water for this hot, exposed trail.

For groups with small children, going to the first switchback offers a good experience without subjecting little feet to the steeper bits just ahead. For those not looking to do a full 12-mile (19 km) hike, going to Indian Gardens offers great views and a nice stopping point before turning around. There is water to refill your canteen and even a ranger on duty most of the time. Indian Gardens is 9 miles (14.5 km) round trip. If you decide

*From the bottom of the canyon*

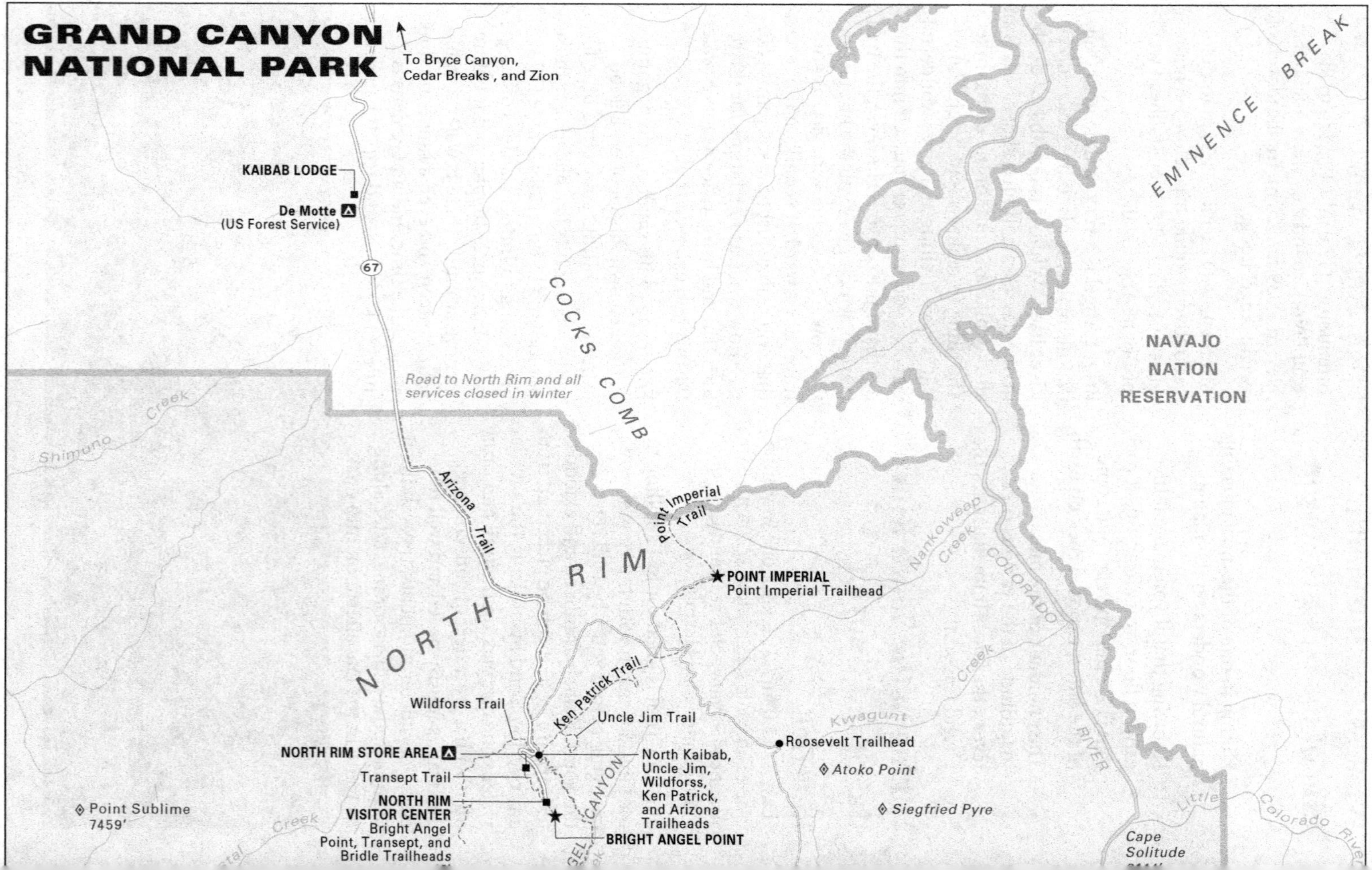
GRAND CANYON NATIONAL PARK
To Bryce Canyon, Cedar Breaks , and Zion
KAIBAB LODGE
De Motte
(US Forest Service)
67
COCKS COMB
Road to North Rim and all services closed in winter
EMINENCE BREAK
NAVAJO NATION RESERVATION
Shimuno Creek
Arizona Trail
Point Imperial Trail
NORTH RIM
POINT IMPERIAL
Point Imperial Trailhead
Nankoweap Creek
COLORADO RIVER
Ken Patrick Trail
Wildforss Trail
Uncle Jim Trail
Kwagunt Creek
Roosevelt Trailhead
Atoko Point
Siegfried Pyre
NORTH RIM STORE AREA
Transept Trail
NORTH RIM VISITOR CENTER
Bright Angel Point, Transept, and Bridle Trailheads
North Kaibab, Uncle Jim, Wildforss, Ken Patrick, and Arizona Trailheads
BRIGHT ANGEL POINT
CANYON
Point Sublime 7459'
Creek
Little Colorado River
Cape Solitude

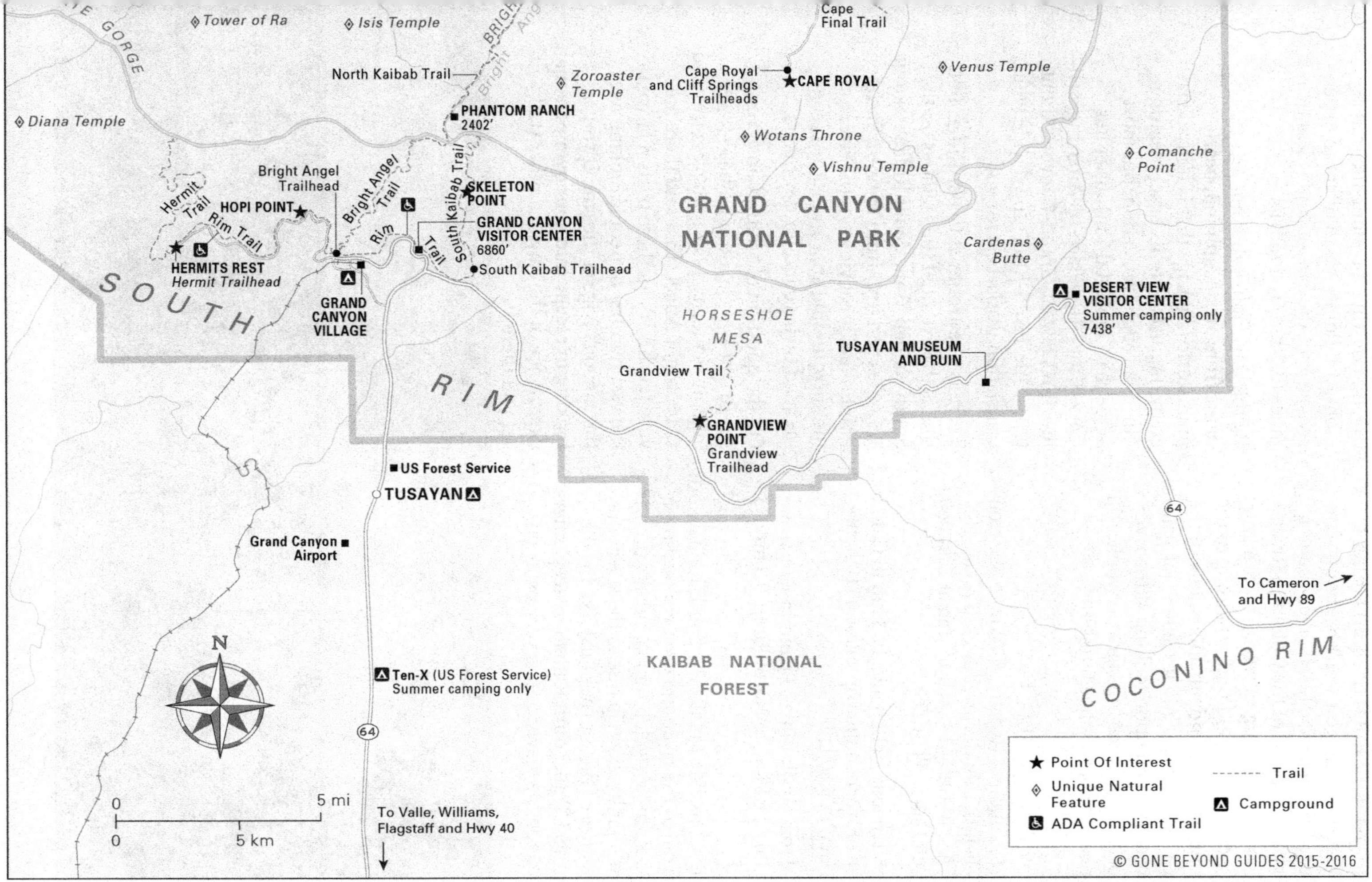


## Grand Canyon - South Rim

to go the 1.5 miles (2.4 km) farther to Plateau Point, you won't be disappointed. This fairly level trail takes you to a nice viewpoint of the Colorado River and surrounding canyon. This is a great spot to get a good understanding of the immensity, grandeur, and beauty of the Grand Canyon. You'll see how far you've traveled, and upon looking at the river below, you'll see how far you would still need to go, which is humbling.

## South Kaibab Trail

Strenuous – (6.0 mi / 9.7 km to Skeleton Point), round trip, allow 4 -5 hours, elev. Δ: 2,011 ft / 613 m, trailhead at Yaki Point off Desert View Drive

Strenuous – (12.0 mi / 19.3 km to Colorado River), round trip, allow 8 -10 hours, elev. Δ: 4,800 ft / 1,463 m,

From South Rim to Phantom Ranch: 6.9 mi / 11.1 km, to North Rim: 20.9 mi / 33.6 km

It is possible to take the South Kaibab Trail to the river and even connect over to Bright Angel, but most people do this as a multi-day trip due to the strenuous nature of the journey. Just like Bright Angel Trail, South Kaibab is steep, offers incredible views, and is very exposed.

The first destination along the trail is Ooh-Ahh Point, which offers an expansive view of the canyon and is less than 2 miles (3.2 km) round trip.

By the way, Ooh-Aah Point gets its name from an uncommon, nearly prehistoric language that is hotly debated by linguists as to its exact meaning. This is a rough translation, but most agree that "Ooh-Aah" means either "Wow!" or "The-Place-of-Amazing-Selfie-with-View-of-Grand-Canyon-About-One-Mile-From-Rim." You decide which translation works best for you.

There is a restroom at Cedar Ridge, but that is the extent of the facilities on the South Kaibab Trail. Cedar Ridge is about 1.5 miles (2.4 km) from the rim. Skeleton Point offers great views of the river and the surrounding area and is the recommended turnaround for day hikers.

On the question of South Kaibab versus Bright Angel, South Kaibab's fewer amenities means it is slightly less traveled than Bright Angel. That said there are very few hikers on these trails relative to the vast number of people looking over the canyon's edge at the rim. If you are looking to escape into your own personal experience of the canyon, either trail will get you there.

## Hermit Trail

Strenuous – (17.8 mi / 28.6 km to Colorado River), round trip, allow 8-12 hours, elev. Δ: 4,340 ft / 1,323 m, trailhead at Hermits Rest

The Hermit Trail begins at Hermit's Rest and, like all the trails described here, is accessed via shuttle. This trail is great for many reasons if you are an experienced hiker looking for something a little more rugged. It was originally built by horse thieves during the nineteenth century and is today considered a threshold trail, which means the National Park doesn't actively maintain it. There is water to be found along the trail, but it needs to be treated. Some of the trail has rutted out in areas and, in some cases, rock slides covering the trail require one to do a little scrambling to navigate around them. The point here is, if you are an experienced hiker, the Hermit Trail offers just about everything, including an endpoint worthy of the journey. It is 8.9 miles (14 km) down to the river, but if you are able to make it, you are rewarded with Hermit Rapids, perhaps the strongest hydraulics and biggest waves of any set of rapids in the canyon. The Hermit Rapids help to motivate any hiker and do not disappoint. You hear them before you see them and in seeing them there is nothing but gushing awe and respect.

It cannot be overstated that this is a trail to be taken seriously. Plan—bring the right gear, including plenty of food and water, and start early if you do plan to take on this all-day hike. There is a primitive campground at the river's edge and most folks do this as an overnight trip.

## Grandview Trail

Strenuous – (6.0 mi / 9.7 km to Horseshoe Mesa / Toilet Junction), round trip, allow 4-5 hours, elev. Δ: 2,500 ft / 762 m, trailhead at Grandview Point along Desert View Drive

Grandview is one of the quickest ways to get down into the canyon. It is very steep in some places and during the winter is dangerously icy. Crampons or some other means of traction for your footwear is required in winter. The trail offers deep views into the canyon as well as ruins of historic mining structures. Another feature of the trail is the placement of log "cribs" in some of the vertical sections of the Kaibab/Toroweap section. Many of these log supports were swept away during a landslide in the winter of 2005, but there are a few examples of these historical trail structures still around.

*Panorama of the Grand Canyon*

The Grandview Trail is not as well maintained as either Bright Angel or South Kaibab Trails. There are steep drop-offs in some areas. Use caution when hiking this trail.

## River Rafting

Rafting down the Colorado is not only a popular activity, for many it is a bucket list item, something they have to do before they head on to the big national park in the sky. As a result, don't expect to show up and get on the river. Rafting is by permit only in the Grand Canyon and, depending on the activity, can take one to two years to receive a permit. The Park has made an effort to streamline the types of trips available and the permitting process for each.

That said, rafting down the Colorado through the Grand Canyon is truly a defining moment in anyone's life. It is an experience that moves beyond words, resets your definitions of awe and wonder, brings a restful peace to the soul and at times puts you in moments of unholy terror that—on getting to the other side of—help remind you just how awesome it is to be alive. It is worth the planning and the wait.

### One Day Commercial River Trips:

Half day and full day smooth water river trips are available through park concessionaire Colorado River Discovery. You can purchase tickets at any of the park's lodges. The smooth water river trips are the only trips that do not require a permit and as the trip never encounters rapids, is open to all ages from four years old and up.

While these trips are gentle and without the excitement of white water, they are a great way to see the park and are highly recommended. Bring food and water, sunscreen, a hat and, of course, your camera. On a side note about the camera, yes, it's okay to bring a camera on the trip that isn't waterproof as it is unlikely you will get wet. That said, use caution. In the summer, you won't need a towel as in the heat of the day you will dry off pretty quickly. In the spring and cooler seasons, bring layers. As you will be entering at the Glen Canyon Dam, which is inside the protection of Homeland Security, you will be checked for weapons, including pepper spray and pocket knives. These will not be allowed, so don't bring them. Transportation from the lodge to the Dam is included.

### 3- to 18-Day Commercial River Trips

For those who are looking for white water rapids and adventure, there are hosts of river concessionaires that provide full service guided trips. Each company offers its own suite of trips and many cater to the different experiences visitors are looking for. Trips can last for as little as a few days to up to 18 days.

*A dory in Hance Rapids*

The upside of a guided trip is that, first and foremost, you don't need to become an expert in white water rafting. The domain of the rafter is a world unto itself. They have their own language, and while they are a friendly, tightly knitted group, it's an investment of time and money to enter their world and walk, err—paddle—among them. A guided trip comes with the security that you are riding down the Colorado with an expert at the helm. Plus, the thoughts of where to camp, what to eat, and even where to do your business are pretty much taken care of for you. The downside is the cost and the fact that reservations need to be made one to two years in advance.

Details on what trips are offered, in what type of raft, duration and other amenities are numerous. The best place to start is the Grand Canyon NPS page, which lists all of the river concessionaires. Go to: http://www.nps.gov/grca/planyourvisit/river-concessioners.htm

### 2- to 5-Day Noncommercial River Trips

Permits are available to the general public starting one year in advance and are assigned on a first come, first served basis. Two noncommercial permits are authorized each day launching from Diamond Creek. Each trip is limited to a maximum of 16 people. There is no fee for the permits and they can be obtained by filling out a permit application and mailing it to the NPS permits department. While the NPS does not charge a fee for the permit, the Hualapai Tribe does charge a fee for crossing their land.

The permit can be found by going to: http://www.nps.gov/grca/planyourvisit/upload/Diamond_Creek_Application.pdfYou can also call directly: (800) 959-9164 or (928) 638-7843.

As mentioned above, you are crossing both National Park Service land and Hualapai tribal land. Hualapai means "people of the tall trees" in reference to the Ponderosa Pine. This small community of about 2,000 individuals primarily bases its economy on tourism. One way they do that is to charge a fee for each person (including drivers) and each vehicle traveling Diamond Creek Road, which they own. Cost is $64.20 for each person and vehicle, (example: 16 passengers, 2 drivers and 2 vehicles will cost $1284 total). Camping on the south side of the river (river left) above the high water mark will also require a permit from the Haulapai. More information can be had by calling the Haulapai directly at (928) 769-2219.

The NPS permits authorize you and your group to travel for 2 to 5 days from Diamond Creek in the Lower Gorge of the Colorado River. This 52-mile (84 km) section is spectacular and includes both smooth water and some decent rapids to shoot as well as culturally significant areas. River users are asked to treat these cultural areas with respect so that future generations can enjoy them. Camping is limited but is free on the north side (river right).

One word of note: acceptance. The river has changed since the days of Powell. You will be sharing the river with many other users, especially at the launch and take-out areas. You will find motorized upstream and downstream travel from Lake Mead and even see a helicopter or two. There will be moments that are all yours, but there will also be moments that are shared with others

### 12- to 25-Day Noncommercial River Trips

This type of self-guided river trip travels among the rugged section between Lees Ferry to Diamond Creek and is for those fully experienced in river rafting. The permits are made available through a weighted lottery. For more information, start here: http://www.nps.gov/grca/planyourvisit/overview-lees-ferry-diamond-ck.htm.

## Mule Trips

The mule rides offered by park concessionaire Xanterra are a classic way of seeing the Grand Canyon. The day trips offered change seasonally, and new offerings open up at the whim of the concessionaire. Most rides are typically 3-hour, 4-mile (6.4 km) rides. You don't need prior experience riding a mule, and your tour will include a fair amount of interesting interpretation about the geology and human history along the trail.

Overnight tours are also offered, and this ride is on par with rafting down the Colorado River in terms of generating incredible memories. You will ride your mule to Phantom Ranch located near the river. Lunch is provided and the steak dinner at the ranch is hearty and very welcome after the day's journey. As with the day trips, the overnight trips are full of interpretive narration on nearly all aspects of the park. The overnight trip to Phantom Ranch has been a high water mark for many visitors.

The downsides to the mule trips are the expense and the fact that you need to reserve the event well in advance. There is a wait list for day-before cancellations; however, the chances of people canceling are very slim. As of June 2014, it cost $548.84 for one person or $960.01 for two to ride a mule to Phantom Ranch and spend the night there.

Mule rides from the South Rim can be reserved through: Xanterra Parks & Resorts (303) 297-2757, (888) 297-2757

## Virtual Caching

For those who have never heard of this, virtual caching is the delightful marriage of treasure hunting and technology. Specifically, a "cache" is a term that denotes a bunch of stuff stowed somewhere in the wilderness. With virtual caching, a visitor uses his or her GPS system to find the cache. The reward is in part the journey and in part finding the cache, which— being virtual—means what you find is a cool location.

The National Park Service has done a wonderful job of offering an interesting way to explore the park.

You will need a GPS device (or smart phone with GPS), the park map, which is located inside the park's official newspaper, The Guide, and a copy of the instruction sheet, titled "Story of Grand Canyon." The instructions can be picked up at the Grand Canyon Visitor Center, where different coordinates are listed.

Input the coordinates into your GPS device and take the shuttle or walk to the various destinations. None of the virtual caching is done off trail; everything can be found on the paved rim of the park and on the trails. Along the way, the instruction sheet acts as an educational pamphlet on different aspects of the park. Virtual caching is a cool way to discover new things about the park, and if you are navigationally challenged, perhaps a way of discovering a bit about yourself as well!

You will need to keep a record of all your coordinates, which will be necessary to solve the final clue. It takes about 4–6 hours to complete this puzzle, and the tour will take you over a good deal of the park along the way. You can, in the end, receive a certificate of completion. See the visitor center for more details.

## Driving Around

Like Zion NP and Bryce NP, Grand Canyon receives too many visitors to make driving around the park practical. The NPS offers a fairly robust shuttle system to get you around, and it is not only highly recommended to use the shuttle system; it is the only method year round for some roads and during peak season for others.

In general, the shuttle system is divided into two loops, the Village Route and Kaibab Rim Route. The Village Route goes to the west and stops at Mather Campground, Trailer Village, Market Plaza, Grand Canyon Visitor Center, Shrine of the Ages, Train Depot, Bright Angel Lodge and Trailhead, and Maswik Lodge. The Village Route also stops at the Hermit's Rest Transfer, which is where you pick up the Hermit's Rest shuttle during peak season.

The Kaibab Route winds to the east and stops at the Grand Canyon Visitor Center, South Kaibab Trailhead, Yaki Point, Pipe Creek Vista, Mather Point and Yavapai Geology Museum.

You can drive on Hermit's Rest Road during the winter months and, to the east, the Desert View is a wonderful drive that ultimately takes you to the East Rim of the Grand Canyon.

*Grand Canyon with clouds overhead*

## There is so much to do in the South Rim of the Grand Canyon

There is a tremendous number of things to do and see, more than this little all-inclusive guidebook of seven National Parks can manage to describe in detail. Here are a few places worth exploring further:

### Kolb Studio

Art gallery, photo gallery, bookstore and place of historical interest run by the Grand Canyon Association. Near the Bright Angel Lodge

### El Tovar Hotel

Built in 1905, this hotel is on the National Register of Historic Places. It is noted for its Arts and Crafts as well as Mission style interior and exterior and is an incredible example of early twentieth century National Park lodge architecture.

### Yavapai Geology Museum

A great place to learn everything you wanted to know about the geology of the Grand Canyon. Many exhibits, three dimensional models and photographs along with the outdoor nature and geology "Trail of Time" where each meter traveled on the trail represents one million years of the geology of the Grand Canyon. If you think about it, the "Trail of Time" took about 2 billion years to make, so it is well worth seeing.

### Desert View Watchtower

Located on the East Rim of the park, the four story, 70-foot-high (21m) stone building was built in 1932 by Fred Harvey Architect Mary Colter. Mary Colter designed many of the buildings in the Grand Canyon, including Hopi House, Lookout Studio, Bright Angel Lodge, the Phantom Ranch buildings and Hermit's Rest (but not El Tovar Lodge). Patterned after the Pueblo kivas and watchtowers, the watchtower has a unique touch in its design.

### Skywalk

The Skywalk is managed by the Hualapai Tribe and is located on their tribal lands. It is a horseshoe-shaped walkway securely bolted into the canyon walls such that is juts out over the canyon itself. With the floors and sides made of glass, the structure juts out about 70 feet (21m) from the canyon rim, giving the feeling that you are suspended in air over the canyon. It is one of the most famous attractions within the western portion of the Grand Canyon. There is a separate fee for this attraction. Skywalk reservations: 1-888-868-9378 or 1-928-769-2636

*Desert View Watchtower*

# Grand Canyon National Park - North Rim



## Quick Facts

*View from the North Rim*

**Official Park Website:** http://www.nps.gov/grca

**Visitor Center:**

- General Visitor Information: (928) 638-7888
- Backcountry Information Center: (928) 638-7875

**Park Accessibility:**

- Okay for 2WD and RVs
- Day and Overnight Use (seasonally)

**Experience Level:**

- Family Friendly – Backcountry Hiker

**Camping in Park:**

Reservations strongly recommended at (877) 444-6777 or online at the http://www.recreation.gov/

- North Rim Campground: 90 T/RV, seasonal (closed in winter), drinking water, flush toilets, pull-thru sites, no hookups, dump station, group sites available.

**Lodging in Park:**

- North Rim Lodge, closed in winter. Reservations strongly recommended at (877) 386-4383.

**Dining in Park:**

- Multiple dining options and market at North Rim Lodge, closed in winter.

**Nearest Town with Amenities:**

- Jacob Lake, AZ is 44 mi / 71 km from park

**Getting There:**

- From St George, UT: take I-15 North to UT-59 South to AZ-389 East, turn right onto US-89A South to AZ-67 South to North Rim park entrance

## What Makes the North Rim of the Grand Canyon Special

- The less crowded, more intimate side of the Grand Canyon
- For those that have done the South Rim, knowing you are about to hike new trails within one of the most scenic places on earth
- The better side to start a "rim to rim" day hike because the longer of the two sides is downhill if you come from the North Rim

Granted the North Rim is a bit harder to get to and is closed during the winter season, but the reward is far fewer people. It brings the ability to see the Grand Canyon more on your terms and pace, receiving around 500,000 visitors annually. The North Rim is higher in elevation and thus can be cooler. This side of the canyon is up to 1800 feet higher, making day trips down to the river and back longer than the South Rim.

## Hiking the North Rim of the Grand Canyon

### Bright Angel Point Trail

Easy – (0.5 mi / 0.8 km), round trip, allow 30 minutes, elev. Δ: 200 ft / 61m, trailhead near visitor center

Bright Angel Point is a nice walk from Grand Canyon Lodge and nearby visitor center. There are examples of marine fossils within the rocks along the way. Be sure to pick a park brochure, which shows the location of the fossils and gives a good historical backstory of the lodge and this historic trail.

### Transept Trail

Easy – (3.0 mi / 4.8 km), round trip, allow 1 - 2 hours, elev. Δ: 150 ft / 46 m, trailhead near North Rim Lodge

The Transept Trail starts at the Grand Canyon Lodge and follows the rim of the canyon to the North Rim Campground. Great views along the way.

*North Rim with cloud play*

## Ken Patrick Trail

Strenuous – (10.0 mi / 16.0 km), one way, 5 - 6 hours, elev. Δ: 600 ft / 183 m, trailhead north of visitor center at North Kaibab trailhead

The Ken Patrick Trail is named after a ranger killed in the line of duty. He is buried within the Grand Canyon, but worked at Point Reyes National Seashore and was killed by poachers in 1973.

This there and back trail is best accomplished with two cars. Starting from the North Kaibab Trailhead, the Ken Patrick Trail starts off clearly for the first 2 ½ miles but can become very difficult to find after reaching the Old Bright Angel Trail sign post. If you are an experienced hiker and this sounds appealing, simply keep north and don't go too far from the rim. Once you pick up the Cape Royal Road, the trail becomes easier to find and maintains close to the rim all the way to Point Imperial.

*Lower Ribbon Falls*

## Uncle Jim Trail

Moderate – (5.0 mi / 8.0 km), round trip, allow 2 - 3 hours, elev. Δ: 100 ft / 30 m, trailhead north of visitor center at North Kaibab trailhead

This trail starts from the same parking lot as the North Kaibab Trailhead and meanders through the Kaibab Plateau forest to Uncle Jim's Point, which overlooks Bright Angel, Roaring Springs and an overall spectacular view of the canyon.

## Bridle Trail

Easy – (1.2 mi / 2.0 km), one way, allow 1 hour, elev. Δ: 161 ft / 49m, trailheads at viewpoint at North Rim Lodge and at North Kaibab Trailhead

A gentle trail that parallels the road from the Grand Canyon Lodge to the North Kaibab Trailhead. The Bridle Trail is a great after dinner hike to take in the peace of the canyon.

## North Kaibab Trail

Strenuous – (14.0 mi / 22.5 km), one way, allow 6-10 hours, elev. Δ: 5,780 ft / 1,762 m, trailhead north of visitor center at North Kaibab trailhead

Note that while the total distance to the river is shown, it does not include the distance back. This is because the total distance to the Colorado River and back is 28 miles and is definitely not recommended as a day hike. Folks do use the North Kaibab Trail as the starting point for a rim-to-rim hike, primarily because the trip for the longer leg of the two sides is downhill if you start on from the North Rim.

The North Kaibab Trail is special because it is starts at a higher elevation than either South Kaibab or Bright Angel trails. The 1,000-foot increase in elevation is such that a hike down the North Kaibab Trail to the Colorado River means you will pass through every ecosystem found between Canada and Mexico. It is the least visited of the maintained trails and is also the most strenuous. It is definitely a serious day hike at 28 miles (45 km) round trip and is typically done as a backpacking trip. There are a few restroom facilities and seasonal water available, though the water will need to be treated.

The trail heads steeply down at first until it flattens out a bit as you enter into the base of Bright Angel Canyon. At 5.0 miles (8.0 km), you encounter Roaring Springs, which is a short side trip that is easily visible from the trail. Here you can see water coming directly out of the cliff, typically with a nice flow, creating a little island of moss and ferns within the desert. Roaring Springs flows into Bright Angel Creek as you continue down the trail. This is an important water source, delivering the drinking water for every visitor within Grand Canyon NP. If you make it to the Colorado River, you can see the pipe going over the river on the underside of Bright Angel Trail's Silver Bridge.

Just a little farther down at 5.4 miles (8.7 km) is a structure known as the Pumphouse Residence, or Aiken Residence. From 1973 to 2006, Bruce Aiken was an artist, NP employee, and pump master, overseeing the water supply for the park. He and his wife Mary raised three children at the canyon bottom and lucky hikers were greeted with lemonade from the children from time to time. Aiken's work reflects a fine-tuned harmony with the area of the Grand Canyon. Working mainly in oil, the light, balance, and overall portrayal of rock and water are testimonies to living within the Grand Canyon, raising a family and experiencing nearly each day of one's life for 33 years inside its walls.

Another treasure on the North Kaibab is Ribbon Falls at 8.5 miles (13.7 km). It is a little grotto in the desert cascading gently on the west side of Bright Angel Creek. It is a great place to get out of the heat of the day, which can be intense in the summer. Between the Cottonwood Campground and Bright Angel Campground, you enter the Inner Gorge, which is a narrow canyon of the 2 billion-year-old Vishnu Schist. If you make it this far, you are now walking among rock roughly half as old as the earth itself. You can connect to either the South Kaibab or Bright Angel Trail over the two bridges that cross the Colorado at the canyon bottom.

*South of Point Imperial*

At this point you may be thinking North Kaibab is a gem of a trail, (which it is), and thus wondering if you could do a rim-to-rim adventure. The good news is you can. Trans Canyon Shuttle offers two rim-to-rim shuttles daily (go to http://www.trans-canyonshuttle.com for more info). The not-so-good news is getting reservations at one of the primitive campgrounds is a challenge. In addition, the shuttles depart early morning and early afternoon, so factor in an overnight stay at the opposing rim or hoofing it out to make the shuttle on the last day.

## Widforss Trail

Strenuous – (10.0 mi / 16.0 km), round trip allow 4 – 5 hours, elev. Δ: 400 ft / 122 m, trailhead north of visitor center west of North Kaibab trailhead

The Widforss Trail may just be the longest interpretative trail in the entire Grand Circle. Be sure to pick up a brochure at the trailhead. The trail hugs the canyon rim for the first half of the hike and then heads into a forested area to end at Widforss Point. The expansiveness of the Grand Canyon from this vista is impressive and it was a favorite of Gunnar Widforss, an early twentieth century landscape artist.

## Arizona Trail

Strenuous – (12.6 mi / 20.3 km), one way, allow 5 - 6 hours, trailheads at North Kaibab trailhead and Kaibab National Forest boundary

The Arizona Trail is an 800-mile adventure that starts in Mexico and heads northward until it ends in Utah. A part of the trail leverages the existing north and south rim to rim trails of Grand Canyon NP. From the North Kaibab Trail, it continues through the park for another 10 miles before hitting the park's boundary. This portion roughly follows Highway 67, traveling through forest canopy and the Harvey Meadow.

## Point Imperial Trail

Easy – (4.0 mi / 6.4 km), round trip, allow 1.5 - 2 hours, elev. Δ: negligible, trailhead at end of Point Imperial Road

This is an easy hike through an area recovering from a wildfire in 2000 and is great way to take in the tenacity of nature recovering from devastation. On the way, one will see young Aspens and innocent wildflowers starting anew from the aftermath of the fire. This is a great hike for a sunrise at Point Imperial.

## Roosevelt Point Trail

Easy – (0.2 mi / 0.3 km), round trip, allow 30 minutes, elev. Δ: negligible, trailhead at Cape Royal Road

More of a pleasant walk than a hike, this little ditty leads to a nice bench with great views of the canyon.

## Cape Final Trail

Easy – (4.0 mi / 6.4 km), round trip, allow 1.5 - 2 hours, elev. Δ: 150 ft / 46 m, trailhead at Cape Royal Road

An easy trail that ends at one of the higher elevation views of the Grand Canyon at Cape Final. As this trail is not often used, it provides good promise if you are looking for a secluded and peaceful hike. Cape Final is at 7,850 feet. Be careful if you decide to go onto the ledge's edge, it's a long way down.

## Cliff Springs Trail

Easy – (1.0 mi / 1.6 km), round trip, allow 45 – 60 minutes, elev. Δ: 150 ft / 46 m, trailhead at end of Cape Royal Road

A refreshing hike through a wooded ravine to a rocky overhang containing a seeping spring. The water is not suitable for drinking directly as tempting as it may seem. The spring holds an ecosystem for ferns and moss and can provide some nice shade from the day's sun. Look for the remains of a granary from the original inhabitants of the area early into the hike.

## Cape Royal Trail

Easy – (0.6 mi / 1.0 km), round trip, allow 30 minutes, elev. Δ: 40 ft / 12 m, trailhead at end of Cape Royal Road

An easy, flat walk that allows views of Angels Window arch, the Colorado River, and if you look through the arch at the right angle, you can see both at the same time! Great photo opportunity and easy to access. There are interpretative markers along the way.

*Ewe in the canyon*

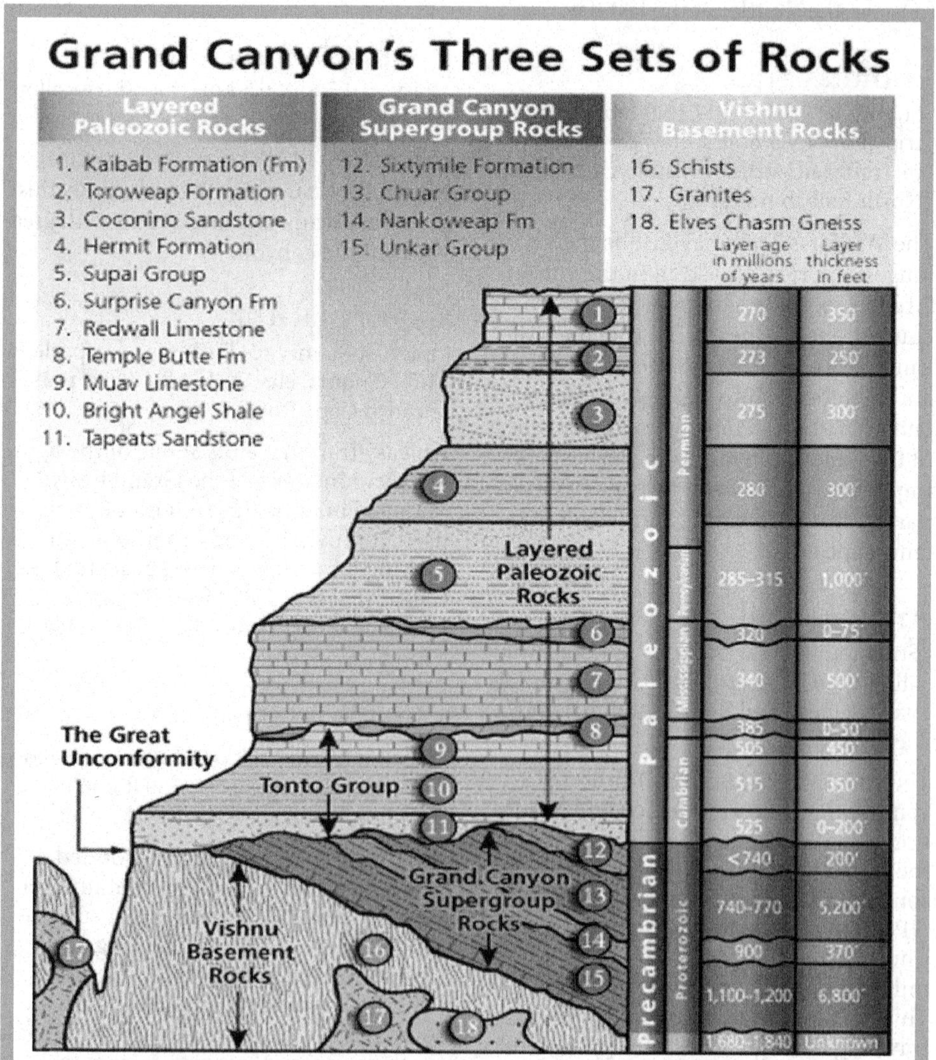


*The geology of the Grand Canyon*

## Quick Facts

**Official Park Website:** http://www.havasupai-nsn.gov/tourism.html

**Visitor Center:**

- Contact Havasupai Tourism at: P.O. Box 160 Supai, AZ, 86435, Phone: (928) 448-2121 or (928) 448-2141, (928) 448-2174, or (928) 448-2180

**Park Accessibility:**

- Okay for 2WD, RVs not recommended
- Primarily Overnight Use

**Experience Level:**

- Casual Hiker, some exposure

**Camping in Park:**

- Havasu Falls Campground: Reservations required, call Havasupai Tourism numbers listed above, (keep trying if no answer), 250T, drinking water, restrooms, no campfires, day ranger on duty in season

**Lodging in Park:**

- Havasupai Lodge, located on the trail 8 miles from trailhead in the town of Supai. Reservations required: (928) 448-2111 or (928) 448-2201.

**Dining in Park:**

- Supai Café, near Havasupai Lodge

**Nearest Town with Amenities:**

- Besides Supai, which is along the trail, Seligman, Arizona, 91 mi / 146 km from trailhead

**Getting There:**

- From Flagstaff: take US I-40 west to Historic Route 66 west at Seligman and turn right onto Indian Road 18 for 65 miles to trailhead at Hualapai Hilltop.

## What Makes Havasu and Mooney Falls Special

- Soft turquoise waters leading to healthy flowing 100 foot and 210 foot waterfalls in a peaceful canyon setting
- Ability to swim, camp and chill in this amazing area
- Getting a postcard to your family and friends partially via mules!

Within the entirety of the Grand Circle, Havasu and Mooney Falls are arguably the pinnacle of destinations. It is the soul of the Southwest, willing to accept all those that travel to it and yet the area continues to retain a serene simplicity and purity. If ever there should be an item at the top of your bucket list of places to go within the Grand Circle, this is that place.

## Hiking Havasu and Mooney Falls

### Havasu and Mooney Falls

Strenuous – (24.0 mi / 38.6 km), round trip, 2-day backpacking trip

First things first, get reservations and pay the fees. One will need to pay a $35 entrance fee plus an environment fee of $5, (each fee is per person). Camping is an additional $17 per person per night. Your entire party will be billed double this amount if you come without reservations, assuming there is availability. There is also a 10% tax on all purchases and a $5 Environmental Care Fee. Total for one night camping is $62.71 per person and $81.41 for two nights. The season opens on February 1st each year and 300 permits are given each day.

Now that you know the particulars on permits and camping, the next thing you will need is luck. The word is out on Havasu Falls and it is very difficult to get a permit. The best approach is to mark your calendar for February 1st and then start dialing every number listed repeatedly until you get through. It is not unheard of for multiple folks trying from different phones to take several days to finally get through. As rough as this sounds, many do get through on the first day. The only good news here is this is the same process whether you are hiking alone or are booking for a professional tour company.

If you do have a group helping you to get the permits, have a plan A, B and C for dates and make sure you have a communication system for when you finally do get through. The season usually books out within weeks, but there is always hope that there will be a cancellation if you don't want to wait until next February to get in line.

Located within the Havasupai Reservation, the trip does get a lot of visitors during peak season. Start by finding a parking spot near the trailhead, which is situated about 1,000 feet off the canyon bottom. Right from the trailhead, you will see you are in a special place. The views down and around are amazing.

The hike heads steeply down to the valley floor via a series of switchbacks. There are plenty of mules along this trail and one needs to be especially diligent on this part. If you see mules coming, stick to the canyon wall side and not the cliff side. The mules often travel at a decent clip giving the backpacker little time to react. Hugging a wall in these instances tends to fair better than clinging to the edge of a cliff. This is especially true in a narrow section later on. The mules have the right of way on this trail.

Most of the hike travels along the wash, with great views of towering orange-red walls on either side. At about mile 7 into the journey, the trail narrows. Be especially aware of mules here. The hiking here is shadier and thus cooler unless you are doing this stretch at high noon.

The slot canyon opens into Havasu Creek and shortly thereafter to the peaceful village of the Supai People. The town holds 208 residents, give or take and is officially the most remote inhabited community in the lower 48. Besides flying in by helicopter (or as the locals call it, "cheating"), the only way in is via the Havasupai Trail. It is the last community in the United States to have its mail delivered by mule.

Havasu Falls are 2 miles from the town of Supai. These two miles deeper into the canyon are utterly sublime. The water is a light blue green turquoise. The distinctive hue comes from the strong reflection of the underlying limestone creek bed. It's not just the falls that are this color, the entire creek from Supai on are a gem like color of paradise found.

Havasu Falls and Mooney Falls further on are tall, roaring sheets of water and simply beyond words. Both are amazing and both must be seen. Getting to Mooney Falls requires a Class 3 descent to the bottom, some 210 feet below. Aids include a tunnel, ladders, handholds, railings, and footholds. This section is quite steep and exposed in areas and not for those that have a fear of heights. In addition, these areas become bottlenecks and one may have to stand in place as they wait for folks to come up or down. Finally, it should not be attempted when the conditions are wet or otherwise unfavorable, as sections can get very slippery. There is a campground in between the Havasu and Mooney Falls.

If you do want to send a post card home from Supai, note that the post office is closed on weekends. If you do go on a weekend, some locals are willing to mail it for you for a nominal fee. The novelty of mailing anything from the community is knowing that the first leg (pun intended) is by mule, the last community in the United States to move mail in this manner.

*The sublime waters of Havasu Falls*

# Photo Attributes

Attributions and permissions given where indicated.

- All Grand Circle Maps and Park Maps copyright Gone Beyond Guides

## Front Cover

- Upper Muley Trail, Capitol Reef, by John Fowler for NPS, CC-BY-2.0

## Back Cover

- All Grand Circle Maps and Park Maps copyright Gone Beyond Guides

In order of appearance.

## Title Page

- Sunset at the Dollhouse - Maze District, NPS photo by Kait Thomas, CC-BY-2.0

## Table of Contents

- Grand Canyon, by Chensiyuan, CC-BY-SA-4.0,3.0,2.5,2.0,1.0

## General Information

- All Grand Circle Maps copyright Gone Beyond Guides
- Thors Hammer, Brcye Canyon NP, by NPS, PD US NPS
- Tower of Babel, Arches NP, by Shannon Martin, CC-BY-3.0
- Temples and Towers of the Virgin, Zion National Park, by John Fowler, CC-BY-2.0
- Canyonlands, by NPS, PD US NPS

## Southwest Utah

- Kolob Canyons, by Gmhatfield, CC-Zero

## Zion National Park

- Zion Narrows, by Jon Sullivan, PD-author
- Sunrise in Zion Canyon, by Stuart Seeger, CC-BY-2.0
- Waterfall at Emerald Pools Trail, by Stuart Seeger, CC-BY-2.0
- Climbing up Angels Landing, by Alex Proimos, CC-BY-2.0
- Zion Colors, by NPS, PD US NPS
- Into the Narrows, by Ada Be, CC-BY-2.0
- West Temple, by Ranger Bryanna Plog, PD US NPS
- Subway, by God of War, CC-BY-3.0
- Kolob Canyons, by Gmhatfield, CC-Zero
- Kolob Arch, by NPS, PD US NPS

## Quail Creek State Park

- Quail Creek Reservoir, by Fredlyfish4, CC-BY-SA-3.0

## Sand Hollow State Park

- Sand Hollow, by Dylan Duvergé, CC-BY-2.0

## Coral Pink Sand Dunes SP

- Coral Pink Sand Dunes, by Eric Henze, copyright Gone Beyond Guides
- Sunrise in Zion Canyon, by Nandaro, CC-BY-SA-3.0
- Coral Pink Sand Dunes, by Eric Henze, copyright Gone Beyond Guides
- Coral Pink Sand Dunes, by Eric Henze, copyright Gone Beyond Guides

## Snow Canyon State Park

- Snow Canyon SP, by AJA, CC-BY-SA-4.0
- Snow Canyon SP, by Óðinn, CC-BY-SA-2.5-CA

## Gunlock State Park

- Gunlock SP, by NPS, PD US NPS

## Frontier Homestead SP Museum

- Front of Frontier Museum SP, by NPS, PD US NPS

## Cedar Breaks NM

- Cedar Breaks, by Michael Gäbler, CC-BY-3.0
- Cedar Breaks Panorama, by LeavXC, CC-BY-SA-3.0
- Cedar Breaks, by LeavXC, CC-BY-SA-3.0

## South Central Utah

- Bryce Canyon Sunrise, by Christian Mehlführer, CC-BY-2.5

- Navajo Trail, by Jesper Rautell Balle, CC-BY-2.0

## Bryce Canyon National Park

- Bryce at Sunrise, by Eric Henze, Copyright Gone Beyond Guides
- Tree in canyon, by unknown, CC-BY-SA-3.0-migrated
- Bryce Canyon Sunrise, by Christian Mehlführer, CC-BY-2.5
- Hiking in Bryce, by Eric Henze, Copyright Gone Beyond Guides

## Grand Staircase-Escalante National Monument

- Wahweap Hoodoo, by John Fowler, CC-BY-2.0
- Lower calf falls, by Nikater, CC-BY-SA-3.0-migrated
- Devils Garden at Night, by John Fowler, CC-BY-2.0
- In Coyote Gulch, by Kerkphil, CC-BY-SA-3.0
- Little Death Hollow, by Greg Willis, CC-BY-2.0
- Cottonwood Canyon Road, by Umberto Salvagnin, CC-BY-2.0
- Paria Rimrocks, by daveynin, CC-BY-2.0
- Harris Wash, by Greg Willis, CC-BY-2.0

## Escalante Petrified State Park

- Petrified Wood Specimen, by Aneta Kaluzna Qbek, CC-BY-SA-3.0

## Kodachrome Basin SP

- Sand Pipe, by Fredlyfish4, CC-BY-SA-4.0

## Capitol Reef National Park

- Butte, by Wolfgang Staudt, CC-BY-2.0
- Gifford Barn, by Eric Henze, copyright Gone Beyond Guides
- Hickman Bridge, by Aneta Kaluzna Qbek, CC-BY-SA-2.5
- Cassidy Arch, by John Fowler, CC-BY-2.0
- Golden Throne, by Qfl247, CC-BY-SA-3.0
- Cathedral Valley, by Greg Willis, CC-BY-2.0
- Old Ford, by Eric Henze, copyright Gone Beyond Guides
- Waterpocket Fold, by NPS, PD US Government
- Upper Muley Twist, by John Fowler, CC-BY-2.0

## Glen Canyon NRA

- Rainbow Bridge, by Jason Hickey, CC-BY-2.0
- Horseshoe Bend, by Luca Galuzzi, CC-BY-SA-2.5

## Southeast Utah

- Dead Horse Point, by Jean-Christophe BENOIST, CC-BY-SA-2.0
- Beehive Arch, NPS photo by Kait Thomas, CC-BY-2.0

## Goblin Valley State Park

- Goblins, by CGP Grey, CC-BY-2.0
- Goblin Valley, by Aaron D. Gifford, CC-BY-SA-2.5

## Canyonlands National Park

- Canyonlands, by Phil Armitage, PD-author
- Mesa Arch, by Michael Rissi, CC-BY-SA-3.0-migrated
- Aztec Butte Trail, by Ronnie Macdonald, CC-BY-2.0
- Upheaval Dome, by Doc Searls, CC-BY-2.0
- Needles Overlook, by Alex Proimos, CC-BY-2.0
- Needles, by Jesse Varner, CC-BY-SA-2.5
- Druid Arch, by RichieB_pics, CC-BY-2.0
- Druid Arch Trail, by RichieB_pics, CC-BY-2.0
- Great Gallery, by Scott Catron, CC-BY-3.0

## Dead Horse Point State Park

- Dead Horse Point, by Clément Bardot, CC-BY-SA-3.0
- La Sals and Dead Horse Point, by Jean-Christophe BENOIST, CC-BY-SA-3.0

## Arches National Park

- Delicate Arch, by National Park Service Photo, PD US NPS
- Courthouse Panel, by NPS, CC-BY-2.0
- Double Arch, by Flicka, CC-BY-2.0
- Landscape Arch, by Daniel Mayer i, CC-BY-3.0

## Edge of the Cedars State Park

- Sun Sculpture, by Scott Catron from Sandy, Utah, USA, CC-BY-SA-2.0

## Natural Bridges NM

- Delicate Arch, by (NPS photo by Jacob W. Frank), CC-BY-2.0
- Horsecollar Ruins, by (NPS photo by Neal Herbert), CC-BY-2.0
- Kachina Arch, by (NPS photo by Neal Herbert), CC-BY-2.0
- Sipapu Arch, by (NPS photo by Jacob W. Frank), CC-BY-2.0

## Hovenweep NM

- Cutthroat Unit, by (NPS photo by Andrew Kuhn), CC-BY-2.0

## Four Corners

- Four Corners, by Rich Torres, CC-By-SA-3.0
- Canyonlands - Needles District by Famartin, CC-By-SA-3.0

## Goosenecks State Park

- Goosenecks State Park, by Gernot Keller, CC-By-3.0

## Southwest Colorado

- Cliff Palace, by Ben FrantzDale, CC-By-3.0

## Mesa Verde National Park

- Cliff Palace, by Tobi 87, CC-BY-3.0
- Cliff Palace, by Ben FrantzDale, CC-By-3.0
- Kiva, by Ken Lund, CC-BY-2.0
- Weatherhill Mesa, by Ken Lund, CC-BY-2.0

## Yucca House NM

- Entrance, by Nationalparks, CC-BY-SA-2.5

## Northern Arizona

- Grand Canyon, by Chensiyuan, CC-BY-SA-4.0,3.0,2.5,2.0,1.0

## Monument Valley

- Monument Valley, by Luca Galuzzi (Lucag), CC-BY-SA-2.5

## Navajo National Monument

- Betakin, by Diego Delso, CC-BY-SA-4.0,3.0,2.5,2.0,1.0
- Betakin Ruins, by John Fowler, CC-BY-2.0
-

## Antelope Canyon

- Antelope Canyon, by Moyan Brenn, CC-BY-2.0
- Antelope Canyon, by Moyan Brenn, CC-BY-2.0
- Antelope Canyon, by Eric Henze, copyright Gone Beyond Guides
-

## Vermilion Cliffs NM

- Coyote Buttes South, by John Fowler, CC-BY-2.0
- Condors on the Rise, by Bob Wick, BLM California, CC-BY-2.0
- The Wave, by Lobineau, CC-BY-SA-3.0-migrated-with-disclaimers
- Vermilion Cliffs, by Bob Wick, BLM California, CC-BY-2.0
- Sunrise at Cottonwood Cove, by Bob Wick, BLM California, CC-BY-2.0
-

## Grand Canyon National Park

- Canyon Mid Day, by Realbrvhrt, CC-BY-SA-3.0-migrated
- Grand Canyon Panorama, by Roger Bolsius, CC-BY-SA-3.0
- North Rim, by Scott Catron, CC-BY-SA-3.0-migrated
- Grand Canyon North, by Khlnmusa, CC-BY-SA-3.0
- Lower Ribbon Falls, by Kkaufman11, PD-self
- South of Point Imperial, by NPS, PD US Government
- Ewe in Canyon, by Ronthemon2, PD-self
- Grand Canyon Geology, by NPS, PD-USGov

## Havasu Falls

- Havasu Falls, by Moondigger, CC-By-SA-2.5

## Acknowledgments

- Antelope Canyon, by Moyan Brenn, CC-BY-2.0

# FIND YOUR PARK

## In Celebration of a Birthday

In 2016, the National Park Service will turn 100 years old. The national parks have always held a very special place in my heart. They represent some of the best of the best in terms of the natural wonders that America holds. I like the robustness that a national park offers, being fully wilderness in so many different ways, the architectural and historical significance of its buildings, and the educational aspects that the rangers play; including the junior ranger and other programs. Each park protects something that is unique to the world, continually inspiring poets, painters, and patrons every single day. They bring that amazement to all that visit them and connect in a way that we should experience more often.

There was an ask of the national park system to share something and bring a gift to this grandest of birthday celebrations. These books are my gift. Happy birthday NPS, for me you represent America at its best! Here's hoping we can continue to enjoy and protect these lands as a nation for many centuries to come.

## The Grand Circle Series Project

This series of hiking guides started from a passion for the area itself. I started visiting the Grand Circle while still in diapers, coming along with my dad on fishing trips up Oak Creek Canyon in the 60's. I have lived within the Grand Circle for much of my life and have hiked many of these places multiple times and through all seasons. I have explored this land for over three decades and each time I went out on a trail or off trail; it was with the same childlike wonder. If a person can fall in love with a place, that is me. Each time I went out, I wanted to share the experience. This sharing started with my friends and then my family, but still, I continued to want to share. Therefore, in that spirit of sharing, I decided to write about my experiences.

The project started by writing my first book on the area, called ***A Family Guide to the Grand Circle National Parks***. This travel guide describes a vacation around seven national parks, Zion, Bryce Canyon, Capitol Reef, Canyonlands, Arches, Mesa Verde, and the Grand Canyon. I had fun with the book. I worked with the rangers on the park descriptions and even wrote semi fictional stories to go along with each park. It was great fun sharing the Grand Circle with others.

Describing the national parks along the "main route" was awesome, but I had this larger idea. What if I described every park within the Grand Circle? I had no idea how large such a project would be or how long it would take. I simply started by writing about every park I knew of and then followed up with firsthand accounts for the ones that I hadn't. I received multiple accounts for each trail. Where I had hiked, I wrote my account, researching, and fact checking along the way. Where I hadn't hiked, I worked with others who had, incorporating firsthand accounts from a strong and amazing network of hiking experts and other folks passionate about the area. A tremendous amount of fact checking and support went into this work because while it is nearly impossible for one person to have hiked every trail in this book, I wanted to make sure every trail was described accurately and robustly.

The intent of this work is simple. The Grand Circle Series attempts at gathering every trail for every national park, national monument, national historic park, national recreation area, tribal park, and state park within the Grand Circle. I am certain that there are trails and possibly even parks yet that need to be included. The Browns Canyon National Monument is a great case in point. It was just recently added to the national park system in 2015. That said, after describing nearly 500 trails and after crossing the 100,000-word mark, I realized I was at a stopping point. (This was my 'Forest Gump at Monument Valley' moment).

When it was all done I had described 12 national parks, 31 national monuments, including national historic sites and preserves, 3 national recreation areas, 29 state parks and 4 tribal parks. These 79 parks in all cover 480 hikes and the truth is there are still hikes left to be defined, especially in the larger and more remote parks. I left out unofficial hikes within parks and also left out secret areas only known to locals, as I believe some land is so special that it should be preserved, that if it wants you to visit it, it will call you, it needs no introduction.

So what to do with all these trail descriptions? The intent originally was to put everything into one book, but then I realized that wouldn't be very useful. It would be too big to fit into a daypack and most folks would not make full use of a book covering such a large area. In the end, I decided to split the content into four guides, one each for Nevada, Utah, Arizona and finally one more collectively covering Colorado and New Mexico. These four kept everything to a manageable area of interest.

Each book spills over in its surrounding states just a bit, because that's how I would use such a book. This way if you are planning to hike Black Canyon of the Gunnison National Park using the Colorado/New Mexico trail guide, you can read on to the chapter that describes Canyonlands National Park in nearby Utah, because it's just as amazing, but in a completely different way. For the one person who buys all four books, first off, thank you! Secondly, hopefully you understand why you have four copies of the Four Corners Monument chapter.

I am always looking for feedback on improving these books and for any accuracy, misspellings, gripes, wants, and of course kudos. Please send to gonebeyond-guides@gmail.com. I write, design, and publish these works myself.

Happy hiking!

## Acknowledgments

First off, I want to thank MRoy Cartography for their wonderful map making, headed by Molly Roy. I came in with a request to make these the best maps out there and she fully delivered.

I am extremely thankful for the constant ebb and flow of feedback from my growing focus group, whom I used day in and day out as a sounding board for ideas, research, and pretty much for every aspect of this book. This is never a one-man shop; I couldn't do what I do without them. These include Ernie, Chris, Frank, Joel, George, Geoff, Jeff, Peggy, John, and Angela.

A special thanks to the National Park Service and its employees. There has never been a time when you weren't able to support this effort, which is remarkable given how much you all do. I truly appreciate all that you do for us as a nation and for all the help and assistance you have given me. To NPS - - Happy 100th birthday!

I also want to thank the states of Utah, Arizona, New Mexico, Colorado, and Nevada. Each of you protects some of the best and most remote lands in the United States. Each state, I commend you for your efforts here.

To my wife Angela and two boys, Everest and Bryce, thank you. The time you have given me to create these books is a true blessing, both in the adventures we have taken and in the many hours writing and editing away you have given me.



You can reach the author through our FaceBook page:

www.facebook.com/GBG.GoneBeyondGuides

**ISBN-10: 0-9971370-2-9**

**ISBN-13: 978-0-9971370-2-6**

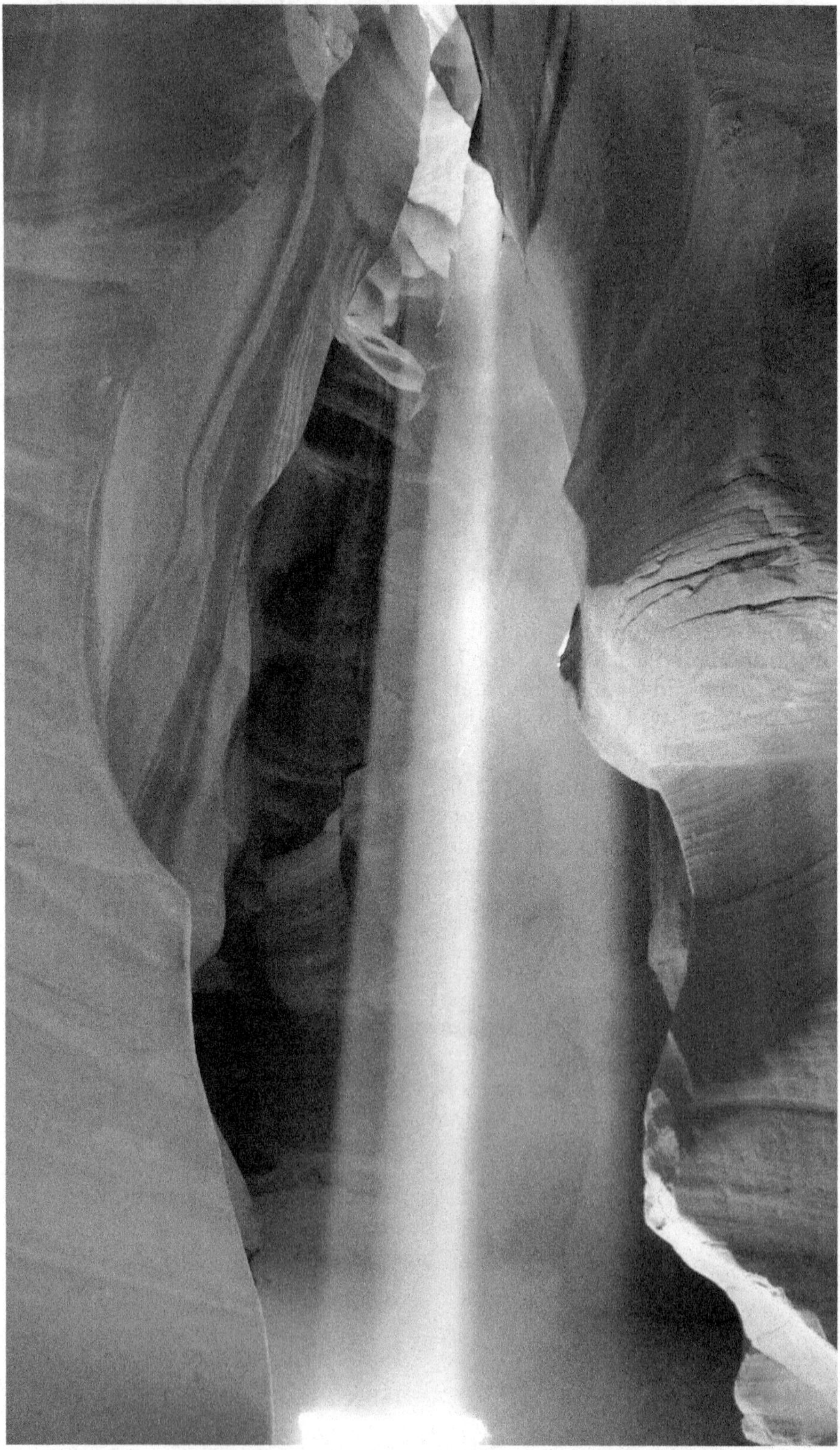

Eric Henze began his writing career at the age of twelve with a sci fi short titled "5:15", tackling a plot around a timepiece that could end the world. His passion for hiking started in Sedona, Arizona where he lived in his youth. It expanded to peak bagging in the Sierra Nevada Mountains and then the Andes of South America, where he lived as a Peace Corp volunteer for two years, climbing many of the peaks of Ecuador and Peru. A highlight was climbing Sangay, an active volcano that often shoots VW size rocks at climbers to maintain their attention. In his own words, "It was a delight".

His passions for writing, hiking, and adventure have led to a series of guidebooks for both the National Park Service and the California State Parks. A portion of the proceeds of all of his books will go towards directly supporting these parks.

By day, the intrepid author works for a Fortune 50 company helping large enterprises navigate towards, within and beyond the digital revolution. He is lives his family, two awesome boys, a lovely wife, and a blue-eyed merle named Sedona.

His children have noted that his last words will be while driving through the Southwest and seeing some point of interest. Those last words will be, "I'll be right back, I'm going go check that out".

## Also Available Within the Grand Circle Series

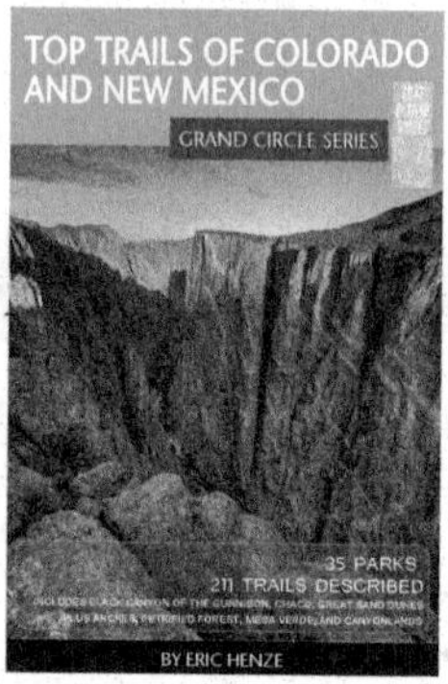


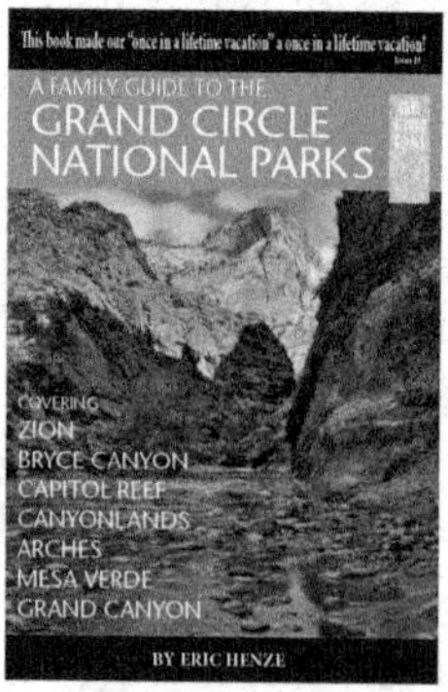


Top Trails of Utah

Top Trails of Arizona

Top Trails of Colorado and New Mexico

A Family Guide to the Grand Circle National Parks

Follow us on Facebook and Twitter!

facebook.com/GBG.GoneBeyondGuides

twitter.com/GoneBeyondGuide

All titles published by Gone Beyond Guides

CPSIA information can be obtained
at www.ICGtesting.com
Printed in the USA
FSOW04n0832170816
23763FS

9 780997 137026